Praise for
Good Morning, Beautiful Business

"Judy Wicks's brilliance redefines what a business can be. The White Dog Café models what commerce will become if we are to create a livable future. This is business as spiritual practice, business as kindness, business as community, business as justice, joy, transformation, leadership, and generosity. There is nothing here you will learn in business school, because the White Dog Café is not in the business of selling life; it's in the business of creating life. How blessed is Philadelphia and the world for her presence and prescience."

—PAUL HAWKEN, author of *Blessed Unrest*

"Judy Wicks is one of the most amazing women I have ever met. She ran the legendary White Dog Café with passion, heart, common sense, and financial success. And she continues to blaze new paths on the road to a truly sustainable people-centered economy. This is a must-read book."

—BEN COHEN, cofounder of Ben & Jerry's

"Wow. What a woman, what a book. In it, you enter the life of someone who, even as a child, learned that she could create—that she could make things and make things happen. We need Wicks's confidence and courage now more than ever. So read it and you'll get some. Her spunk is contagious."

—FRANCES MOORE LAPPÉ, author of *EcoMind: Changing the Way We Think, to Create the World We Want*

"Judy Wicks set out to create a business that expressed her values, served her community, and fed her family. She ended up leading a national movement to build local economies that are inclusive and resilient, provide green job opportunities, and conduct business sustainably and responsibly. *Good Morning, Beautiful Business* is an inspiration—a living, breathing tale of the new American dream in action."

—VAN JONES, author of *Rebuild the Dream*

"Guided by her own powerful activist sensibility, Judy Wicks beautifully conveys the important influences that a restaurant, or any business, can have within a community—politically, economically, and socially."

—ALICE WATERS, owner of Chez Panisse and author of *The Art of Simple Food*

"Beware. This is a business book like no other. It will change how you see the world, America, business, and the economy and should be required reading in every school of business and department of economics. Judy Wicks teaches us how to succeed at business while managing from the heart, having an outrageously good time, and measuring success as contribution to healthy communities and a world that works for all. Those who take Wicks and the White Dog as their model change the world one beautiful business at a time."

—DAVID KORTEN, cofounder of *YES! Magazine* and author of *Agenda for a New Economy: From Phantom Wealth to Real Wealth* and *The Great Turning: From Empire to Earth Community*

"Judy Wicks is one of our great leaders and visionaries, and this book makes clear why. She thinks about traditional subjects—'business,' 'economics'—in fresh, practical, real, and powerful ways. Read it and then live it yourself!"

—BILL McKIBBEN, author of *Deep Economy: The Wealth of Communities and the Durable Future*

"If there ever is a Nobel Prize in planet-saving, Judy Wicks deserves to be the first recipient. Besides creating one of Philadelphia's most popular restaurants (the White Dog Café), her legacy includes Pennsylvania's local food movement, America's fastest growing network of independent businesses, and entrepreneurs worldwide—especially women—whom she has inspired to make business the leading edge of social change. In this riveting, funny, and moving autobiography, Judy also reveals herself as a superb storyteller and a sharp policy critic. Her life story, which unfolds from the Arctic to Chiapas, shows how one passionate person really can bend the arc of history toward justice."

—MICHAEL SHUMAN, author of *Local Dollars, Local Sense: How to Shift Your Money from Wall Street to Main Street and Achieve Real Prosperity*

"Judy Wicks's journey is potent medicine for a culture that falsely separates personal life and work, self and community, business and environment, and entrepreneurship and activism. Anyone who wants to engage their full entrepreneurial vision, and find their own unique path that may combine seemingly disparate goals, can take heart: this remarkable story is a visionary beacon and joyful read."

—NINA SIMONS, cofounder of Bioneers

"Judy Wicks is something rare, invaluable, and essential in our time: a visionary artisan of cultural renaissance. Read this book. Learn what she's done and, even more important, how she became who she is. Let her story inspire you more fully into your own cultural artistry."

—BILL PLOTKIN, author of *Soulcraft*

Good Morning,
Beautiful Business

Good Morning, Beautiful Business

The Unexpected Journey of an Activist
Entrepreneur and Local Economy Pioneer

❧ JUDY WICKS ☙

Chelsea Green Publishing
White River Junction, Vermont

Editor: Joni Praded
Project Manager: Patricia Stone
Copy Editor: Eric Raetz
Proofreader: Eileen Clawson
Indexer: Shana Milkie
Designer: Melissa Jacobson

Printed in the United States of America.
First printing February, 2013.
10 9 8 7 6 5 4 3 2 1   13 14 15 16 17

Our Commitment to Green Publishing
Chelsea Green sees publishing as a tool for cultural change and ecological stewardship. We
strive to align our book manufacturing practices with our editorial mission and to reduce the
impact of our business enterprise in the environment. We print our books and catalogs on
chlorine-free recycled paper, using vegetable-based inks whenever possible. This book may cost
slightly more because it was printed on paper that contains recycled fiber, and we hope you'll
agree that it's worth it. Chelsea Green is a member of the Green Press Initiative (www.green-
pressinitiative.org), a nonprofit coalition of publishers, manufacturers, and authors working to
protect the world's endangered forests and conserve natural resources. *Good Morning, Beautiful
Business* was printed on FSC®-certified paper supplied by Maple Press that contains at least 30%
postconsumer recycled fiber.

Library of Congress Cataloging-in-Publication Data
Wicks, Judy.
  Good morning, beautiful business : the unexpected journey of an activist entrepreneur and
local economy pioneer / Judy Wicks.
     p. cm.
  Includes index.
  ISBN 978-1-933392-24-0 (pbk.)—ISBN 978-1-60358-499-9 (ebook)—
ISBN 978-1-60358-505-7 (hardcover)
  1. Wicks, Judy. 2. Restaurateurs—Pennsylvania—Philadephia. 3. White Dog Cafe
(Philadelphia, Pa.) 4. Community development—Pennsylvania—Philadephia. I. Title.

TX910.5.W47A3 2013
647.95092—dc23
[B]
                              2012043523

Chelsea Green Publishing
85 North Main Street, Suite 120
White River Junction, VT 05001
(802) 295-6300
www.chelseagreen.com

MIX
Paper from
responsible sources
FSC® C068106

For my children, Grace and Lawrence

And in memory of their father,
Neil Schlosser

Contents

When the power of love overcomes the love of power,
then we'll have peace.

—Jimi Hendrix

Preface

It was 1983 when I first opened the doors to the White Dog Café on Philadelphia's Sansom Street, then a collection of somewhat run-down row houses that had just been saved from demolition by its residents, including me. From the first time I saw the Street, some ten years earlier, it had captured my imagination. Its lively sidewalks and graceful if neglected buildings invited me. Its characters fascinated me. It was a place that I had found myself lying down in front of a bulldozer to save. Yet even as I lay spread-eagle on the pavement and wondered just how close the huge earth-moving machine would come, I hadn't remotely suspected that Sansom Street would become the epicenter of my life. Or that the act of saving our community from destruction to make way for a mall of chain stores would become a lifelong passion.

I would have been as surprised as anyone to learn that I would someday start a restaurant there and raise my family in a home above it. And I would have been even more surprised to learn that the restaurant would gain international acclaim as a socially responsible business serving farm-fresh local food, take me to political hot spots around the world, and play a powerful role in building what has come to be known as the local living economy movement.

Even by the time I was adjusting the blue-and-white checkered curtains and welcoming my first customer, I felt like a more-or-less accidental restaurateur. As a girl, I had vowed never to cook, and as a young college grad I had eschewed the concept of profit. But I was absorbed by the challenge of creating an outstanding restaurant on the block I had helped to save and intrigued at the prospect that it could be used as a meeting place for the community and a vehicle for good works.

Perhaps that's why, several years after I opened my restaurant, I hung a sign in my bedroom closet in my home above the White Dog Café—right where I would see it each morning. Good morning, beautiful business, it read, reminding me daily of just how beautiful business can be when we put our creativity, care, and energy into producing a product or service that our community needs. I was just beginning my journey. I didn't know then what I do now: that when you connect head and heart in business, you can transform not just business as usual, but the economy in general. You can find a way to make economic exchange one of the most satisfying, meaningful, and loving of human interactions.

The sign would stay there for the next fifteen years and would often make me think of my own business, and how the farmers were already out in the fields harvesting fresh organic fruits and vegetables to bring into the restaurant that day. I would think of Judy Dornstreich picking rose geraniums at Branch Creek Farm and how she once told me that when she picked it, she would imagine our pastry chef James Barrett making rose geranium pound cake for our dessert menu. I would think of the farm animals out in the pastures—pigs, cows, goats, chickens—enjoying each other's company in the warm morning sun and fresh air. And I would think of Dougie Newbold, the goat herder, who claimed that when she kissed her goats' ears it made their cheese better. And I'm sure that's true.

I would think of our bakers coming in early in the morning to put bread and pastries into the oven for our customers to enjoy that day, and of our property manager, Long Pham, who for over twenty years arrived before daybreak to make repairs and oversee cleaning before our guests arrived. And I would remember the Zapatistas down in Chiapas, Mexico, growing the organic coffee beans for my morning cup.

Business, I learned, is about relationships. Money is simply a tool. What matters most are the relationships with everyone we buy from, sell to, and work with—and our relationship with Earth itself. My business was the way I expressed my love of life, and that's what made it a thing of beauty.

The world, though, isn't always a beautiful place. Not yet, anyway. There is a news photo of a little girl that not only proves that point, but also still haunts me. Though I saw it years ago, I vividly recall how vulnerable she looked in a tattered pink dress, standing on a garbage dump in Haiti, looking for food. The image hovered above a front-page *New York Times* article telling of a global food crisis, and speculating about the causes for the rise in food prices that had left this little girl and millions like her hungry. Was it the drought in Australia? Or the diversion of corn to ethanol in the United States? Or the increase in meat eating in China? I read the whole article and found no mention whatsoever about the failure of the industrial global food system itself.

The year was 2007, and by then it had become clear to me that to rescue that vulnerable little girl from hunger or, worse yet, abuse and exploitation, we would need to do far more than examine a few episodic causes here and there. We would need to change our failed economic system from one dominated by transnational corporations to one based on local self-reliance—one in which the inevitable fluctuation of prices in the global marketplace would have little effect.

Ideas like that were still far from making it to the front pages of major dailies. But a growing network of people around the world were showing how building strong local economies—rather than relying on transnational ones—could empower communities to feed, clothe, and care for their children and meet the basic needs of all their people. And the effort wasn't just to end hunger or rein in poverty or challenge corporate power. No, ultimately, building local food, water, and energy security provides the foundation for lasting world peace.

This book is the story of how I arrived at that conclusion—from growing up in a small town, to a short but unforgettable experience living with indigenous people, and most of all to creating, over the course of twenty-five years, the White Dog Café. It's also the story of where that café led me as I worked with others to build a local food system and then a whole new local economy for our community. It's about how I finally joined with my colleagues across North America in an effort to help relocalize economies and enliven communities across the nation and around the world.

But it is also the story of my own awakening from a girl who denied all things feminine, and refused to wear pink, to a businesswoman who found strength in her feminine energy—a quality that's available to both men and women. I used that energy to build caring business relationships, make heart-based decisions, cooperate with my competitors, and ultimately work collaboratively to build a compassionate and caring economy.

I started my work to build that new economy in the year 2000 with the simple premise that an environmentally, socially, and financially sustainable global economy must be comprised of sustainable local economies. Rather than a global economy dominated by mammoth, and often unnecessary, transnational corporations, I envisioned a global economy as an intricate network of small-to-small, win-win business relationships connecting communities that were self-reliant for their basic needs.

A year later, I cofounded the Business Alliance for Local Living Economies, known as BALLE. If you are wondering just what a "living" economy is, it's one that supports three areas of life—healthy natural life, vibrant and culturally unique community life, and long-term and just economic life. Examine a thriving local living economy and you'll find a multitude of locally owned, human-scale businesses committed to the health of their community and their ecosystem. They produce basic needs locally, export the surplus, import—through fair-trade practices—goods not available locally, and develop products unique to their region for exchange in the global marketplace—be it a fashion design, fine wine or cheese, artwork, entrepreneurial innovation or any of the many other things that celebrate what it is to be human.

This book is more than a memoir. It is a survival manual. It is certainly not about a utopian dream. Rather it is about solving deep problems unique to our time—and the need is urgent. Today, we are confronted with crises the world has never faced before: a depleted natural environment no longer able to sustain our materialistic society; increasingly severe and erratic weather brought on by global warming; a declining oil supply that will likely, in time, make global transport prohibitively expensive—if burning the oil does not destroy us first. There is growing wealth inequity; an American political system increasingly controlled by corporate interests; and escalating global violence, social upheaval, and environmental destruction over control and extraction of the remaining oil, freshwater, and other natural resources. It doesn't have to be this way.

I imagine a future where the little girl in the pink dress is in a different photograph. She's smiling over an abundant meal of organic locally grown food seated along with the rest of the world's happy people at what I've come to call the Table for Six Billion (or maybe seven or eight). And where are the transnationals who claim we need their mono-crops, fossil-fuel-based pesticides and fertilizers, genetically modified seeds, cruel animal factories, and long-distance transport to feed the world? They are not in the photograph. Turns out we didn't need them after all.

This book is both a love story and a business book. It's about a love of life, nature, animals, community, and unique local culture, a love of good food and family farms, and a love of democracy—all being threatened by a global economic system driven by profit. It's also about a deep love of business, and how we can embrace a way of doing business that is beautiful, that nurtures all that we cherish, and that furthers the creation of a whole new economic system based on caring relationships.

Though this new economy is global in vision, my story and the story for each of us begins right at home in our own community—and with our own capacity to recognize and protect what we truly care about.

I have always loved a window, especially an open one.
—Wendell Berry

❈ I ❈
My First Place:
Growing up in Ingomar

I BUILT MY FIRST FORT when I was nine. I called it a fort because I made it from upright logs like a Western fort in the cowboy movies. Each spring I dismantled the last year's fort and built a more elaborate version, a process that went on every year until I went off to college. I continued to call them my forts even though I abandoned logs as a building material and began using discarded boards salvaged from around the neighborhood, often scraps left over from the new houses popping up in the open fields at the outskirts of Ingomar, the small town where I grew up in western Pennsylvania. Every year for my birthday in May, beginning when I turned ten, I asked for a bag of nails and a roll of tar paper, then headed for the woods with my new supplies, along with a hammer and saw, to begin a new fort.

I have always had a strong sense of place. Much of this book, though not all of it, is about a place in Philadelphia—the 3400 block of Sansom Street where I lived, worked, created a business, and helped build and maintain a community. I cared for that place for almost forty years. But other places came first.

I chose my first place in the woods behind the house I grew up in, where we moved in 1953 when I was six. Walking across our sunny yard and stepping into the shady woods that bordered it was like entering a magical world—one of adventure and imagination where anything was possible. When my father, Jack Wicks, cleared a field for our family's house to be built, he stacked the small trees he had cut down, largely slender sassafras and sapling oaks a few inches in diameter, into a big pile on the edge of the woods. One day, while playing on the stack of wood, I thought what a good fort the logs would make.

I found a place in the woods where there were four medium-sized trees growing about six feet apart in a square. Then I sawed four saplings into seven-foot lengths and lashed them to the trees horizontally to form a square outline of the fort about five feet high.

As my pet beagle, Peppy, looked on, I began sawing more saplings for the walls. My light brown hair pulled back from my freckled face was braided into pigtails hanging down my back just past my shoulders. Sawing the saplings was slow going, especially with the thicker pieces, so I recruited my first employee, a neighborhood boy about eight years old, to take the other side of a two-man saw I found in Dad's toolshed. With much effort, we cut the saplings for the sides and lashed them upright to the horizontal bars, first digging a trench in the ground to hold the bases in place. After that, I found discarded lumber in my neighbor's backyard and built a roof, leaving a hole for a hatch door on the top.

One reason I had chosen this spot for my fort was that there was an oak tree nearby that had cracked in the middle—perhaps struck by lightning or snapped by a windstorm—so that the top, still partially attached to the trunk, had fallen over to form a giant arch. It was under the arch that I built my fort. While I was just finishing the roof, some boys came by who lived behind our woods and teased me, telling me how they had built a far better playhouse in their woods with large windows on all four sides made with real glass, while my fort had no windows at all.

When I came up to the woods the next day, I was crushed to find that the large broken tree branch that arched over my fort had been pushed over onto the roof, smashing it in. I knew right away that the boys had done this and raced through our woods and into theirs, my sneakers pounding along the dirt path with Peppy and my pigtails flying behind. I found the playhouse they had bragged about, picked up a big stick, and smashed all the windows to smithereens. I ran home and never heard from them again.

As my forts developed, I would add more touches, laying a brick path leading up to the entrance and planting flowers along it. Occasionally, I found a treasure to add amenities to my forts—linoleum flooring left over from kitchen remodeling and large metal pulleys from a junkyard that I used to raise a sliding door. Inside, I took great care in making comfortable places to sit, and hanging pictures and curtains—just the sort of thing, it turned out, one might do in a restaurant. When it rained for the first time, I would sit in my finished fort and feel very proud if the roof didn't leak.

But once the fort was built and weather tight, I didn't actually spend much time playing inside. It was much more fun to ride bikes or hike down to the creek to hunt salamanders and crayfish. What was fascinating to me was the process of building—imagining something in my head and then making it happen.

One day, while working on what must have been my third or fourth fort, when I was twelve or thirteen years old, I felt a strange wetness "down there." I went to the house and in the bathroom was astonished to find a bright red stain on my underpants. At first I was in denial that I had gotten my period—that I was really a girl, something I always tried to forget—and went back up to the woods to keep building. Finally, I gave in and went back down to the house to tell my mom. She patiently fitted me with an elastic "sanitary belt" that held up a big white sanitary pad on metal hooks in the front and back. The pad felt so bulky and awkward between my legs, and it was humiliating to wear this contraption under my jeans. I went back up to the woods hoping that no one would come along and somehow know. I hammered the boards on my fort all the harder.

When I was twenty and a sophomore in college, it was in my fort that I made love for the first time with a young man who had been my boyfriend in fifth and sixth grade. Many years later, when I told a girlfriend about losing my virginity, she clarified: "You didn't lose anything, Judy. You invited him into your fort!"

After our college graduation, when my childhood sweetheart and I were married, I created a place for the ceremony where a favorite fort had once stood. I even had the organ from our church hauled up to the woods, where the organist complained of his fear of spiders, and the minister read a passage I had chosen from *Midsummer Night's Dream*. Dressed in a traditional white wedding gown, with our parents and family gathered around us, I married my first love in the place I loved most in the world.

Beyond the woods was a larger place I grew to know well—my hometown of Ingomar. Growing up in a small town was a great exposure to the way local businesses wove through community life. Across the street from Ingomar Elementary School, Marie's candy store was the favorite after-school destination, where we would stock up on treats like root beer barrels and cherry pop-cycles, my favorites. Marie didn't just sell candy. Peering through her thick glasses with eyes slightly cockeyed, she made sure each of us was polite, waited our turn, and threw our wrappers in the trash can.

In the same one-story building was the Ingomar post office, where Benny, the dad of the Benscoter kids, was the town postmaster. Next to the post office, along Ingomar Road, was Steve's Meat Market, where my mother and grandmother claimed they got the best cuts of steak, and where they always let Steve know how our Thanksgiving turkey compared with last year's.

Many of my friends' parents owned or worked in local businesses. I met Greg Otto in first grade, and his father's business, Otto Milk Company, delivered milk to our house in glass returnable bottles. Ray, our milkman, came right into our kitchen and checked our refrigerator to see how much milk and cream we needed, making sure Mom got the quart of buttermilk he knew she enjoyed. To make friends with family pets, Ray kept a pocketful of dog biscuits. My second dog, Pooie, also a beagle and a bit overweight, would be sure to get hers, and then follow Ray around the neighborhood, begging for more at every stop. Sometimes she would go hunting for treats on her own, and I once found her dragging a whole ham up our driveway—her stolen loot from an unsuspecting neighbor.

Small businesses were scattered through town, and one way or another I had a connection to all of them. My friend Peggy's dad was the town doctor, and the dad of my sister's friend owned Thomas's Service Station, the town's only filling station in the early years, where my parents had a charge account before the time of credit cards. The Steigerwald kids grew up on a farm on the outskirts of Ingomar raising pigs and chickens. Another close friend, Gail, who lived in a rural area farther away, had a summer job every year at her uncle's roadside farm stand selling fresh fruit from their orchard, starting the season with strawberries. Of course, we had no cell phones to keep up with the latest news about boyfriends and goings-on at the local swimming pool, so I would get newsy letters from Gail handwritten from the stand and covered with strawberry stains.

I had my first cherry coke, not the bottled version of today, but one mixed at the soda fountain, at Richie's Pharmacy on Harmony Drive near the intersection with Ingomar Road, our busiest corner—though not busy enough for a traffic light. Another close friend, Barb, got a job from Mr. Richie in high school. I thought it was so cool that she got to make the sodas, mixing the cherry and cola syrups and adding carbonated water. Barb could even get a peek at the adult magazines Mr. Richie kept behind the counter, so the younger kids couldn't get into them. After his retirement, Dad walked down to Richie's every morning and sat at the counter for a cup of coffee to talk sports and trout fishing with other retirees, who each had a mug hanging with their own name on it.

Across Harmony Drive from Richie's was the Ingomar Fire Hall where the dads who worked in the town's small businesses made up the volunteer fire department. On special occasions, the fire engine was moved out and the hall was used for square dances, Halloween costume parties, wedding receptions, and Ingomar's very first rock 'n' roll dance. Next to the fire hall was the beer distributor, where the favorites were Iron City from Pittsburgh and Rolling Rock from nearby Latrobe. Down Harmony Drive on the other side of Ingomar Road was Joe Heinregle's grocery store where I often went with my mom to do the weekly shopping. Mr. Heinregle knew all his customers by name and threw an annual Christmas party for the whole town.

Like most women in my hometown, my mom, Betty Wicks, was a homemaker during my growing-up years, though when I went off to college she returned to teaching third grade to help with my tuition. It was through her work in community service that Mom became my role model for what came later in my career. A great outdoorswoman, she was leader of our town's Girl Scout troop and the director of our summer day camp. She led us on camping and white-water canoe trips into the wilds, teaching us how to build a fire and pitch a tent, how to fend for ourselves and how to work in a group. I watched as she conducted the morning program at camp and organized work assignments for each unit, always with fairness and enthusiasm.

Mom and Dad were nature lovers and enjoyed the out-of-doors. They took our family on many camping trips, including expeditions to a remote Canadian island they had first discovered before I was born. Using a map and compass, Dad navigated the motorboat with a chain of canoes strung behind carrying our gear and family members, including my younger siblings, Diane and John, as well as my aunt, uncle, and six cousins. Mom did the planning for our trips, packing supplies for two weeks and cooking meals for thirteen people over the campfire.

When it came to cooking, campfire cooking was the only form I would take part in because it was not sissy stuff. While growing up, I much preferred to play in the woods than cook in the kitchen. Even though I would not be caught dead showing an interest in homemaking, I learned the importance of good food from my mother and grandmothers.

Bringing people together around food was a tradition for the whole family. As far back as I can remember Mom and Dad entertained with summer picnics on the patio, campfire sings up in the woods, and their monthly Friday night Hungry Club, a potluck dinner tradition they formed with close friends the year I was born, 1947. Visiting my maternal grandmother Grace Scott, in Winter Haven, Florida, I remember her most in the kitchen, cooking up big meals for our family, sometimes of fresh fish she had caught in the lake and always with the favorite home-baked sticky buns that she constantly nibbled. By comparison, my paternal grandmother, Eleanor Wicks, whom I called Nana, was much more formal though no less social. She set the perfect table at the many elegant dinner parties she hosted in her big house in Pittsburgh, where she would ring a small crystal bell to summon the maid. It was from Nana that I learned to appreciate the details of fine service.

My mother took interest not only in creating tasty meals, but also in providing the maximum nutritional value, using books like *Let's Cook It Right* by the popular nutritionist Adelle Davis. Mom and Dad planted a good-sized family garden every year, which they tended faithfully, while I always managed to take off on my bike rather than help with the weeding—though I did enjoy picking tomatoes, beans, squash, and corn from the garden, which Mom would use for dinner that very night throughout the season.

On special occasions, Mom made her namesake dish, Betty's shish kebabs—skewers of marinated beef, fresh tomatoes, peppers, and onions that Dad grilled over charcoal. Nana was an excellent pie baker, with flakey crusts holding a fresh fruit filling—strawberry, cherry, peach, blueberry, or apple—as each came into season. When she arrived at our house with her pie basket, I could not wait to find out what kind of pie was inside. Her strawberry pie, made every June, was a recipe Mom and later my cousins all kept in their recipe boxes. I got a kick out of whipping the cream and plopping big snow-white spoonfuls onto the bright red fruit of the open-faced pie.

Even in winter we enjoyed frozen and jarred homegrown vegetables. I remember how Mom and Nana spent the hottest days of summer in the kitchen jarring applesauce and stewed tomatoes and making jams and jellies. I was curious to watch as they lifted large sacks of cheesecloth dripping with dark juice from big pots, straining preserves all made from fresh fruits bought at the local farmers markets. A special treat at the market was ice cream made from seasonal fruits. I longed for peaches to ripen, so I could have my favorite—fresh peach ice cream.

By the time cold weather came, our freezer was chock-full of vegetables from the family garden and frozen fruit pies that we hadn't already gobbled up during the summer. Glass Mason jars of canned foods lined the shelves in our storage room and would last us through the winter season, until Nana made the first pie of the spring—fresh rhubarb—and Mom would serve fresh local asparagus, which usually arrived in time for Easter dinner.

Back then, it came naturally to enjoy fresh produce just when it was in season rather than eating the same fruits and vegetables all year shipped in from South America. Except for cold-stored apples, fresh fruit was mostly citrus in the winter when it came into season in Florida. I can remember my excitement as a child when we returned home from the train station carrying a big crate my maternal grandfather, Armor Scott, the vice president of a citrus nursery, had shipped from Florida. On the floor in the kitchen we would open the crate, and the smell of Florida oranges filled our house as though the warm air of the South had blown our way.

Many of the fathers in Ingomar commuted the fifteen miles into Pittsburgh to work each day, including my dad, who was a lawyer, like his father before him. Dad picked up things in the city that we couldn't find in Ingomar, and I remember jumping for joy at age eleven when he arrived home with my very first record, one I had asked him to find for me—a single 45 called "I Got Stung by a Sweet Honey Bee" by Elvis Presley.

Twice a year, in the spring and fall, Mom and Nana would take my sister Diane and me into Pittsburgh to shop for clothes at two family-owned department stores, Horne's and Kaufmann's. These stores were almost an extension of Ingomar to us because of the personal relationships we had there. Nana knew all the saleswomen by name, and they guided us to the style of clothes they knew we preferred. If something didn't fit exactly right, Nana had alterations made, and I stood up on a riser and turned slowly around while the seamstress at the department store pinned my hem to the right length.

Mom was an excellent seamstress herself, and each fall made a few new school outfits for Diane and me. When I couldn't find the dress of my dreams for the senior prom, she made me a gown just as I described to her with a blue satin top and a layered white lace skirt.

I was raised a patriotic American by my parents and by Ingomar. On the Fourth of July, I woke up to the sound of Dad playing John Philip Sousa marches, which he blasted out through the front door for the whole neighborhood to hear. Leaping out of bed, I dressed up in red, white, and blue clothes and hurried outside. With the American flag held high, I marched around the yard to "The Stars and Stripes Forever" while Diane and John followed along, banging on pots and pans.

My father had been a naval officer during World War II, serving as captain of a patrol boat in the Pacific, where he rescued downed pilots. Like most kids growing up in the 1950s, I thought the United States was the best and bravest country in the whole world. I believed that ever since defeating the Nazis and Japanese, our government had been defending the world from the communists. During air raid drills in elementary school, we students were instructed to hide under our desks in case of a nuclear attack by the Soviets, which gave us the clear impression that the communist nation, and anyone who sided with them, was our enemy. I was proud to be anticommie like the rest of Ingomar and was convinced that my country was a generous one that went around the world bringing democracy and providing aid to help other peoples.

Like many small towns, the Ingomar of my childhood changed over time, swallowed up by suburban sprawl. When I was in high school, shopping centers began to spring up along the highway between Ingomar and Pittsburgh. The Northway Mall opened up with great fanfare as one of the first malls in the country, and next door our first McDonald's soon appeared. I was excited by the new developments and was drawn to fast-food and chain stores at the mall where we teenagers began to hang out. At the time, like most others in Ingomar, I saw all this as an improvement over small town life. After all, I could find the latest fashions and buy my own records without relying on a trip to the city with my parents.

As the farms, woods, and fields surrounding Ingomar, where I hiked and rode my girlfriend's horse, gave way to housing plans, the stores in town gave way to malls. The first to go was the hardware store on Ingomar Road with a big front porch and wide wooden steps, where the men used to gather on Saturday afternoons. Before the malls arrived, I thought of business owners as neighbors and parents, who helped keep an eye on us kids, and who sponsored the scout troops, the Little League, and the annual fireman's parade and carnival. Those days lasted long enough for me to become aware of the many ways that local businesses helped create a sense of place, local identity, and a feeling of belonging for all the townspeople. Though I lived in a typical small town, I was a kid from Ingomar—and that was a place like no other.

During the time I grew up in the 1950s and 1960s, a career in business was not even considered for girls, at least not in the small towns where I attended high school and college. I certainly never gave a thought to being a businessperson. Yet from a young age, I continually created primitive forms of business to attract and entertain the other kids in the neighborhood.

I had just turned six when my family moved into our new house with a big front lawn on Woodland Road, a quiet lane on the edge of town. On the first day in my new community, I collected all the extension cords I could find and connected them down the driveway where I set up my little child-sized dining table with two chairs and plugged in my toy record player. Turning the volume up full blast to play "How Much Is That Doggy in the Window?" I sat down at the table to see who might come along. At last I spotted a neighborhood boy about my age walking up the road and watched expectantly as he neared our house. I still remember the glee I felt when Johnny Baker stopped, hesitated, and finally turned up our driveway, walking slowly toward me in his pigeon-toed oversize sneakers to take a seat at my table. Though I hadn't yet any food to serve, he was my first restaurant customer.

Another early "start-up" involved making paintings on scraps of wood I'd collected, and selling them from my wagon along Ingomar Road. My first store! Making money was not always part of the plan. I simply enjoyed using whatever resources I could find to create something of value and have some fun doing it.

Each summer I converted our garage into a theatre, making stage curtains with the matching twin bedspreads from the room I shared with Diane. My younger siblings and the other neighborhood kids were the actors in the skits I wrote and directed, with silly titles like *The Day Dirty Dan Bumped Off Grandma*. We invited the mothers in the neighborhood, all stay-at-home moms, and sat them in chairs we dragged from the house out onto the driveway. Between the chairs, I set up folding tray stands to hold their glasses of ice tea and ashtrays (yes, in those dark days, most moms and dads smoked).

When I was in junior high, I built a five-hole miniature golf course in the woods near my fort, with a maze of ramps, tunnels, and hills, using emptied frozen orange juice cans to line the tunnels and holes. I so enjoyed being in the woods, working with the moist soil hidden under layers of fallen leaves on the forest floor. I breathed in the rich earthy smell as I formed the soil into valleys and hills, packing it flat so the balls would roll smoothly on its dark surface. I was so excited to witness the fun the miniature golf course provided the neighborhood kids—the same excitement I would relish years later in creating events for the customers and employees in my restaurant.

The freedom my parents gave me growing up allowed me the opportunity to do my own thing—to concoct a plan in my mind and make it happen without the help of adults. I have no doubt that this freedom to create at an early age has carried through my whole life, and as I grew older actualizing my ideas into real life led to larger and larger projects.

There was nothing I enjoyed more than creating a charming place where people liked to gather—from the miniature golf course, to the summer plays, to the forts I continued to build in the woods.

The older I got, the more often I ran into disappointments because I was a girl who had interests and abilities that presumably were only fit for boys. I longed to take wood shop in school to learn how to use different building tools to improve my forts and design new projects, but to my dismay girls were not permitted. I'm sure there were boys in my class who would have rather cooked than hammer nails, while I was required to take home economics. Stubbornly, I swore I would never learn to cook.

My passion for baseball brought my biggest disappointment. Growing up in western Pennsylvania, I was a Pittsburgh Pirates fan, and I decorated my room with pictures of the players and kept their batting averages posted on my wall. Dad played on his college baseball team, and though I was a girl, he taught me to play. I earned money selling greeting cards door-to-door to buy my very own baseball mitt, signed by Dick Groat, shortstop for the Pirates and my favorite player.

One eventful morning in fifth grade, our gym teacher announced, "It's the first warm day of spring—time to start softball practice." I jumped out of my chair with great excitement, ready to go. Then I heard, "Boys, down to the field. Girls, go over there somewhere and practice cheerleading." I couldn't believe my ears! How could this be? I was dumbfounded, but too shy to object. Of course, nowadays the teacher would be sued, but back then it was the way things were.

I refused to cheerlead and just stood dejectedly behind the backstop watching the boys play, and looking down on myself and the other girls simply for being female. I thought to myself, *Girls are losers. Boys play the important roles, and girls just stand by to cheer them on.* My sense of self seemed to evaporate. The experience hit me hard but was an important lesson in understanding the destructive effects of discrimination. It also taught me how the whole community loses when some are left out. After all, I really was a good ballplayer, and the team would have been better, I was sure, if I had been allowed to play.

There was one person who saw the importance of allowing girls to play—the janitor at Ingomar Elementary School, Joe Bullick. At recess, he organized a softball game that included the girls. Though it did not make up for the gym class exclusion, it helped me see that there were possibilities, that other men along with my own father saw things differently, and that I was important to them. When I graduated from grade school, I collected money from the kids in my class. At the jewelry store at the mall, I dumped a jar of coins onto the glass counter and bought Joe a watch. On graduation day, I told my teacher that I wanted to present a gift on behalf of our class. She assumed it was for the school principal, but when I got up on the stage I asked Joe the janitor to come up and gave him the watch and a big hug.

Joe went on to become the supervisor of maintenance for the whole school district and started the first girl's softball team at Ingomar Junior High, and later a girl's golf team. In time, under Joe's coaching, the Ingomar girl's softball team became state champions. (Joe came to my sixtieth birthday party, and around the campfire we told our intertwined life stories of being an inspiration to each other. And he still has the watch!)

But unfortunately, there were other times that confirmed the treatment I received from the gym teacher on the softball field. In seventh grade I won a second prize in the Ingomar Junior High Science Fair. I had always enjoyed mechanical things and was good at putting them together. I invented a device using my little brother's Erector Set. A series of pulleys attached to an electric motor in the back of my display made several arrows move around in circles to demonstrate the process of evaporation and precipitation in a papier-mâché landscape that I had molded from newspaper. It had not occurred to me that girls did not play with Erector Sets, nor that we were thought to be clueless when it came to mechanical things, so I was taken aback when my science teacher questioned me about whether my father or brother had helped me with my project. I explained that my brother was only seven years old and that while it was his Erector Set, he had not yet used it, and that I had done the project without anyone's help.

The story doesn't end there. During the science fair, when all the parents came to view the exhibits and celebrate the winners, a classmate came running to find me, saying that my teacher had sent for me because my science project was broken. I went straight there. A crowd had gathered around my project with its big red ribbon, where my teacher stood with a "gotcha" sneer on his face. I opened up the back of my exhibit to find that someone had taken the bands off the pulleys. I quickly put them back into place and started the motor again. My teacher looked stunned and then very sheepish. I could just tell from his face that he had done it and what he had been thinking—that because I was a girl, he couldn't believe I had built the project myself and assumed I must have been lying.

Even before these disappointments, I shunned things feminine as sissy stuff. I even ran away in third grade because my mother wanted me to wear a dress one day a week instead of my favorite flannel-lined jeans with suspenders, leather fringe jacket, and cowgirl boots. But after the experience of being excluded from softball, my negative feelings grew stronger and I developed contempt for girls—I'd even go so far as to say self-contempt. I looked down on what I considered weakness in myself, in other girls, and also in boys—leading to an incident that I later came to regret.

I had a childhood friend, a boy around my age, maybe a year younger, who liked to dress up like a girl in our summer plays. I had enjoyed casting him as a comic ballerina dressed in a pink tutu and red wig. We had fun playing together with my sister, Diane—not only with the skits, but also with board games on rainy days and pestering his mother in the house across the street for a glass of punch they called Kick-a-Poo Joy Juice. One day when we were about twelve or thirteen, for no reason that I can remember, I started picking on him—punching him in the upper arm and taunting him, "What's the matter, sissy, you afraid to fight?" He moved across our lawn toward his house as I followed along, continuing my taunts and occasional jabs to his arm. He disappeared into his house and never came back to play.

I missed him. I felt ashamed of hurting someone I had perceived as less powerful. From that experience, I became conscious of how and when I used my power, careful not to take advantage of my size or age, and fascinated to observe how various people used power constructively or abused it.

As I grew older, I was able to see that my abusive behavior on that day was about scorning the part of myself that is vulnerable and soft. I didn't want to be a sissy. At the time, I didn't even want to be a girl because I saw girls as less worthy. To attack my friend was to attack that part of me. Today I understand that men or women who reject their feminine side, just as I had rejected mine, can be potent bullies—lashing out against women, children, animals, or boys and men who reveal their vulnerability—for the very same reason: a self-hatred of the softness within.

Age brought me other insights about power, as well, that would play out in the worldview that came to shape my business. One of those was that power comes with an obligation to protect and support those with less of it. That is a lesson I learned, as many do, by falling in love with an animal.

From the days when I played "How Much Is That Doggy in the Window?" on my toy record player as a six-year-old, I begged my parents for a dog. Three years later, perhaps as a substitute for the buckets and tubs of snakes, crayfish, and salamanders I kept in my bedroom, my parents consented to getting a dog and we picked out Peppy from a litter of beagles. He followed me everywhere while I built my forts and explored the woods, and I learned to feed and care for him. When ants got into his dog food dish, I made a moat by pouring water in a pie pan placed under his dish. Unfortunately, unlike most beagles and likely caused by a birth defect that caused him pain, Peppy had a short temper at times, usually when kids I didn't like much were around. After he bit a few of them, the police told my parents we had to have him put to sleep. I cried for him almost every night until I grew up and left for college, even after my parents brought home a second beagle puppy.

In sixth grade, I wrote a story about the last time I saw Peppy. When the teacher asked me to read it to the class, I was astonished that my story made the kids cry. Some time around then, I received a solicitation in the mail. I still don't know how they got the name of a ten-year-old, but it was a powerful message that has lasted to this day. The solicitation was from an antivivisection society, and it showed a photograph of a beagle, just like Peppy, strapped down on an operating table. I sent in my allowance and have been a contributor ever since after learning that beagles are the most commonly used dog in medical research and consumer product testing, where they suffer needlessly.

After being kept off the softball team because I was a girl, it really took me till my thirties to begin recognizing and honoring the nurturing qualities in others and myself, and to stop buying into the "stiff upper lip" approach to success in the business world. Eventually, I came to realize that the feminine qualities I often tried not to reveal as a child and youth were the very qualities most needed in building a more caring economy in today's world. But first I had to learn to value those qualities in myself.

Most of us have had the experience of being left out of something we wanted to do, feeling separated and marginalized because of our class, race, age, gender, sexual orientation, or cultural background—or for our lack of knowledge or money. Overcoming such experiences to value our gifts, to find our true purposes, and to believe in ourselves can take a long time—as it did for me. Later in life, I came to see how important diversity was to the strength of any group of people, as it is in nature. Society is weakened when feminine energy is repressed in men and women both, and when people, whoever they are, are excluded for their differences rather than given the opportunity to contribute their unique gifts. Finding a way for everyone to play the game became an important part of my business philosophy.

But back in fifth grade, when I was rejected on the softball field, I accepted my fate. Like most other girls raised in the 1950s, it became clear to me that since girls couldn't play ball, the next best thing was to marry the best ballplayer. I picked my future husband that day in fifth grade. Dick Hayne was the pitcher and a great hitter, too—an unusual combination of skills. From the ball field, I went back to my desk in the classroom, crossed *Judy Wicks* off my tablet, and wrote *Mrs. Richard Hayne* all over the cover.

Twelve years later, my childhood fantasy became reality—I married my fifth-grade sweetheart and became Mrs. Richard Hayne.

Jensen: Does the universe then have a purpose?
Berry: The purpose is simply existence. And the
glory of existence. That's the ultimate
purpose of everything—existence and
self-delight in existence.

—Derrick Jensen interviewing
Thomas Berry in *Listening to The Land*

❧ 2 ❧
A Culture of Sharing:
Life with the Eskimos

THE WAR IN VIETNAM was raging when Dick and I graduated
from college in the spring of 1969 and married that summer in the
woods behind my house in our hometown of Ingomar. I had lost
my John Philip Sousa patriotism. No longer did I believe that the
United States was always right. Dick's college deferment from the
draft ended on graduation day. If we didn't find a draft deferrable
job, he could end up in Vietnam, a war we both strongly opposed.

We thought of joining the Peace Corps, which would have
solved the problem, but the admissions process was lengthy, so
we signed up for the domestic alternative—Volunteers in Service
to America (VISTA)—and requested an assignment to a large
eastern city. I had long dreamed of living in a big city, after
growing up in Ingomar. But the government assigned us to an
Indian reservation in the Midwest instead and sent us for training

in Oregon. During our orientation, our class of several hundred volunteers was asked if a married couple among us was willing to serve in a remote Eskimo village in Alaska for a year. *Why not?* we thought. It turned out that Dick and I were the only ones to raise our hands. So after our training—which included a grueling three-day wilderness backpacking trip to weed out the fainthearted, with one night when we were each left on a chilly mountaintop alone without a tent, sleeping bag, or any supplies other than one pack of matches—we were sent to Chefornak, Alaska, population 120. Not exactly the big city I had dreamed of.

There were no roads leading to this isolated village perched on the bank of the Kinia River not far from the Bering Sea, a town far smaller and more remote than Ingomar ever was. The nearest airport, hospital, and phone were all a hundred miles away in a town to the northeast—Bethel, population 1,600. In summer, boats could navigate the rivers, and in winter the dogsleds made the hazardous journey across the unmarked, frozen tundra. We traveled as passengers on the mail plane that carried supplies and letters from Bethel to the scattered Eskimo villages of southwestern Alaska. The river served as the runway, where the planes used pontoons in the summer and skis after freeze-up.

Our ride to Chefornak in the mail plane began with a harrowing takeoff from the river in Bethel, still unfrozen on an early September day. I sat next to the bush pilot with Dick behind me amid boxes and mailbags piled to the ceiling. As we roared across the water on pontoons, the plane struggled to lift off, its doors rattling as though they might fall away any minute. From the front seat, I watched the shore come closer and closer, and just as I thought we would surely run smack into the trees looming up ahead, the pilot suddenly cut the engine and headed back to the dock. He nonchalantly threw some boxes off the plane and tried again, this time with success as we lifted from the water and soared over the trees into the sky.

There was an air of the Old West about the rugged bush pilot. Just as the stagecoaches of frontier days served the scattered Western settlements, mail planes were the primary contact with the outside world for the remote Eskimo villagers, bringing a letter from a child in the Indian high schools of Oklahoma or Oregon, a sister who had married into another village, a son in California for National Guard training, or a spouse being treated in an Anchorage hospital.

As we looked down from the air, Chefornak was easy to miss. A wooden boardwalk running the length of the village from the schoolhouse at one end to a church at the other connected less than two dozen small houses. As we landed on the river and taxied to the dock, it seemed the whole village of 120 people came out to meet us. A new neighbor greeted us and showed us to our tiny one-room cabin, which was not much bigger than my childhood forts. Like all the other cabins, it was pieced together with old scraps of wood wrapped in tar paper and heated with an oil stove. The furnishings were as sparse as the landscape: a kitchen sink, a bed, and a little table with several chairs. There was no bathroom, no shower or bathtub, only an outhouse—a frightening thought considering the subzero temperatures to come. But I soon learned that it was only a place to dump what was called a "honey bucket" after it was used indoors.

The cabin's real surprise, though, was the thirty or so empty, giant-sized peanut butter jars stacked on the shelves lining the walls, apparently left by the volunteers that had spent the previous year there. I remember wondering just how anyone could eat so much peanut butter in one year. But I would soon feel the same craving for fat once the cold weather set in. At twenty-two, I still held to my home economics class rejection of cooking, but in Chefornak I made my first exception, quickly learning how to make bread in the oven of our iron-topped stove. Then Dick and I smeared thick slices with lots of peanut butter, jar after jar.

Following our active college days, the pace of village life initially felt painfully slow. Our VISTA projects teaching preschool and adult education took up only about twelve hours a week, and Dick's main project to help the men assemble new pre-fab housing did not begin until the spring. There was so little stimulus that I sometimes found myself sitting still and watching reruns of my life in my mind. The biggest diversion was the mail plane. In our first weeks, I was surprised to see how all the villagers dropped what they were doing and ran excitedly down to the river at the first sound of the motor's hum, rushing to be the first to point out the distant spot of the approaching plane in the sky. It was not long, though, before I joined the stampede down to the river and across the frozen ice to greet the plane along with them, eager for news from home.

Another diversion came in early fall, when most everyone would head to the river again, but for a different reason. For just a few days, the river ice was strong enough to hold people, but not too thick to cut through, so it was perfect for ice fishing. Dick and I tagged along and learned to fish with a circular rod that looked more like a mobile than a fishing implement, with strings to hold it from the top and several hooked lines dangling off it. The idea was to take the rod in one hand, lower it down through a hole cut just to its size, then yank it up. In the other hand we held a round net, also the size of the hole in the ice, waiting to scoop up the snagged fish. At that time of year, shad ran so thick under the ice that it was hard not to get any snagged on the hooks. We were amazed to see the piles of fish grow bigger and bigger next to the Eskimos as they snagged more and more, until each had caught hundreds, enough to last through the winter after drying over smoke. Struggling to get the hang of it, Dick and I finally caught a dozen or so shad before heading in out of the near-zero-degree cold.

Except for the ice fishing, where some of the best catches were made by women, most of the activities of the village were largely segregated during the day, with the men outside hunting, fishing, making repairs, taking steam baths, or hanging out someplace where the women weren't. The women stayed indoors visiting each other in groups, tending babies and young children while doing beadwork, sewing clothes, and weaving baskets from field grass. Naturally, I hung out with the women, especially Jane, who was my age and spoke English. Every day at her house we would talk over hot tea served with large soda crackers called "pilot bread" spread with jam as we kept our eye on her two young children. When I managed to weave a small basket, Jane teased me that it looked like a whiskey bottle.

One of my favorite times of the week was gathering in the house of Leon, the jolly postmaster, who was among the few adults who spoke English, which he learned while he was in California for tuberculosis treatment. A representative of each family sat on the floor of Leon's house while he passed out the mail, making jokes about what each letter or package contained. Joking was an art form among the Eskimos, and Leon was a master. I only wished I could have spoken the language to understand the roars of laughter as each letter was distributed, but I began to realize that most of his jokes were about sex.

He also found great humor in the little golden puppy that Dick and I had taken in and named Augeyak, the Eskimo word for star. Though most families had sled dogs, pets were rare. Every once in a while, thanks to a lone short-haired dog someone had brought to Chefornak long ago, a dog would be born without the thick coat needed to survive the harsh, often subzero winters chained outside—as the dogs in the village were. Augie, as we came to call him, was one of those, and we had taken him in to make the place seem a little more like home. When I brought him out to the mail gatherings, I kept him nestled in the front of my parka. Leon thought it hysterical that a dog would be held against the breast and took great delight in calling Augie my "baby." "Won't your husband provide you with a real baby?" he would tease me.

It snowed almost daily, and the strong winds blew drifts that covered our little house. When we opened our door in the morning we were greeted by a wall of white. We dug ourselves out each day and cleared our one window to let in the scarce light. I gradually adjusted to the pace and spent hours examining patterns of frost on the window and sitting outside in my down parka stirring a container of condensed milk and sugar, delighted that it would turn into ice cream in the frigid temperature. Sometimes it was so cold that Augie's water bowl on the floor of our cabin would freeze. Our bed was up on stilts to bring us as close to the ceiling as possible, the warmest place in the cabin.

But I couldn't quite leave the world I knew behind me. During the long, dark days of the Arctic winter, when daylight was only a dusklike gray haze at noontime, I recognized my attachment to technology. For only two hours a day we had something wonderful called electricity. I had never realized my dependence on electricity until I went twenty-two hours a day without it. Despite my pleasant times drinking tea with the women, I found myself waiting in eager anticipation for those two gleeful hours.

In the late afternoons, I prepared for the moment in early evening when the electricity would come on. I found a toy record player among the preschool supplies and each day set it up on the table and plugged it in. There was only one record, left by past volunteers. I placed it on the tiny, motionless turntable, set the needle on the edge, and turned the volume knob to high. A little radio sitting silently on the shelf above me was set on the only station we could pick up—a Soviet one from across the Bering Sea. That volume knob also was set to high. In the stillness, I sat at my table by candlelight, staring at the bare lightbulb hanging above me, waiting for it to go on and listening intently for a distant sound.

At last I heard it—the faint sputter of a motor on the other side of the village, then a growling hum rising and falling, growing louder and faster, faster and louder as the generator picked up speed. The lightbulb began to flicker, the radio crackled, and the turntable slowly began to move. As the hum in the distance became a roar, the turntable gained speed, and Russian voices came from the radio. The distorted moaning from the record player grew into a voice I knew well. "Everybody, let's rock . . . dancin' to the Jailhouse Rock," belted the King. I jumped to my feet and danced about the cabin. If you're living in a remote Arctic village and you only have one record, *Elvis Presley's Greatest Hits* was the best I could imagine. I could hear the washing machine of my next-door neighbor, Maria, cranking up to wash the clothes of her six children. At that point in my life, I didn't think about where electricity came from—oil, nuclear power, hydroelectric dams. I wasn't aware and wouldn't have cared. I just wanted to enjoy it.

My family sent care packages on a regular basis, and a group of teenage girls would inevitably follow me home from the postman's house to see what had come. I opened a mild Swiss cheese my mother had sent, and the girls were repulsed, feeling nauseous at the smell and the very idea of aged milk. That was strange to me until the situation was reversed one day when the girls came into my cabin holding their hands over their mouths and giggling. "Whatever is the problem?" I asked. "Stink heads," they replied sheepishly. They had been eating stink heads, and knowing how the smell would offend me, were covering their mouths. "Stink heads" were made by stuffing the heads of raw fish into the extracted stomach of a seal, and then burying the tied bundle in the ground. After a few weeks, when the stink heads had become stinky enough, the delicacy was ready to eat. Rancid seal oil, a source of fat that was also aged in buried stomachs, was squirted on dried fish and on everything else, too. Much like catsup in the lower forty-eight, it was the favorite condiment in Chefornak.

"Seal party, seal party!" came the invitation, along with an eager knocking. Opening my cabin door, I was greeted by a wide grin encircled with fur. Maria, our next-door neighbor, had on her dress-up *kospok*, a colorful cotton dress worn over a long fur parka with a hood trimmed in fox fur. She beckoned me to follow, as she turned to join the other village women hurrying across the snow in sealskin boots (called *mukluks*) with pails swinging from mittened hands. Their festive *kospoks* were bright swatches of color against the pure white landscape, stretching flat and treeless to the distant horizon in all directions. I pulled on my *mukluks*, slipped on my *kospok* that Maria had made for me out of bright green corduroy sent by my mother, and joined the party.

A blue, cloudless sky domed over this speck of a village in early spring with the temperature barely above freezing. After winter temperatures as low as thirty-five below, the spring air felt warm and inviting. The Eskimo women gathered outside the doorway of a simple wooden cabin almost buried in snow, the home of Florence and George Billy, parents of my friend Jane. George had just caught his first seal of the season, a time for celebration. Tradition called for the wife to divide the meat among the families in the village, who in olden times would have had little left to eat at winter's end. Florence dropped a large slice of dark red seal meat and a chunk of blubber (another source of fat) into each of the women's pails. After the meat was distributed, the tradition was to hand out things the family had accumulated during the year that were not needed for survival, such as furs, fabrics, buttons, and canned goods. As a grand finale, small items like hard candies were tossed into the air. Laughing and cheering, moon-shaped faces shining up toward the sun, the women caught the prizes in the outstretched skirts of their *kospoks*. It was a form of wealth redistribution served out in buttons and bubble gum. I joined right in, hoping for my favorite—root beer barrels—and eager for merrymaking in the sunshine after the long, dark winter.

I had never seen anything like this kind of sharing. Ingomar was a warm and caring place. But in my society, what one earned belonged to the earner. Here, in Chefornak's indigenous culture, what was caught from nature's bounty belonged to everyone. Chefornak's subsistence economy was based on sharing, cooperation, and frugality.

If you admired something an Eskimo had, the person would give it to you. This meant I had to be careful with compliments. Once I said, "I really like your necklace," and an Eskimo woman took it off and handed it to me. The Eskimos of Chefornak had no concept of envy or ownership, giving freely what was desired—a dramatic contrast to the competitive consumer economy I had grown up with, one where advertising created envy in order to increase spending. Ads made women feel they had to buy another dress, or yet another shade of lipstick, to be attractive. Men had to have a new car or smoke a certain brand of cigarette, or they were made to feel inadequate. In this faraway land, free of television and the advertisements and billboards that proliferated in my environment at home, I began to understand more about how the values of my society were shaped. Along with other girls of my generation, the first to grow up watching television, I had been programmed to be a good consumer, moving on from my tomboy days to desire the clothes, body shape, and lifestyles of glamorous models. Here with the Eskimos, none of that mattered.

The Eskimos viewed hoarding as deviant, which by contrast made me realize how my own society rewarded greed. Rather than seeing it as destructive behavior, we actually admire those who hoard the most—those who use up the most natural resources on big houses, big cars, big wardrobes, and other accumulations of material wealth. The Chefornak Eskimos, on the other hand, valued people and nature more than possessions. That lesson was one that I would try to carry with me as I crafted my own life and business in later years. But other lessons that would shape my life still awaited me in Alaska, and one of those was about the power of community.

At the time we first arrived, Eskimo village life was still largely communal, with concern focused on the well-being of the group rather than on individual achievement. Traditionally nomadic, the Eskimos were lured by the government to settle in one place by a promise that the Bureau of Indian Affairs (BIA) would provide a school in each village to educate their children. Cultural differences became apparent when children shrank from the praise of white schoolteachers who rewarded good work with the proverbial star on the forehead to single out superior students, an embarrassment in the cooperative Eskimo society.

But just as I had seen change come to Ingomar, I saw it come to Chefornak even more starkly.

The Eskimos have a long oral tradition, and their history and culture had been passed down through storytelling in the Yupik language. But ever since the village had settled around the BIA schoolhouse some years ago, the younger generation from my age down now spoke English. Every Friday night an American movie was shown, and through these movies the Eskimos were educated in the lifestyles of Western culture. Already, one family had put in a wooden floor covered with linoleum, which they kept clean with Spic and Span, replacing the bare dirt floors that had provided the warmth of the earth. Rubber boots from Sears catalogs were replacing the cozy and warmer sealskin *mukluks* with inner soles of coiled field grass.

Cultural change was also creeping in as young Eskimo men joined the National Guard, as nearly all of them did, believing that they were protecting our shores from the Soviets across the sea. Returning to the village after basic training, they brought new habits that conflicted with village life—drinking; chain-smoking; swearing; and loud, boisterous talk, all of which were frightening to the girls. Like many indigenous people, Eskimos have a low physiological tolerance for alcohol. After some incidents when alcohol turned normally loving and peaceful people into abusers, the village voted to become "dry." But alcohol was still an occasional problem.

This hit me personally when a drunk driving a snowmobile purposely ran down Augie, snapping the tendon of a back leg so that it hung limp and useless. The closest veterinarian was in Anchorage, way too far to travel, so I took the mail plane back to Bethel and walked to the hospital, where I pleaded with a doctor to operate on my dog. A young physician about my age, stationed in Alaska to do community service, kindly agreed. I'll never forget the sight of Augie being wheeled down the hall to the operating room, unconscious under a white sheet. The operation was a success, and we left with a big cast on Augie's leg and instructions for how I would remove it back in the village, along with the stitches, when the leg healed.

Although there were different opinions in the village, the group now leading the village council felt their future lay in adapting to the white man's ways and forgetting about the culture of their ancestors. This was never clearer to me than when I was helping a group of teenage girls plan some events and educational projects. I suggested that they document the stories of the village elders in English and hold traditional Eskimo dances, but the village council denied permission to publish the stories and to hold traditional dances.

While some villagers were embarrassed about being Eskimo, there were still some who remained proud of their culture. But the tide was shifting to the West. With the money from jobs on fishing boats and canneries, an increasing number of village men were showing off the latest models of snowmobiles. When we arrived in the village only two families had snowmobiles, while the other eighteen families had dogsleds. When we left close to a year later, only one family still had a dogsled, and the rest were now dependent on gasoline-driven snowmobiles.

So much was changing so fast—dependency on gasoline, rubber boots and coats from the Sears catalogs, jobs in the global economy: Western culture had come to Chefornak right before my eyes. It seemed to me that as people began accumulating possessions, the feelings of competition and envy, once virtually unknown, became more common.

During the ten months I spent in the village, I witnessed the disintegration of a culturally beautiful, environmentally sustainable society that had lasted for thousands of years. For some of the villagers, this was welcomed progress, while others felt sadness and a loss of a way of life they cherished. One man, whose five children were among our favorite visitors, refused the Western ways and continued to live simply and cooperatively. When he went hunting or fishing, he would often share his catch with us, stopping by our cabin to drop off a duck or fish. During our stay, he became ill and lay on the table in his house, surrounded by his wife and children until he eventually died. I can't help but think that his death was in some way a refusal to live in a changing society that no longer practiced the values he upheld.

One day as the Eskimo girls watched me unpacking a box from home, I unwrapped a pair of pink satin slippers, a gift from Nana (who had not yet given up on making me a lady). I'll never forget how strange and out of place those slippers looked in my primitive cabin in Alaska. The shiny pink shimmered and glowed like the magical slippers of a princess from a faraway land. The girls *ooh*ed and *aww*ed over them. Because the slippers weren't appropriate for the weather and conditions, I told the girls I was putting them away. They looked disappointed and perhaps ashamed, and I suddenly realized they thought I was saying that their village was not good enough for the delicate pink slippers, where most of the houses still had dirt floors.

What could I say to explain to the girls how much more I appreciated the warm sealskin *mukluks* trimmed in beaver and beads that Maria had made for me than the silly pink slippers? How the simple earth floors in their homes were actually cleaner than white linoleum washed with cleaning products full of chemicals? How could I explain to them, as I felt even then, that the "pink slipper society" was destroying the earth and that we had to become more like them, not they like us? Yet I could not blame them for wanting to have things they saw in magazines and movies, things they admired and had never experienced. How could we deny them what we ourselves continued to use? I soon gave the pink slippers to one of the girls when she got engaged to be married, and she was tickled to have them.

Changes were also coming back home. While we were trudging through snowstorms in subzero temperatures halfway around the world, others of our generation were fighting and dying as soldiers in the tropical jungles of Vietnam. By this time, the draft system had ended the unfair deferment for college students and volunteers in community service programs such as ours and began a lottery system based on birthdays that treated all young men equally, whether or not they had the money to go to college or the connections to find deferments. Luckily for us, Dick's birthday drew a high number, but other volunteers, along with college students, suddenly became eligible for the draft.

We became aware of the turmoil at home when we learned that four students were shot dead and two severely wounded by national guardsmen who opened fire on an antiwar demonstration at Kent State University in Ohio. What was happening in our country? In recent years, Martin Luther King, Jr., and John and Bobby Kennedy had all been shot—and now innocent nonviolent students had been shot dead on a college campus. We were shocked by the news. I had not been a social activist before joining VISTA and had never participated in an antiwar demonstration during my college years. In the small women's college I attended in a conservative Ohio town, not much different from Ingomar, the only demonstration at my college was to protest a new rule that we could not put our feet up on the coffee tables in the library lounge. That lack of activism in my life, though, was about to change.

There were other VISTA volunteers, also recent college graduates, who had come straight to Alaska from leadership positions in university antiwar protests. If the government thought that placing activists in remote villages across Alaska would put them out of commission, they guessed wrong. By mail (we had no phones, faxes, or e-mail) the activists began to organize all the volunteers in the state. It was from them that I learned how to take action about what really mattered. Led by the experienced activists, we VISTA volunteers in Alaska took a stand on Alaska's local issues of the day—opposition to the construction of the oil pipeline across the state, support for Eskimo land claims, and resistance to the war in Vietnam. We also objected to the fact that, unlike other states, where the administrative jobs overseeing the VISTA program went to local citizens, in Alaska they went not to the indigenous people but to white men. We volunteers living among the Eskimos in Alaska suggested that these well-paying jobs be given to the people in the communities we served. In essence, this meant we were suggesting that our bosses be fired. Instead, all the VISTA volunteers in Alaska were fired.

The write-up in the newspaper explained that the VISTA program in Alaska was being restructured. Shortly before our firing, the newly elected President Nixon appointed a new director of the US Office of Economic Opportunity, the agency that oversaw VISTA. The new director was Donald Rumsfeld. The newspaper article reporting on our firing said that Rumsfeld believed that VISTA should be about providing social services and not about social change. In time, I saw that my life would, in fact, be about social change, so it was very fitting that I was fired from my first job by Donald Rumsfeld.

Our abrupt departure did nothing to change how much I was influenced by my time in the village. The Eskimos believed in the abundance of the universe—that there is enough for all if we are willing to share. As a society, the Eskimos as I had first found them are still the happiest people I've ever known—showing such delight in the smallest things. They had a sense of their place in the world, in the web of life, based on who they were, not what they had. Their happiness and security did not depend on money and material possessions, but on community and their relationship with the land and knowledge of nature. Despite great hardships, there had been a joyfulness among the Eskimos, lost to so many of us, a delight in simply being alive on this beautiful planet. I learned from them that a sustainable economy could be based on sharing and cooperation rather than on competition and hoarding.

Living in a culture grounded in the knowledge that all life is spiritually and environmentally interconnected helped me to recognize and articulate this belief and then make it the foundation for my work to come, the work that this book ultimately is about—helping to build a compassionate and caring economy.

As a young person questioning my own society, I began to ask: Why couldn't we build an economy that combined modern technology with the indigenous philosophy of living coopera- tively with people and with nature? With all that humankind has accomplished, couldn't we learn to live inclusively, simply, and sustainably, and still have lights and record players available for all who wished to enjoy them?

In late July 1970, Dick and I (along with Augie) left Chefornak, riding off in the mail plane that had first brought us. As our Eskimo friends waved good-bye from the shore, our plane rattled and roared across the river and up into the boundless blue sky. Looking down at the tiny village that had been our home for ten months, the sadness over leaving was tempered with an eagerness to see our families back home. But beyond that we had no idea of where life would take us next.

Tell me, what is it you plan to do
with your one wild and precious life?

—Mary Oliver

❧ 3 ☙

My First Business:
The Story of
Free People's Store

RETURNING HOME from Chefornak was a culture shock. Dick and I hadn't seen a car, eaten french fries, taken a shower, or soaked in a hot bath in ten months. Even in our peaceful hometown of Ingomar, life seemed so noisy and fast—and hot. Augie had to get used to meeting strangers and crossing busy streets. But we adjusted within weeks, and for the time being all I had learned from the Eskimos receded to the back of my consciousness as I turned my attention to what we needed to do right away—find jobs.

It didn't take us much riffling through the help-wanted section of the *Pittsburgh Post-Gazette*, and a few interviews, to realize that working for someone else wasn't right for us. The obvious answer was to start our own business. But what? I suggested we open a retail store—the next step after selling merchandise from my wagon as a child. "What could be so hard about running a store?" I asked. "You buy something at one price and sell it for a higher

33

price. It's that simple." True enough, and even though we didn't know much about business, we did know what was appealing to our generation. I thought that selling things we liked to people our age—like a general store for the 1960s generation—would be a fun idea. What more did we need to know?

So just after our first wedding anniversary, Dick and I drove around Ingomar looking for a location for our store-to-be. The malls along the suburban highways had become the popular shopping areas, but that did not do it for us.

Soon after, we were visiting college friends in Philadelphia, and we told them our idea for the store—selling hip clothing and apartment furnishings to the under-thirty crowd. (We had taken the 1960s truism "Don't trust anyone over thirty" one step further—we would not *sell* to anyone over thirty.) Our friend, Scott Belair, who was in graduate school at the University of Pennsylvania, pointed to the lack of stores for students in the university neighborhood and suggested that it would be a great location for the kind of store we wanted to open. A store in Philadelphia—of course! It didn't take us long before we found an available storefront, only a few blocks from campus. All of a sudden, we were just about in business.

While Dick dealt with the rental logistics, I drove the three hundred miles back to Ingomar to pick up our few belongings. I packed our suitcases of faded jeans and T-shirts; Augie and a new mixed-breed puppy, Jessica; and two white pet doves and a stereo with Dick's collection of Bob Dylan albums into a used Volvo station wagon—our wedding gift from Dick's father—and moved from Ingomar to our new home in Philadelphia. Without funds to rent both an apartment and a retail space, the storefront at 4307 Locust Street in West Philadelphia became both our business and home, though we had to go to Scott's apartment to take showers.

The neighborhoods to the west of the university where we now lived offered modest rents and housing prices, and residents were a mixture of students, faculty, and progressive intellectuals along with middle- and working-class white and African American families. Our block had several shops, including a popular Jewish deli called Koch's, a Laundromat, and an Acme grocery store across the street that was frequented by residents from our neighborhood, as well as people living farther to the west and north where there was little access to fresh groceries. Though we were oblivious to it at the time, the poverty rate rose dramatically toward the west, north, and southwest of our block. Leaving behind the stately Victorian houses surrounding the campus in what was once an elegant suburb of Philadelphia, the neighborhoods became increasingly dilapidated with empty lots, trash-strewn streets, and boarded-up houses deserted by those lured to the new housing developments in the booming suburbs. Then these neighborhoods were redlined by banks unwilling to give mortgages to African Americans.

The Vietnam War was winding down, but it had greatly influenced our views not only of government but also of business. We had come across President Eisenhower's infamous warning, issued nearly a decade earlier, about the dangers of the military-industrial complex and the undue influence it could exert over politics. I was awakening to the fact that corporations could wield their powers in ways that threatened our freedom and our democracy, and I blamed corporate interests for the war. Dick and I distrusted all profit-making business. The profit-at-any-cost value system of corporate America wasn't us. We decided that our business would be different— we would operate like a nonprofit. By that we simply meant we planned to make just enough to earn a living, but not more than we needed. Though my understanding of profit and my concept of how much it takes to "just make a living" have changed in different stages of my life, I continue to believe, as I did at the idealistic start of it all, that we should constantly challenge ourselves and our business and our society with the question, "How much is enough?"

We wanted to give the store a name that expressed our antiwar, antiestablishment values and decided on "Free People's Store." We were acting as "free people" in at least two important ways—by opposing our government's war in Vietnam and by creating a business that was an alternative to the dominant corporate model. We were sure the store would attract other freethinking people who shared our outlook.

Dick cut a piece of plywood in the shape of a dove, and we lettered it with "Free People's Store" and hung it out front. With no merchandise to display, we turned the front window into one huge birdcage for our pet doves, with tree branches and a birdbath. As the war continued to take lives in Vietnam, the dove, symbol of peace, became our logo and mascot. Even before we opened the doors or had anything to sell, our first business clearly expressed our values.

We started Free People's Store with what we had—our ingenuity and the three thousand dollars that was our combined stipends from VISTA. Our rent and living expenses during the two-month transition between Alaska and setting up life in Philadelphia had used up any other savings we had. Determined to get the business open and money flowing without taking out a loan, which we would not qualify for, we had to find every possible way to cut start-up costs. With an empty store to furnish, we set out to forage on garbage days, when trash was set out on the curb for pickup. We particularly searched the streets in Philadelphia's Chinatown for discarded wooden crates used for shipping goods from China to the local stores. I put my fort-building skills to use, constructing shelving by hammering the crates together and arranging them like staggered building blocks across the wall. I left some in the natural wood still stamped with Chinese lettering, and painted others in bright orange, yellow, and blue.

Dick found another use for the crates: mounted on sawhorses, they were just the right size for record bins. He also salvaged a large wooden spool used to store electric cable and put it in the middle of the room to display stacks of T-shirts. I painted the walls of the store in swirling super graphics like a giant paisley. (A couple of years later, I used my super graphics talent to decorate Philadelphia's "McGovern for President" headquarters, and we hung a poster in our store announcing that with every purchase from Free People's Store, we would make a contribution toward the election of the antiwar candidate, George McGovern.)

At last, the store was ready for some merchandise. Dick and I took as much cash as we could spare and drove to New York City. We had never heard of gift shows or showrooms (that would come later), nor would it have done us any good if we had since we couldn't afford the minimum purchases necessary to open vendor accounts. Arriving in Manhattan, we parked as soon as we saw an empty phone booth and looked up *Importers* in the Yellow Pages, figuring that imports would be cheapest. Noticing that many importers were located in the same area on lower Broadway, we drove straight there.

Climbing stairs to third- and fourth-floor offices crammed full of goods from faraway places, we explored this exciting new world of buying wholesale. I had no consciousness then about "fair trade." I didn't stop to think about who made the products and whether they were paid fair wages or if the production process was healthy to workers and the environment. If I had stopped to think about it all, I probably would have thought we were helping people in less-developed countries by buying their goods, rather than understanding that we may have been supporting a system that enriched factory owners while exploiting workers.

We loaded the station wagon to the brim with a cargo of madras bedspreads, long print skirts, carved wooden boxes, and barrettes from India; dangly earrings, block prints, and throw rugs from Thailand; beads and incense from Pakistan; woven fans, baskets, and leather neck wallets from Africa; and hand-blown glasses, pottery, woven shoulder bags, and peasant blouses from Mexico— all items that we felt would appeal to our 1960s generation.

Back in Philly, we found sources for books like *Diet for a Small Planet* by Frances Moore Lappé and *Be Here Now* by Ram Dass; T-shirts; jeans; records by Bob Dylan, The Rolling Stones, and James Brown; and houseplants that we displayed with a corny sign that said BRING SOME LIFE INTO YOUR APARTMENT. From local craftspeople we bought hand-dipped candles, macramé belts, and wooden kitchen utensils. Paper lanterns and tea sets came from

Chinatown. An old glass display case served as a counter, which we filled with jewelry along with a small supply of rolling papers and pipes—though despite our tattered jeans and long hair Dick and I were pretty much small town straight arrows when it came to pot. Next to the counter we put a secondhand old-fashioned cash register, and nearby we placed a big old red sofa where customers sat and talked with us while we worked behind the counter. This area served as our living room, where we spent most of our time, since the small room through the back door of the store where we slept was not big enough to entertain guests.

Finally, in October of 1970, we had enough merchandise to make a go of it and opened the door of Free People's Store for business. We barely had enough merchandise to cover the shelves, but as we took in cash, we immediately bought more, gradually filling the store to the brim. So that no one would have to leave the store empty-handed for lack of money, we created a "Free Bin" full of old clothes discarded by college students.

I quickly became comfortable with the unexpected nature of city life. A frequent Free Bin "shopper" was a neighborhood bag lady who quacked uncontrollably while flapping her arms like wings when she wanted to "say" something. My initial encounter came on one of my first mornings in Philadelphia when I was having breakfast at the corner diner. Sitting across from me at a long table full of customers, the person I came to know as Duck Woman suddenly put both hands into her fried eggs and smeared them around on her plate and all over the table while quacking. Amazingly, no one else at the table paid any attention, continuing to eat breakfast. It was just Duck Woman doing her thing, I learned, and I would get used to her. Weeks later Duck Woman was trying on clothes from the Free Bin when she got stuck with a dress over her head in our tiny dressing room. I went to help her, and frantically struggled to pull down her dress, almost overcome by her body odor as she thrashed against the walls, quacking loudly. Life in the city was sure different from Ingomar. I was fascinated to see who would come through the door next.

Our friend, Scott, now a Wharton business school student, made an investment in the business and became our partner. He helped cook up ideas like having a loss leader—in our case, popular record albums that we sold around cost at $2.75 to draw customers to the store, hoping they would buy more when they came inside. We began to stretch our dollars by buying inexpensive merchandise and finding creative ways to get a high markup. From our T-shirt wholesaler, we bought long white underwear and underwear tops with three buttons at the neck. I went across the street to the Acme market for fabric dye and a plastic garbage can and went about dyeing the underwear bright colors, stirring the hot cauldron with a mop handle. The tops cost us around a dollar apiece, and after dyeing we sold them for six dollars. I hung one pair of long johns I had dyed bright pink in the window of the front door, unbuttoned the rear flap, and hung our OPEN sign there. At closing time, I buttoned the flap and flipped the sign to CLOSED.

Vintage clothing provided another big markup. Dick found a dealer who sold used clothes by the pound. Usually the owner sold the clothes in very large quantities, often by the ton, to be shipped overseas. But he took a liking to us and gave us the liberty to pick through the old clothes to find choice items. I remember climbing into huge bins in his warehouse filled twelve to fifteen feet high with used clothes. Dick and I sat on the mounds of clothing, digging through many useless items. We were on a treasure hunt to find the occasional old velvet dress, silk slip, fur coat, or leather jacket that could bring a high price in the store. We bought these at a few dollars a pound and sold them for twenty-five to fifty dollars apiece. This more than made up for the loss-leader record sales.

Some of those old dresses and jackets became my personal favorites, especially an old leather pilot jacket with a hidden inside breast pocket that proved helpful. As soon as we sold enough merchandise, Dick handed me one thousand dollars in cash, which I stashed in that hidden pocket before heading back to New York City to buy more merchandise. After the first trip, I did most of the New York buying of international crafts and other imports and also bought locally made crafts and did the decorating and display, while Dick purchased most of the clothes, records, books, and plants and—with some assistance from Scott—handled the financial affairs.

In the beginning we couldn't buy our jeans from a big brand name company like Levi Strauss & Co. because we couldn't make the minimum order. All we could afford was to buy three pairs in three sizes from a lesser-known brand. Once we splurged and bought three pairs of purple velvet bell-bottom jeans, a big investment for us. They were the most expensive items in the store, and we were eager to sell them so we could buy six more pairs, then twelve, and so on.

The purple velvet jeans led to something we hadn't yet thought about. One day when I was in the store alone, a group of ten or twelve high school girls descended on the store all at once. I was trying desperately to keep my eyes on each of them as they asked me questions to draw me to different parts of the store. Suddenly they all left as they came, at once, and I noticed with dismay, as they hurried out the door, that one of the girls was wearing a pair of the purple velvet jeans!

"Stop, they're my jeans!" I cried out, and they took off running. I locked the door and gave chase. Up the street and around the corner we went, dodging traffic across a busy thoroughfare. I was gaining ground, and as the group reached the parking lot of the supermarket at the corner of 44th and Walnut, I lunged and tackled the culprit to the ground. Without thinking, I unzipped the jeans and yanked them off her. As she lay on the sidewalk in her underpants screaming, I ran back to the store and triumphantly returned our purple velvet jeans to the shelf. I was determined that we would sell that pair, and more and more and more until someday Levi Strauss & Co. would be very glad to sell to us.

Meanwhile, my tackle didn't stop unwanted visitors. Not long after the jeans episode, when I was alone in the store again, a teenage boy walked out with his shirt looking suspiciously bulky. "What do you have on there?" I asked, and he suddenly raced down the street. I had learned to wear sneakers when working in the store, and I raced after him. At twenty-three, I was in great shape—but could I catch a fourteen-year-old boy? He ran into a back alley with me speeding behind, and leaped over a fence. I did what he did, only to find that he was cornered against the back of a building. He had a knife in his hand, and we stood facing each other, both of us gasping for breath.

"Just give me back my shirts," I said as calmly as possible. We stared at each other for what seemed like a full minute. At last he threw down the knife, and began removing his shirt, and then another, and another. I could not believe the number of shirts he had stolen as he dropped one after another onto a pile on the ground. Finally he stood bare-chested. "Thank you," I said, scooping up the shirts and racing for home.

I still hadn't learned the obvious. One evening, as I was again working the store alone, I noticed a man spending a long time looking at our record collection. When another customer I was waiting on left the store, the man followed close behind with a suspicious-looking bulge under his jacket. I couldn't be sure enough to accuse him, so I locked the store and cautiously followed as he walked up the street, hoping that if he had stolen the records, I might see him take them out of his jacket. I continued following at a block's distance behind, careful that he not see me. Block after block we went, moving westward deep into an unfamiliar neighborhood. It was night, and I was alone, but I was too angry and too intent on my economic survival to think about the possible danger. At last he turned up the porch steps of a row house, and I came closer to watch him from the sidewalk. He opened his jacket and pulled out a big stack of records. I heard myself scream at the top of my lungs, *Give me back my records!* He looked down at me from his porch with complete astonishment and said, "Here, lady," holding the records out to me. I leaped up the steps, grabbed the records, and ran for home as fast as I could.

I returned my prized records to their bins, pondering this latest episode in my new life in urban America. I was beginning to realize that having a store showed that we had more money than many of those in the low-income neighborhoods around us. We were fair game. Until now, except for the Eskimo village, I had lived with people in the same general economic bracket as my own family. I was beginning to experience a new reality.

You would think by that time we would have figured out that we always needed to have two people working at a time. But there was just too much work for each of us to do to have both of us in the store all the time, and we couldn't afford to hire employees to provide a second person. Scott was in school full time, and Dick was often out picking up merchandise or over at Scott's apartment in the evening talking about the business. Scott's girlfriend, Mary, and a friend named Barbara helped us tend the store on occasion, but I still often worked alone and continued to think nothing of it. I thought I could handle anything. I had so far, hadn't I?

The shoplifting efforts so far had been a kind of high-voltage game, with me tearing down the streets to corner the culprits. The next incident was more serious. One afternoon, while I was alone in the store as usual, two young men came in. One of them called me over to ask the price of an item on a bottom shelf toward the back of the store. As I bent down to check, an arm came around my neck, yanking me up. From the corner of my eye, I saw his accomplice emptying the cash box behind the counter.

"Don't make a sound," my assailant said roughly. He held a large knife to my throat. "What's through that door?"

"The basement."

"Open the door," he demanded as he pushed me toward it. I did as he asked, and he shoved me through the door and locked it behind me. Stumbling down the steps, I regained my footing and ran across the basement, where I flipped open the hinged metal door leading to the sidewalk and climbed out. I spotted the robbers walking down the street and followed them. I realized I couldn't run up to them—at least one of them had a knife—so I walked a safe distance behind, pointing at them and yelling to every passerby, "Those men just robbed my store! Call the police!"

The two of them continued to walk nonchalantly along, as though they were completely innocent and had nothing to do with me. Would anyone take me seriously, or was I seen as just another crazy Duck Woman?

Then a police car came along, and the two men took off running in opposite directions. The officer was able to catch one of them, the one who held the knife to my throat, but unfortunately he was not the one with the cash. We had lost more than one hundred dollars, a lot of money to us.

When the man came to trial, I felt conflicted. I was a progressive child of the times, and I had no faith in the dehumanizing criminal justice system that I had studied and read about in college. I decided that sending the offender to jail could turn a young man with problems into a hardened criminal. After prison, I surmised, the life of the next victim might end with a slashed throat. I didn't think of another possibility: that if the young man didn't go to jail, he might feel emboldened and take his knife to rob again, maybe this time drawing blood.

At the trial, I went over to the defendant's mother and told her I did not want to cause her son to go to prison. I explained what had happened—that he had held a knife to my throat and stolen my money and that I hoped he would straighten out if I gave him this break. When the judge asked me if the man who committed the crime was in the room, I said I wasn't sure, and he was set free. It was not the perfect solution, which would have been found in a community-based system committed to rehabilitation, one that would have helped him deepen his humanity, not destroy it. But as far as I was concerned, it was the better of the two choices I had—prison as it was or no prison.

The impact of this experience, which gave me the capacity to send someone to prison, stayed with me for a long time. It was one reason that years later, when I was developing educational programs at the White Dog Café, I sponsored tours to prisons, hired people coming out of jail, brought in speakers to lecture on restorative justice, and invited exoffenders to tell their stories.

As I soon discovered, being the victim in the assorted efforts to rob Free People's Store had also installed in me an element of prejudice that I had not yet been aware of. I was walking along on a sidewalk one day when a car jumped the curb just in front of me. The driver hopped out yelling, "Stop, thief!" Ahead I saw a young black man running, and I immediately chased after him, assuming that he was the thief. Down the sidewalk and around the corner I ran, but suddenly I stopped in my tracks and, to my amazement, burst into tears. I went home, sobbing all the way. I threw myself on the bed and couldn't stop crying. What had come over me? Why was I so terribly upset? I felt like a racist because I had immediately believed the driver of the car—a white man—and started chasing the black man without questioning who was right.

I had grown up in a sheltered all-white world where I had encountered only a few black people in my entire youth. Now I had been experiencing crime for the first time, and all the perpetrators happened to be black. Had my experiences made me prejudiced? I felt terrible, as though grieving over a loss. But what loss?

Finally, I came to understand my grief. In this urban neighborhood where I now lived, it was indeed more likely that a black youth would be poorly educated, raised in poverty, a victim of violence and theft, jobless, and—yes—therefore more likely to commit a street crime than the average white who lived here. This was heartbreakingly sad to me. I was grieving for the ideal America that I was gradually losing—a country I had believed in as a child, one that was based on principles of equality and fairness, where all children were given a quality education, a safe environment, decent housing, medical care, and a pathway toward successful careers. I now saw, in my own naïve but heartfelt way, that the richest, most powerful country in the world—a country I loved and believed in—had failed to achieve its ideals and that, as a society, we all suffered for it. I longed to help build a more equitable society, and I believed, as the Eskimos had shown, that one's survival depended on the well-being of everyone in the community.

Despite the challenges, I enjoyed living in the city. Growing up, I had always yearned for more excitement and diversity, and now I was fascinated by the variety of people and cultures around me and by the many choices of things to do. I thrived on the fast pace, the feeling of never knowing what I would find around the next corner, and perhaps most of all, the activism concerning issues important to me—peace, civil rights, and economic justice. We didn't talk much about these issues back in Ingomar. Living in a small suburban town separated its occupants not only from the richness of a diverse community, but too often from active engagement in building a better society. Now, here I was in Philadelphia. What could I do to support all the many inspiring progressive activities going on in my new home city?

An idea soon began to form. Our store had become a popular hangout, like the forts I once built in the woods. The red sofa by the cash register was always full of people when it wasn't monopolized by our dogs. Just as I first imagined the mix of our merchandise to be like a general store for people our age, so too we cultivated an old-time general store atmosphere—a place where people stopped to discuss the issues of the day. We had a bulletin board by the door where notices were hung about a peace march, a co-op forming, or free classes, and we saw how our store had become a place to share information. In a small town like Ingomar, everyone knew what was going on, but in a city the size of Philadelphia, so much was happening that there needed to be a vehicle for better communicating how to get involved, how to find resources and services, how to solve a problem, how to work together to bring change. (Remember, this was decades before the Internet.)

Dick and I had seen a publication from Boston called the *People's Yellow Pages*, which listed all the counterculture organizations in town. We liked the basic idea but didn't want a book that further divided people by appealing only to the counterculture. Why not make a book that would bring people together, embraced by everyone from the Black Panthers to the Gray Panthers and even the business community?

We decided to form a nonprofit publishing company (a legally certified nonprofit this time) so we could receive contributions to support the work. Dick named it Synapse, referring to the neural communications circuits in the brain.

We rounded up a few others to join our effort and Free People's Store became headquarters for researching and publishing the *Whole City Catalog*, a resource guide that listed and described every community action group, service organization, do-it-yourself, and alternative enterprise that engaged people in their communities—from grassroots groups to government agencies. Though I didn't think of it this way at the time, I was taking an inventory of the resources my new city had to offer. In later years, this was exactly what I advised communities to do when they were beginning work to build a local economy—start by taking an inventory of what you have.

I had been an English major in college and relished having a writing project. By researching all the subject areas I was interested in, I learned a tremendous amount about my new home city. When I heard about an interesting project or group, I set up an interview with the leader, and from these people I connected to other groups and activists, so that I built a network of friends and contacts engaged in the issues I cared about. Many of those relationships last to this day.

Listings in the *Whole City Catalog* were a reflection of all that was happening in Philadelphia in the early 1970s—including, in no particular order, the Ecology Food Co-op, Health Law Project, Philadelphians for Equal Justice, Mt. Airy Baby Sitting Co-op, Black Political Forum, Casa Del Carmen, Radical Jewish Community, Architect's Workshop, People's Bail Fund, Imprisoned Citizens Union, Indian Rights Association, Citizens Council for Clean Air, Philadelphia War Tax Resistance, Women's Strike for Peace, Pennsylvanians for Women's Rights, Gay Activists Alliance, People's Painting Co-op, Movement for a New Society, People's Video Center, Philadelphia Free Press, Philadelphia

Resistance Print Shop, Black People's University, and Canadian groups to which Philadelphia's draft resisters could go (such as the Vancouver Committee to Aid American War Objectors). The listing for Free People's Store read, "Keeps us alive while we're doing things like the *Whole City Catalog*."

Volunteers contributed their time to work on the *Catalog*. Sometimes a customer would walk in the door and offer to research an area we needed help on, and another would offer to type. (It's hard to imagine that we used typewriters back then.) We gathered photographs, drawings, and quotes to sprinkle throughout the book that expressed both our disillusionment with our society and our hope and inspiration in bringing change by working together. I chose a quote from Black Elk, the great Sioux healer and visionary, which read

> I could see that the *wasichus* [white people] did not care for each other the way our people did before the nation's hoop was broken. They would take everything from each other if they could, and so there were some who had more of everything than they could use, while crowds of people had nothing at all and maybe were starving. They had forgotten that the earth was their mother.

Black Elk continued to be a guide for me, and some forty years later, when speaking at a conference, I would again quote the prophetic Sioux leader. Black Elk envisioned a future when the hoop would be reconnected and the world reunited—just as those of us in the local living economy movement were hoping to do, community by community, as we built and connected just, sustainable and humane economies.

Funding for printing the first edition of the *Catalog* came serendipitously. One day when I was taking a photograph of artists painting a mural to use in the *Catalog*, the director of the Philadelphia Museum of Art's Department of Urban Outreach,

David Katzive, stopped by to watch, and we began chatting. He was enthusiastic about the idea of the *Catalog* and made an unsolicited grant toward its printing. Our first grant! I was so excited. Other acquaintances connected us to two additional funders, the Religious Society of Friends and the Philadelphia Gas Works, which completed our funding along with a generous printer who agreed to print fourteen thousand copies at cost and to wait until sales picked up before collecting the bill.

When it was time to lay out the pages of the *Catalog*, we closed the store for a week during the slow summer month of August to provide space to do the work. Locking the front door, we set up several old doors on sawhorses to be used as tables arranged across the store. On these we placed rows of blue-lined paper (undetectable to the printer in the old-fashioned offset printing process) that provided a guide for gluing onto the pages hundreds of little typed pieces of paper, along with photos and drawings. We had no air-conditioning and could not even open a window or use a fan because the moving air would have blown the paper all over the place. Dick and I tied bandanas around our heads in an attempt to keep our sweat from dripping onto the pages. It was back-straining work to lean over those tables for a week in a closed room that smelled of sweat and rubber cement. But we finally finished the first *Whole City Catalog*, which we published in 1973.

Though I never had any interest in business while in college and imagined a career in the arts, I began to change from my naïve days as a reluctant businessperson who believed that profit was a dirty word. Working in the store pretty quickly helped me see the need for a reasonable profit and I came to understand how profits ensure the health of a business, allow ideas to grow, and can be used as contributions to community nonprofits—such as our publishing work at Synapse and the many other good works I was discovering through my research for the *Whole City Catalog*.

As my life evolved, the values with which we started the store and my thoughts about the role of business in community life stayed with me. So did my interest in selling what I personally liked to people I enjoyed being around and providing a place to gather and talk about the issues of the day. This was a feature that would blossom fully years later in the White Dog Café, where educational programs inspiring customers to be engaged citizens became a product of the business along with food and service.

From the beginning, business ownership for me meant the freedom to express my creativity. I saw that being a good businessperson was about giving my customers something special and that the uniqueness came from who I was as a person. Besides looking at what product or service was needed in my community, it was also important to look within and see how my business could be a unique self-expression.

Free People's Store was a kind of art form that expressed my personality, like my childhood ventures, but it also expressed my personal values. From then on, having my work truly reflect what I stand for as a person became an essential aspect of my career. The success of Free People's Store taught me not to be afraid to express my progressive values through my business, values that Dick and I shared at the time. I learned that it was possible to develop a clientele of "free people"—a community of customers with shared values—something I would do again successfully at the White Dog Café some twenty years later. I also learned that you can increase the positive social impact of a business by starting a nonprofit affiliate, as Free People's Store did with Synapse and as I would also later do with the nonprofit White Dog Community Enterprises.

But I didn't just learn about business and community during my years at the Free People's Store. I learned a lot about myself, too. I felt the power of my own will and determination, not only to create and build, but also to protect and endure. I realized that being an entrepreneur was about envisioning something out of nothing. Even more, it was about the determination to manifest dreams and persist through inevitable challenges to realize them. Though it may seem like mumbo jumbo to some, I began to believe that when I set my mind to something, committing myself wholeheartedly, I aligned myself with a greater force that gave me courage and strength. The more I believed this, the more doors opened. Was it something I imagined? It seemed that people, even strangers, appeared just as I needed them, bringing assistance, advice, or material resources. Even the unwanted strangers had lessons to teach.

Meanwhile, not all was well in my married life. While Free People's Store continued to grow and thrive in those first couple of years, my relationship with Dick did not. The leadership qualities that attracted me to him as a young girl picking the best boy to marry had now become oppressive. After moving to a big city, starting a business, and testing my strength in the world, being perceived as less worthy or capable because I was female became less and less palatable, and that was the situation I found myself in. Dick and Scott increasingly ignored me as a business partner, keeping me in the dark about our finances, and joking about how *the little woman shouldn't worry her pretty little head about business.* The tone was lighthearted, but it was no joke. I knew it was the way they saw things. I realized that my important contributions in conceptualizing the store were discounted. Same with my work in buying and displaying, and my aptitude for building relationships in the community—all discounted. The "important work" of controlling finances and planning for growth was left to the men. This brought me right back to that ball field in the fifth grade: girls can't play.

I slowly and painfully realized that my place in the world was not at Dick's side. I couldn't be Mrs. Richard Hayne any more. Now it was time for me to challenge tradition in another way and not accept the second-class status they had assigned me for being female. My choices were clear. I could remain in a safe yet constricted role, or take the risk to lead my own life.

Just as all of us, men and women, must overcome the psychological barriers that tell us that we are not capable, that we are not good enough, that we need someone else to be whole, I had to let go of old notions that were holding me back. As scary as it was, I had to give up all Dick and I had built together in exchange for the freedom to follow my own path. My courage came from having learned that when I set my intention, something somewhere provided what I needed to get there. Now I had to find out whatever became of that little girl named Judy Wicks, whose name I had crossed off my tablet in fifth grade.

Dick's and my lives would take drastically different turns. He continued on with Free People's Store, and I had no idea where life was leading when I packed my bags and left my husband, home, and business. I got only a block away when I ran a red light and collided with another car. Luckily, no one was hurt, but the car I was using could not be driven. A passerby offered to help me home.

"But I can't go home. I've just left my husband! My bags are packed, and I've got to keep going!" I poured out as we stood on the sidewalk. "And now I have to find a job fast because I need money to repair the car!"

"Maybe I can help," said the passerby, a very friendly blond, curly-haired young man about my age. "I work in a restaurant called La Terrasse on the 3400 block of Sansom Street near the university, and they have an opening for a waitress."

"I'll take it," I said immediately, as if I was talking to the person who was hiring me.

And so that's how I got into the restaurant business that would be my life for the next forty years—quite by accident!

Yield who will to their separation
My object in living
Is to unite my avocation and my vocation
As my two eyes make one sight.

For only where love and need are one
And work is play for mortal stakes
Is the deed ever really done
For heaven and the future's sakes.

—Robert Frost

❧ 4 ❧

It's Not the Coin that Counts: Learning to Do Business My Way

LA TERRASSE WAS a hard place to find. Sansom Street was only two blocks long in that part of town, largely surrounded by the expanding campus of the University of Pennsylvania. When I finally came upon the 3400 block of Sansom Street and walked down the narrow tree-lined street for the first time, I was entirely enchanted. The row of charming, though slightly run-down, Victorian brownstone houses provided a small oasis from the bleak, unfriendly institutional buildings that surrounded it. Many of the older homes in the university community were being torn down and replaced by stark high-rise dormitories and office buildings, strip malls, and acres of dead zones used as parking lots for the many commuters who drove in from the suburbs. In sharp contrast, these hundred-year-old, three-story row houses on Sansom Street were human-scale—quaint, homey, inviting. The rosy brownstone gave the street a warm glow, and the fringe-like decorative Victorian trim along the cornices added a festive, old-fashioned allure to the block.

Nestled on that magical block, I found the restaurant I was looking for and asked to see the manager. He seemed very eager to find a new waitress as soon as possible, and though I had no experience other than serving cocktails for a summer job in college, I was immediately hired and put right to work. When my first table was seated, I was so hesitant that the hostess had to give me a big push, and I stumbled up to the table to greet my first customers. Not a glamorous beginning to my new career! But I soon got the hang of it.

When taking the waitress job at La Terrasse in 1972, I of course had no inkling that I was beginning twelve years of on-the-job training for opening my own restaurant just down the street. After all, it wasn't that I actually chose the restaurant business after contemplating the career best suited to me. I didn't even like to cook. Rather, I used the cards that were dealt me. When the opportunity presented itself, I went with it, not knowing where it would take me—and for the time being, I was open to whatever might come.

Not long after taking the job, I moved into an apartment just down the street from La Terrasse. On first walking through the door of the house at 3420 Sansom Street, which had a health food store on the first floor and my apartment above, again I could never have guessed that I would live in that building for the next thirty-eight years. But I did immediately feel a connection to Sansom Street and began to make it my home. It was not only the look and feel of the street that I liked, but also the people who lived or gathered there.

Night and day there was activity on the sidewalks—residents coming and going to work or to class and customers going in and out of the shops and cafés. My new neighbors, ranging in age from eighteeen to eighty, included artists, young professionals, students and professors from the University of Pennsylvania, and (like me) employees of the local businesses. One house was still a single-family home, complete with all the original Victorian details, where an elderly woman had lived for more years than anyone could remember. But most of the houses had been divided into several apartments with a few small retail businesses and offices on the first floors that served the local community.

La Terrasse was a neighborhood hangout—a bohemian-style French café with a tree growing right up through the leaky corrugated plastic roof of the covered terrace, and where the Gruyère cheese on the onion soup was so thick it had to be cut with a knife. I joined the staff of flamboyant young waitresses who typically dressed in 1970s-style hot pants and tall boots or long flowing skirts and sheer tops. It turned out that there was only one male server, Skip, the very same blond, curly-haired fellow who had witnessed my accident on Locust Street. Balancing carafes of wine and trays of French pastries, we servers made our way through the crowded dining rooms filled with a hodgepodge of customers dressed in everything from business suits with ties to tweedy jackets with patched elbows to jogging shorts and blue jeans with T-shirts.

Many of the La Terrasse regulars who came almost daily were part of the cultural intelligentsia of the university. Professor Neil Welliver was a painter whose large-scale oils of the Maine woods led him to be called one of the greatest American landscape painters of his generation. Neil was cochair of Penn's Department of Fine Arts along with sculptor Robert Engman, who was my next-door neighbor. I could see through the windows across the light court between our houses into Bob's two-story studio, where he worked on an enormous abstract piece called *Triune*, which would be cast in bronze and placed at a busy intersection near

Philadelphia's City Hall. Bob had a hearty spirit, and I remember him telling the story of feeling so annoyed by the sound of his wife's vacuum cleaner when he lived in the suburbs that he had finally picked it up by the hose, swung it around like a lasso, and let it sail right through a glass window into the yard.

A few doors farther up the street in an apartment above La Terrasse lived another nationally recognized sculptor, Robin Fredenthal. Stricken at an early age with Parkinson's disease that resulted in unsteady hands and erratic motions, Robin worked with the help of assistants who followed his directions in constructing three-dimensional cardboard models in geometric shapes. Some of these models went on to become giant steel sculptures that graced the Penn campus and public spaces around Philadelphia and across the country. A charming and brilliant visionary with the courage to carry on his work despite his crippling disease, Robin attracted many visitors to the apartment studio he rarely left. Friends and fans climbed the narrow wooden steps to the third floor where Robin sat surrounded by thousands of white cardboard models that filled every nook and cranny of the flat he shared with his two cats.

When I first waited on Ian McHarg, esteemed chair of Penn's Department of Landscape Architecture, I was impressed with his elegant manner, long bushy moustache, and kindness toward the staff. But I was too naïve to understand the importance of his recent book, *Design with Nature*, which pioneered the concept of ecological planning. Not until thirty years later, when I was deeply engaged in the local living economy movement, would I come to realize how his revolutionary thinking around humans' place in nature was foundational to our movement's work. Professor McHarg, I saw at that later time, articulated so clearly and profoundly the importance of this era in history—that we are transforming our world from the modern industrial era that he referred to as one of "dominate and destroy" to a new era of "cooperate and restore." But in 1972, I just wanted to make sure I didn't spill his martini.

I soon learned that our Sansom Street neighborhood had its own experience of "dominate and destroy" to deal with. Not long after I settled into my new home and community, I heard shocking news. Our entire block, prized for its location on the University of Pennsylvania campus, was earmarked for the development of a commercial mall. How could it be that the residents and small businesses would be evicted, our community destroyed, and the beautiful brownstone houses demolished to make way for ordinary chain stores and fast-food restaurants? I was outraged.

Determined to help save my newfound community, I eagerly joined the Sansom Committee, whose mission was to stop the demolition and to develop an alternative plan for the restoration of this historic block. Our powerful adversaries included the University of Pennsylvania, their corporate allies in the old boys' network who would benefit from the development, and two government agencies—the City of Philadelphia and the US Department of Housing and Urban Development, which wielded their power to support the university's expansion.

Sansom Committee members included the residents and small business owners of the block, along with the Penn professors who frequented La Terrasse and opposed their employer's demolition plans. The committee was led by Elliot Cook, the rapscallion owner of La Terrasse, who had a fascinating blend of high-minded vision and roguish behavior that often went over the top. What he likely viewed as a harmless prank—making repeated, unpaid-for, long-distance phone calls with an illegal device called a "blue box"—had landed him in federal prison for three months during the seventies. There, he was trained for his job in the prison kitchen by outgoing inmate G. Gordon Liddy of Watergate fame. On the other hand, it had been Elliot's higher self that led the process for creating an alternative plan for our block—a plan that would preserve its historic character while developing a mixed use of unique shops and restaurants as a vibrant retail center with housing for our community on the upper floors. During the fight to save our block, the university offered Elliot a deal that would have saved his own business while sacrificing the rest of the block to the wrecking ball. On principle, and likely also because he enjoyed a good fight, he refused the offer and continued his opposition.

Among the other members of our community group were several graduates of Penn's architecture department, including Sam Little, whose contributions included light studies demonstrating how the towering mall the developers proposed for Walnut and Sansom Streets would leave the Penn Law School, across Sansom Street to the north, in perpetual shade. Neil Schlosser was another architecture school graduate, who like Sam had moved onto the block while attending the university. Neil's firm, SRK Architects, had expertise in historic restoration and provided the Sansom Committee with renderings of the restored block our committee envisioned. I still remember the exact table at La Terrasse, a four-top right next to the tree growing through the roof, where I met the handsome, dark-curly-haired young architect with kind brown eyes—because eventually I would marry him.

My role on the Sansom Committee was building community relations, and I took the lead in organizing an outdoor block party publicizing our "Save the Block" campaign. My research for the *Whole City Catalog* had made me aware of other community groups fighting demolition, and I invited them all to join our event. Each group put up displays about its own David-and-Goliath struggles at our "Save the Block" party amid food booths and live music—the first of many street parties I'd throw on Sansom Street in the years ahead.

During that time of struggle to save our block, I learned from others on the committee about the legendary urban activist Jane Jacobs, author of *The Death and Life of Great American Cities*. At that time in the 1970s, Jacobs had not yet been recognized as a visionary, but for the Sansom Committee she was our guiding light. It was from reading Jane Jacobs, who loved her own neighborhood in New York City as we loved Sansom Street, that I learned the important concepts of "mixed use" and "walkable communities," in which residents prospered from a lively mixture of residences and businesses and could walk to stores and restaurants, to jobs and schools, to parks and theatres. This approach to designing cities and towns became known as the New Urbanism, vitally important today as we struggle to reduce carbon emissions.

The bustle of city life I enjoyed so much was eloquently described by Jacobs as "sidewalk ballet." It was Jane Jacobs who helped me understand why it was no accident that interesting people came to our community. They were attracted to the vibrant character of our block and the unique warm feel of the architecture, the only intact historic block remaining on the campus amid the bleak new institutional development that turned a cold shoulder to the street life Jacobs upheld. Arrested several times for protesting developers, the outspoken Jacobs condemned the urban renewal movement following the end of World War II, when whole neighborhoods were razed, destroying close-knit communities and thriving local economies to build sterile high-rise office buildings. She showed how residents were encouraged to leave the city for the sprawling suburbs where housing developments and shopping malls were destroying rich farmlands for no more than what she scornfully called "cheap parking."

Just as our heroine once presented her arguments to resist a highway proposal to protect her beloved Greenwich Village, the Sansom Committee fought to save our block using Jacobs's work to articulate our case. We hired a top attorney, Robert Sugarman, a lovable yet ferocious crusader known for defending communities and the natural environment against abuse of power, and filed a lawsuit based on the misuse of eminent domain and the lack of the required environmental impact statement. The Sansom Committee architects drew up plans to show how the block could be beautifully renovated to create a unique retail center for the campus and provide urban homes for university faculty who now commuted from the suburbs. We pointed to the vibrancy of other urban campuses, such as Cambridge and Georgetown, which thrived with the mixture of commercial and residential, students and nonstudents. Quoting Jane Jacobs, we showed how mixed-use development keeps neighborhoods occupied day and night, providing more vitality as well as security; the shopkeepers keep watch over the neighborhood during the day and the residents keep watch at night.

In my separation from Dick, we agreed that I would take responsibility for the continued publication of the *Whole City Catalog* and running the nonprofit publishing company Synapse. We also agreed that I would receive a two-hundred-dollar-a-week stipend from the store for one year so that I did not have to work full-time in order to finish the *Catalog*. Though Synapse, as a nonprofit, had no value, it was valuable to me as a way to be involved in the community and bring about positive social change. Because I was ashamed about leaving the marriage—divorce was not common in Ingomar and had a negative stigma attached to it—and because I felt terrible about the hurt that my leaving had caused Dick, it did not seem appropriate to talk about money or how we would split the only thing we owned of real value, the store. I walked away, taking nothing else with me but a verbal agreement from Dick that when he sold the store, I would get my share. Not having a written agreement was a mistake I would make at least one more time.

The first issue of the *Catalog* was finished in 1972, just before I moved to Sansom Street. For the next two years, while I worked part-time waiting tables at La Terrasse, I focused much of my energy on researching, writing, and designing the second edition.

In the spring of 1974, just as I finished the second edition, a newly hired general manager of La Terrasse had sent the restaurant into a tailspin. Elliot, our boss, was living in Boston while attending graduate school, and things were getting increasingly chaotic. Rumor had it that the restaurant was losing money. The cashier, Marge Greenspan—a quick-witted, middle-aged mother of three whose opinion was valued by all—came up with the surprising suggestion that I manage the restaurant. *Me?* Though

I had a tiny bit of business experience from Free People's Store, I certainly had never run a restaurant, nor supervised employees, but Marge must have seen something in me that I hadn't yet discovered. Since Elliot was in the middle of exams, he hadn't much choice and over the phone he asked me to take the job for two weeks until he had the chance to finish his semester and hire a professional manager. This seemed like a wild idea, but why not? I had just sent the second edition of the *Catalog* off to the printer, so had the time.

Elliot flew down from Boston, fired the manager, promoted me, and returned to Boston. Suddenly, at age twenty-seven, I went from being a waitress to general manager of a restaurant with 120 seats and over fifty employees. *What had I gotten myself into?* The previous manager had left his desk totally empty—not one file, job description, form, system, or record other than basic bookkeeping (and that was inadequate, as I soon found out). There was no instruction book, and no one to guide me in this big undertaking. Fortunately, Elliot had also promoted Marge from cashier to bookkeeper, and we shared a second-floor office. With a tremendous sense of humor and motherly warmth, along with a great deal of faith in me to handle the job, Marge provided the support and encouragement I needed to go downstairs and face many difficult situations, which began with having to supervise those who had just been my playmates the day before.

On my first day as a manager, a waitress and close friend picked up a loaf of newly made pâté. Held only by the two ends, the long loaf gave way in the middle and crashed to the floor. There went the profits! What in the world was she doing so carelessly carrying a pâté that had taken the kitchen hours to make? What should I say to one of my friends?

Then there was the incompetent French chef whose Band-Aid I once found in the soup. Not only had he no sense about cooking, but on Sunday mornings—Sunday was his day off—just as the bartenders had a long line of Bloody Marys lined up with condiments of celery stalks and limes awaiting the brunch rush, he would take a shower in his apartment above the bar with his foot clamped over the drain so that the water overflowed through the ceiling and into the drinks. There went the profits again!

One of my biggest challenges was the ferocious lunch chef, Yvonne Lighty, who had terrorized me when I was a new waitress, along with the rest of the staff, with deprecating insults delivered in a thundering voice. The sound of her yelling along with the banging of her omelet pans against the stove carried all the way to my bedroom window six houses down the block. She was scary. The last manager had succumbed to her demands that she be allowed to watch soap operas on television while she cooked lunch. Now I would have to take away the television that she guarded like a mad dog and make peace in the kitchen.

The job of managing a restaurant was not an easy one, and taking the job had certainly not been my conscious choice as a career path, but when it became clear that the Sansom Committee depended on financial contributions from La Terrasse to pay the legal expenses for saving our block, I took up the cause. In order to save my new home and the community I had come to care about, I needed to turn around the failing restaurant and produce a healthy profit. This was profit with purpose—one I committed myself to wholeheartedly.

Although I still saw my job at La Terrasse as temporary, I threw myself into my work learning how to run the company largely by using my common sense and a lot of trial and error. But I did feel the need for more formal education in basic accounting and signed up for an evening class at the Wharton business school. I was surprised when I received an A in a subject I had assumed would be difficult for me, perhaps still clinging to the 1950s notions that girls were not good at math and that financial issues were best left to the menfolk. Now I found myself fascinated to learn about the balance sheet and the profit and loss statement—tools I put right to use at La Terrasse. Who would have thunk it? I customized our financial statements to better serve my decision making, separating the beverage sales and expenses into distinct categories of beer, liquor, bottled wine, and house wine, because different cost-of-goods-sold percentages were expected in each area.

It was an exciting time each month when the financials arrived from the accountant and I could see how we did. Just as I had hung baseball batting averages on my wall as a child, I made charts to track the sales and profit in each category and posted them on the wall of the office I shared with Marge. I was thrilled to watch the steady improvement and kept thinking of more and more ways to increase sales, which I found to be my strong suit and much more fun than decreasing expenses.

Managing people was the far greater challenge. There was no help from Elliot in learning how to be a good manager. When he made an infrequent visit to town from his home in Boston, where he was in graduate school, he often demonstrated how *not* to manage people, though he did inspire a clean kitchen. I once did a drawing of him on his hands and knees inspecting the equipment with white gloves and a magnifying glass.

Despite or maybe because of Elliot's antics and off-color humor, such as pretending to sneeze an escargot out of his nose while seated at the bar, the work environment at La Terrasse when I arrived was lively, and I wanted to keep the informal, eclectic charm that made the restaurant interesting for customers and a fun place to work. Yet I had to create order and discipline to improve the service and food and turn a profit.

This was a big change for me. I had been a person who often made fun of rules. The first thing I did when I got to Girl Scout camp each year was to read all the policies posted on the wall in the bunk room and then vow to break them all before I left. And I always succeeded. Now I had to write the rules—and enforce them. But at least I knew all the tricks. As a waitress, I had gone into the walk-in refrigerator where no one could see me and eaten the forbidden French pastries, washing them down with big swigs of sangria. I knew about the tradition among some of the servers and bartenders to give away free drinks and food to friends. Now it was my job to change the behavior and stop the losses.

Though I had been a natural leader growing up in my neighborhood and among my college friends, it was usually around playing games, planning parties, or getting into some sort of mischief. I had never taken a formal leadership role in school and was repelled by the idea of being a boss—a person I imagined as a large man in a dark suit sitting behind a desk smoking a cigar and looking down his nose at the "help." I still carried a heightened consciousness about the possibility of abusing my power. I even found myself abdicating power when I actually needed it, a problem I experienced occasionally throughout my career both in business and in nonprofit leadership. This was particularly the case when dealing with assertive men, who, perhaps unknowingly, pushed me aside when my own approach appeared less forceful. I needed to learn how to stand up for myself and use my power wisely. Though I never lit up a cigar and looked down my nose, I soon got the hang of being the boss.

My first showdown happened with a big, burly bartender. In order to increase sales, I had come up with the idea of buying a baby grand piano for the dining room, so that we could have entertainment during dinner and also build a late night crowd. After dinner when the dining room closed, the bar was always packed to the gills, and I saw the empty dining room as a missed opportunity. At first, the bartenders didn't see it that way, thinking that my plan to extend the dining hours would take business away from the bar. When the big, burly bartender refused to make drinks for the waitress working the new late shift in the dining room, I realized I had to fire him. I think I was more surprised than he was when I said, "Get out!"

The next big change for the bartenders came when I promoted the only female, Catherine Austin Fitts, to be bar manager. It wasn't because she was female, but because I saw her as being the most capable person for the job. The bartenders soon came around when she implemented some great new ideas and we developed a rocking late night business that totally filled the dining room as well as the bar, dramatically increasing their tips. (Some thirty years later, after Catherine had started her own company, Solari, to guide financial investments, our paths crossed again around our shared interest in small business and building community wealth.)

I began to develop a management style I felt comfortable with, which I came to describe as a balance between freedom and structure, individuality and conformity, spontaneity and discipline. I wanted to create a workplace that provided employees the maximum amount of freedom to be themselves within a clear framework of policies and job responsibilities.

That's how my mother raised her three children, and how she ran her third grade class, which was the noisiest in Ingomar Elementary School—a kind of controlled chaos, where learning could thrive. I later raised my kids the same way, and that's even how I have always treated my dogs—maximum freedom within the confines of what's safe and suitable. (Well, maybe not suitable by everyone's standards.) Most importantly, it's the philosophy by which I try to manage my own life—a balance of freedom to be myself with enough self-discipline and just enough conformity to succeed in society.

My first lesson in balancing freedom and conformity came in kindergarten. On the opening day of school, I was yelled at, very loudly, for eating my cookie and milk before grace was said. I was humiliated by this treatment and unhappy about going to school, so the second day, when Mom dropped me off, I snuck away and hid up on the hill behind the school building. I amused myself by digging up worms and draping them gently over the branches of a small tree I was hiding behind to see which could wiggle off first, but finally I got bored and wanted to see what the other kids were doing. I crept up to the window and peeked in to find they were playing musical chairs—my favorite game—so I ran in to join the group. That was my first experience of giving up freedom for socialization, playing by the rules so I could gain the joy of community. And maybe it was then I became determined to someday have a career that allowed me to eat whenever I wanted.

Now I was applying this theory of balancing freedom with constraint to the restaurant business. I had been in restaurants that exemplified each extreme—too much conformity and structure, which inhibits individuality and creates a stiff, boring atmosphere; or too much freedom and individuality, where things get out of control and you wonder if you will ever get your food. La Terrasse was a bit that way when I first arrived. I remember a time as a waitress when I sat on a customer's lap and drank his gin and tonic! Though riding that edge between control and freedom was not the easiest way to manage a business, for me it was the *only way* to manage.

Years later, I was intrigued to find that this concept exists in nature, which is likely why it came intuitively to me. Sister Miriam MacGillis, the founder and director of Genesis Farm, an Earth literacy center in New Jersey, introduced me to the work of Thomas Berry, the Catholic priest who described himself as an "Earth scholar." Listening to the tapes of his talks at Genesis Farm, I discovered that, according to Berry, the tension between freedom and constraint is, in fact, a natural phenomenon. Berry points out that Earth was created by the perfect balance between the energies within the Earth pushing out and the constraint imposed by gravity that contains that energy holding it all together. A degree of difference one way or the other would either collapse or explode Earth. That perfect tension is perpetuated into infinity, and it is at that point of tension where creativity thrives and we enjoy life on Earth.

That is just where I want to live my own life—at that perfect point of tension between freedom and constraint where creativity lies. And I believe that is the same point at which a business thrives. Oddly enough, I discovered many years later that another hero of mine, E. F. Schumacher, author of *Small Is Beautiful,* had a similar outlook when he said "any organization has to strive continuously for the orderliness of order and the disorderliness of creative freedom."

To explain my evolving management philosophy to my staff, I wrote the *Introduction to La Terrasse for New Staff,* which contained all the rules and regulations I was implementing as well as encouragement to be authentically one's self and to participate in making suggestions for improvements in systems and rules. I wrote a thorough job description for waitressing that even had a table of contents and an index, as I had done with the *Whole City Catalog,* and it was just about as thick. My once-empty desk was soon bulging with job descriptions I wrote for every position as I learned them, along with forms I designed for taking reservations, keeping inventory and ordering supplies, seating charts I drew for each dining room, charts tracking costs in each department, and sales in each category at various times of the day—all this before computers.

I was so happy to see the results of my hard work: The sales that had been stagnant for years were climbing, and costs were coming into line. Most of all, I was proud that the profits I earned were used to defend our block.

Meanwhile, efforts on the Sansom Committee took a big jump from lawsuits to street combat. While the row where I lived on Sansom Street was still occupied, the residents and storefront businesses behind us on the south half of our block, the 3400 block of Walnut Street, had just been evicted. Worse was to come.

Early one morning, I heard a rumbling from behind my row house home. Running to the rear window, open to catch the summer morning breeze, I stuck my head out to discover a bulldozer grinding its way up the back alley. I watched in horror as it began ramming into the rear of a house in the row behind mine. Bricks began to topple, and a cloud of dust partially hid the gaping hole in the wall. The developers were making their move to clear the land. McDonald's and Dunkin' Donuts were at the door.

I flew down the stairs and up the street to La Terrasse. Bursting into the kitchen, I yelled out to Elliot, who happened to be down from Boston and was repairing a stove, to call our lawyer as I raced to the back alley. Rounding the corner, I saw the bulldozer preparing to ram another hole, this time in the back of a building that, until the recent eviction, had housed a locally owned men's clothing store. I ran down the alley yelling and waving my arms and without a second thought lay down in front of the roaring bulldozer, blocking its attack.

Fortunately, the driver stopped and called it a day. How could he not when a twenty-something blonde in cutoff jeans and T-shirt lay in his path? Turns out he had accomplished a large part of his assignment. The developer's strategy, it soon became clear, was to irreparably damage the back of each building on the row before our community group could file for a restraining order. For the moment, I had managed to halt the developer's advance, and we began the long process of legal appeals to save our block.

Tiananmen Square it was not. But, eventually, I came to understand that my act of civil disobedience in our community's struggle to protect our homes and small businesses from the onslaught of chain stores was also a fight for democracy, and an act for peace as well.

Our lawyer succeeded in getting a restraining order to hold off demolition while he filed our appeal. We ended up appealing all the way to the US Supreme Court. When, about a year later, the highest court rejected hearing our case, we lost the fight to save the Walnut Street half of our block, which was demolished to make way for our future neighbors—Cinnabon, CVS, Dunkin' Donuts, and the Gap. But the Sansom Street half of the block was still ours, and we continued to fight on.

Elliot remained wrapped up in graduate studies, and when he was in town he spent his time meeting with lawyers and holding Sansom Committee meetings. Since the business was improving, and I was enjoying my job, he had no reason to hire someone else and gave me the freedom to do things my way—though not until after I had put my foot down in an early exchange. When he came back to Philadelphia for his holiday break the first year I was in the job, he began to question my plans for New Year's Eve, always a crucial night for a restaurant. I told him that I had to do things my way or not at all, and I surprised myself at how sure I was of this. He backed off and gave me that lucky break to prove what I could do in managing the restaurant on my own.

Even though I succeeded and the restaurant prospered, all the while I mentally had one foot out the door. When people asked what I did for a living, I still only talked about Synapse and my desire to build it into a career that combined my interests in community building, social activism, writing, and design. No matter that this was nothing more than volunteer work. Why mention the restaurant? At that point, I didn't realize I'd spend a total of twelve years at La Terrasse, with ten of those years as general manager. To me, La Terrasse was still temporary.

I thought I would soon be finished with my restaurant "project," and that would be that. But slowly I began to see that managing a business was a never-ending process, and there would not be a time when, like publishing, I would say to myself "I've finally got it just as I want it: I'm finished." Even so, I could not imagine that I would continue a career in business, because I had always wanted to do something to make the world a better place, and I still could not envision a career in business as a way to do that.

But one night that changed. I was talking at the bar with a customer about my parents' age, an eccentric character named Isaac who came in almost every night, partly because after the restaurant closed and the other customers were gone, I let him play our baby grand piano. The black sheep of a distinguished Philadelphia family, Isaac was very intelligent and had gone to Princeton, but had a few strange habits such as never changing his clothes. He did take a daily shower at the boarding house where he lived, but then he'd put on dirty clothes, which he rotated but never washed. I don't think he brushed his teeth either. I once made an appointment for him to visit the dentist, and when I arrived to pick him up, he wouldn't come out of his room. After much coaxing, he opened the door and stood there with his eyes closed. I had to lead him by the hand to the dentist's office where he finally opened his eyes and his mouth for a sweet sounding dental assistant.

Isaac appeared in the bar most nights around midnight and enjoyed getting into conversations with graduate school students while he drank beer, smoked Camel cigarettes, and incessantly drummed his figures on the bar, gliding them back and forth as though playing the piano. One couldn't help but notice that Isaac had a missing finger, which he said was lost in an accident. The loss prevented him from becoming a concert pianist, though he hinted that it was self-inflicted. Isaac fascinated me, and we became friends, so I confided in him about my ambivalence toward business. "It's just about money," I complained over a scotch one night. "How can this work have real meaning in my life?"

"Oh, my dear," Isaac replied, "it's not like that at all, not in the way you run the business. When a coin passes from one hand to the next, it's not the coin that counts, but the warmth of the hand." This may have been a corny saying, but it woke me up to something that would guide my career from then on—that business is not about money, it's about relationships.

This simple concept dramatically changed my view of business. My uncertainty about my accidental career began to evaporate, and I turned to my job with renewed energy. About that time, I was offered a job working as an artist designing and painting wall murals, and I wavered a bit before realizing that the restaurant business was itself an art form for me. I was a *business artist*. I finally accepted the fact that I loved the restaurant business, and looked at my position at La Terrasse as more than a temporary job.

More importantly, I began to realize just how much I really cared about the staff and the customers—some became my best friends—and I realized that I had created a wonderful workplace and a warm and exciting place for customers to gather for consistently good food and service. I had fired the "Band-Aid chef" from the kitchen, and after one false start with another chef who turned out to have an alcohol problem and kept a freezer full of carrots he had carved into penises to show off to the salesmen,

I was lucky to find a talented and capable person to take over the kitchen in 1976. Kamol Putlek blended classic French cooking with a splash of the cuisine of his native Thailand, and this delicious food, like sea bass Provençal and Thai noodle salad, so consistently and thoughtfully prepared, finally put La Terrasse on the map as a food destination.

In the beginning, I was often too attached to my employees. I remember the day a favorite waiter, Dean, left to go back home to Texas. I was in tears to see him go. It was something I had to get used to—the coming and going of employees in the restaurant business, notorious for high turnover. I consoled myself by recognizing that each time someone left, I had the opportunity to get to know a new person, and I began to see that as a benefit of the business. For many years after he left, Dean called me from Texas on Halloween to see what costume I was wearing that year, which was always some sort of animal – pig, cow, skunk, raccoon, and, of course, dog.

In time, I learned not to become so attached, but always to care. I took lots of photographs of every employee that worked for me and arranged the photos in albums so that I would always remember each person. I recognized every birthday and, when the occasion arose, threw engagement parties and baby showers. The first new parent among my employees was a blond-haired young man named Tom Slenzate whom I hired as property manager to keep on top of cleaning and repairs—because I knew that was one thing that Elliot would be examining with his magnifying glass! Tom seemed so wet behind the ears that it was a big surprise when he brought in his wife and newborn baby girl to meet everyone. I took photos of Tom with his baby for my album. Tragically, a few years later, Tom passed away. He was the first person I knew to die from AIDS.

I enjoyed discovering underutilized talent and promoting employees into positions where they could shine. I had moved the piano from the bar to the dining room and hired classical pianists to play during dinner and jazz performers to draw a late night business. I noticed that one classical pianist, Pasquale Iocca, whose Chopin was heavenly, also had an aptitude for fine wines. I sought his opinion as I struggled to build our wine list and eventually asked him to be Director of Wine and Music, a position I created just for him. That began a practice I used again over the years for filling management positions: hire a talented person and design the job around that individual's strengths and interests, rather than define the position first and find someone to fill it.

Pasquale tended to be a quiet person without a big social life, and I often dragged him off on adventures. Once down at the shore in Cape May Point, New Jersey, I brought five or six giant blow-up plastic animal-shaped floats for riding the waves. Pasquale had a purple hippopotamus, I took the turtle, another friend took a giraffe, and so on, and we set out to sea. Somehow Pasquale drifted around the jetty and out of sight. When I noticed he was missing, I went to shore and ran down the beach past the jetty to look for him. There I caught quite a sight. A group of nuns from the nearby convent had formed a human chain to rescue Pasquale and his purple hippo who were being dashed against the rocks. The nuns dragged him to shore and took him off to the nunnery to bandage him up. I ran back to tell the others that the nuns had captured Pasquale, and we all went to fetch him. Finally, he emerged from the nunnery covered with bandages but with no serious injury, dragging the purple hippo behind him.

Despite the hippo episode, Pasquale was really quite a sophisticated fellow and went on to become an expert in European wines. When I left La Terrasse and started the White Dog Café, which had an all-American wine list, Pasquale moved to New York City to take a job with the Portuguese Trade Commission, becoming known as the greatest authority on Portuguese wines in the country, writing books and brochures and speaking around the world. We remained dear friends throughout his life. The restaurant industry lost many fine people to the AIDS epidemic. For me it began with Tom in the early 1980s and ended with Pasquale in 1998.

During my inaugural year as manager, my first big outdoor event was the annual Bastille Day party on July 14th. The Bastille Day celebration had already become a tradition at La Terrasse, so I had witnessed both the fun as well as the problems during my waitress days. The previous year, after a wild night waiting tables and joining in the debauchery, I had found myself waking up on the floor of the restroom in the wee hours of the morning. Stumbling into the kitchen, I discovered the dishwasher passed out on the floor, surrounded by heaping piles of dirty pots, pans, and dishes. The whole restaurant was trashed, with furniture askew and overflowing garbage cans scattered about and no other staff in sight. No wonder the restaurant was traditionally closed the day after Bastille Day for cleanup and recovery.

Now it was my turn to manage Bastille Day. I wanted the outdoor party under the stars to be a magical experience—an outrageously good party for my customers to remember. But I was determined to manage the event in a way that did not require sacrificing a day of business. I wanted everything cleaned up so that we were ready to serve lunch the next day.

I began by imagining how the event would look—how I would arrange the tables covered with red tablecloths and decorated with candles and bouquets of red, white, and blue flowers with little French flags; how I would string the red, white, and blue streamers and balloons; and where the serving stations and trash cans would go. I bought some French records, and as I recorded them onto a dance tape, I imagined how I would move the crowd from dining to the dance floor and how they would react to each song. Just after dinner, I would first play "La Marseillaise" and everyone would rise to stand for the French national anthem. Next, while everyone was still on their feet, I would play an irresistible French cabaret-style waltz with accordion and violins. I envisioned the couples taking to the dance floor and whirling about to the enchanting waltz, then dancing to a few fast songs like "Madeleine" by Jacque Brel, before falling back into each other's arms for the ever so romantic "La Mer" with Charles Trenet. After that, a mix of French and American dance songs would keep the dance floor hopping until last call at 2:00 a.m., when cleanup would begin.

When July 14th arrived, I was up at the crack of dawn to begin preparations and could barely contain my excitement as my plans unfolded in real life. After a delicious dinner ending with a red, white, and blue dessert of strawberry and blueberry tart with whipped cream, everyone stood for "La Marseillaise." Then just as I imagined—I couldn't believe my eyes; it really was just as I imagined!—when the waltz began the couples glided to the floor waltzing and swirling and smiling and whirling. I was overjoyed to see the customers having such a marvelous time. I wanted the staff to enjoy themselves, too, and encouraged them to join in the dancing. It was a wonderful party, and at 2:00 a.m. all of the staff pitched in to clean up, folding up the tables and over one hundred chairs and sweeping the street and floors. When everything was cleaned up, to my great surprise and delight the staff lifted me up on their shoulders and carried me through the street in celebration of a triumphant night. I was full of joy and overwhelmed with affection for the customers, the staff, and for La Terrasse. And the next day, we opened on time for lunch, not missing a beat.

Constantly thinking up new ideas to please my La Terrasse customers, I began drawing murals on a blank wall leading from the bar to the dining room depicting upcoming events, and for Valentine's Day dinner posted photographs of couples who had met or courted at La Terrasse and later married, including a growing number of employees. I built a mailing list and began sending a quarterly newsletter, bringing news to my customers about the latest dishes Kamol had put on the menu and special events that became annual traditions—wine dinners to highlight fine vintages selected by Pasquale, Halloween costume parties with a stage for performances, and outdoor festivals like Bastille Day and a new one I called Rum & Reggae, featuring live reggae music and our long list of distinctive rums. Music was an important part of restaurant life for me, and I discovered a most unusual seventy-two-year-old pianist who became a regular performer at La Terrasse and gave me a new perspective on aging. Gertrude Redheffer was in the audience at a piano concert where Pasquale was performing. When we met her at a reception following the concert and discovered that she was a pianist, too, Pasquale and I invited her to come back to La Terrasse with us to see how she liked our Steinway baby grand. We were smitten with Gertrude's charm and her stride-style playing—pounding the jazz of the 1920s, 1930s, and 1940s with tunes like "Sweet Georgia Brown," "I Got Rhythm," and "Stumbling All Around." And always with a big smile and sparkling blue eyes that lit up the room. From that night on, for eight years Gertrude played at La Terrasse every New Year's Eve as well as New Year's Day brunch. During New Year's dinner, Pasquale played classical music for the first set, and then Gertrude would play until midnight, ending with "Auld Lang Syne." One year, a busboy streaked naked through the dining rooms at midnight and I was afraid an elderly lady like Gertrude might be offended by the nudity. That is until I heard her describe the occasion to a friend the next day at brunch. With a giggle, she asked her friend, "And where do you think he tied a big red bow?!"

Soon Gertrude was playing for brunch every Mother's Day and Father's Day and on Easter Sunday, when the serving staff wore rabbit ears or flowered Easter bonnets from the collection I hung on my living room wall. When she was seventy-five, I produced a record called *Gertrude Live at La Terrasse*, recorded by my brother John, who owned a recording studio on the third floor above the restaurant (next to the apartment of the sculptor Robin Fredenthal) called Third Story Recording. I drew a portrait of Gertrude for the cover of the album showing her at the keyboard in her favorite outfit—a red dress with white pearls, and a little black hat with a red feather. Gertrude, a retired telephone operator, told everyone that I had "discovered" her as a pianist when she was seventy-two, beginning her late blooming career as a café entertainer with her own record. In a newspaper article about her record debut, the reporter captured Gertrude's description of the night we met:

> "I played for one and a half hours, dear," she said. "She liked me and she liked my style, and from then on it was parties, parties, parties. Saturday night. Sunday night. Parties, parties, parties. And it was fun, dear. I've made a lot of fun for myself in my life. And they tell me I've made a lot of fun for them, too."

And fun we sure did have! Though we were more than forty years apart in age, Gertrude and I became close friends, and people joked that I turned up at parties accompanied by an old lady, a baby (which I'll get to in a bit), and a dog. The dog was Newman, a part-beagle stray whom I had rescued several years earlier when he was foraging by the garbage dumpster and who reminded me of my childhood beagles, Peppy and Pooie. At the time, I was single, and I named him "Newman," because he was the new man in my life!

Once I felt secure in my career, my mind turned to starting a family. I was thirty-two years old. It was time to get on with it. Neil, the handsome, brown-eyed architect who served with me on the Sansom Committee, shared my values for building a Jane Jacobs–inspired community on Sansom Street. The first person I ever heard talk about solar houses and energy efficiency with concern for the natural environment, he had caught my eye. We were married Labor Day of 1978 in a magical event catered by the staff of La Terrasse, which closed for the day. I could not imagine getting married anywhere but in the woods—a place sacred to me, where tall trees create a natural cathedral. The woods behind Neil's parents' house in the Wissahickon Valley of northwest Philadelphia was the perfect place for both the wedding and gala reception. The waiters, dressed in formal black and white from the neck down, were topped with giant papier-mâché animal heads— a bear, squirrel, rabbit, wolf, eagle, and cardinal—as they walked through the crowd carrying large silver trays of food to the buffet arranged on the dance floor we had laid across the woodland landscape. I hauled the baby grand piano from LaTerrasse into the woods, and of course, Gertrude played a few numbers like "Tea for Two" when the dance band took a break.

Our daughter Grace, named after my mother's mother, was born the next year. The birth didn't come as swiftly as I had hoped. Despite my wild dancing to Motown to get things moving, Grace was three weeks late. I had stopped clearing my desk every night before going home. A couple of weeks later, when my water finally broke about midnight, I insisted to Neil that before going to the maternity hospital, I had to go back to the office to clear my desk. I wrote notes to each of the managers and stopped in the bar to say good-bye to the crowd as Neil waited with the car ready to go. We need not have rushed since it took twenty-four more hours to push out the nearly ten pound baby.

I had planned to take off a few weeks after Grace was born, while Elliot watched over the restaurant, but he was impatient to get back to New York City, where he had moved after finishing school, and he took off after a week. So I went back to work, bringing one-week-old Grace with me. By then I had been managing the restaurant for five years, with full responsibility for the operation of the business, and Elliot had promised me a partnership stake that would be formalized once the fight to save the block had ended and he was able to retrieve the company stock from his older brother, an attorney who was holding the stock in safekeeping from a possible suit by the university. In the meantime, he called me his business partner and I assumed the role of co-owner and proprietress. My new role, coupled with the fact that I wanted to keep the business running well, meant maternity leave didn't cross my mind.

Marge was delighted to look after Grace in the office when I was downstairs, and at night during dinner service I kept Grace in a little basket on top of the piano. The dining room hostesses, beginning with my cousin Debbie, who worked part-time, would amuse Grace by carrying her along while seating the guests, and the bartenders enjoyed having her stationed on the bar, to the delight of their customers.

Lawrence was born two years later, and I went back to work in a week, bringing him along. Once again, it never occurred to me to take a maternity leave, and I didn't feel that I could. It's my one lifetime regret—perhaps like many working mothers—not to have taken more time to focus only on my children during those early years. But at least I kept both children next to me night and day for the first nine or ten months during the breast-feeding stage. One Halloween, when Lawrence was two months old, I fit him into my costume by dressing up as a nursing mother beagle and dressed Lawrence as my puppy. When a customer realized that Lawrence was a real child, she let out a loud scream.

As infants, both children came along with me to community meetings, to parties, and out to dinner at many different restaurants. During the day they were in my office as I went about my business paying bills, writing reports, and meeting with staff as I fed them, changed diapers, and rocked their cradle with my foot. I remember a busboy who many years later told me he was traumatized when I fired him while breast-feeding my baby!

In time I began to represent La Terrasse as the co-owner in the larger Philadelphia community. I sat on the Mayor's Small Business Council for several years where I learned a lot about how city government functions. During that time I experimented with looking more businesslike by going to Brooks Brothers' women's department and buying a navy blue suit, oxford cloth shirts, and those silly bow ties popular with businesswomen in the 1970s who were trying to fit into careers that had traditionally been for men. But I was soon back to jeans and cowgirl boots.

Next, I joined my first board of directors at Business Executives for Nuclear Arms Control (BENAC). Serving on a board provided me with an important experience in learning how nonprofits operated as well as an understanding of how businesspeople can work together for positive change. Most of the board members were men of my father's generation. The founders and board cochairs—John Haas, the CEO of Rohm and Haas, a chemical manufacturing company; and Frederick Heldring, president of Philadelphia National Bank—had previously cofounded an organization of business executives who publicly opposed the Vietnam War back in the 1960s when it was a risky position to take, especially for Fred, who was vying for a promotion to bank president at the time. I greatly admired John and Fred. They were the first to show me how business leaders could demonstrate compassion and use their voice and influence to work for peace and justice.

By 1981, I was accepted into a year-long program called Leadership, Inc. that exposed young professionals to civic needs so that they'd be inclined toward leadership positions in nonprofits to serve their communities. We found ourselves observing city life in diverse ways—even riding around the city all night long in the backseat of a police car. One experience in particular strengthened both my desire to help people in need and my resolve to find a way to build a more just and inclusive community.

It was close to Halloween when a small group of us were driven by van to an inner city neighborhood to meet with leaders of an African American community association. As we walked from the parked van, I noticed that many of the houses in the neighborhood were boarded up or separated by vacant lots heaped with trash. I felt a sense of despair and hopelessness walking along the sidewalks littered with broken glass, imagining that the neighborhood was home to drug dealers and criminals. We stopped before a building that, like many others, had boarded-up windows on the upper floors and looked to be vacant. But as we entered, I heard the sound of music that became louder when the door to the basement was opened and we walked downstairs. The lights were bright in a room adorned with colored decorations and filled with happy children dressed in Halloween costumes laughing and playing. A group of women were serving treats to the kids and leading them in games.

I was astonished by the contrast to the bleak street life outside. Here were mothers doing all that they could to create a wholesome and happy experience for their young children, struggling to create a life rich in love and care within a community suffering the effects of extreme poverty and neglect. How strong these mothers were. How humbled I felt. From that point on, whenever I see neighborhoods with boarded windows and trash-strewn streets, I remember that as in any neighborhood there are loving parents and innocent, sweet children living there—who are, unfortunately, more likely than I to be the victims of crime and violence.

Experiences like this one fed my longing to be of greater service. As much as I loved the restaurant business, I didn't want my career just to be about celebration, the icing on the cake of life; I wanted to bring positive change to the world. Though I was secure and happy in my community on Sansom Street, there was so much suffering in other parts of the city and around the globe. Eventually, a small opportunity entered my life, showing me how I might both run a business and engage in social change at the same time.

It began when a flyer stapled to a phone pole on Sansom Street caught my eye. The poster announced a slide show presentation by activists who had just returned from a fact-finding trip to witness the civil war in El Salvador. I didn't know much about Central America, but I knew there was controversy about President Reagan's policy toward El Salvador, and I decided to attend the talk and find out what was going on down there. After the travesty of Vietnam, I wanted to stay informed about what my government was up to in foreign countries.

The slide show was held in the home of an elderly couple, the Millers, who had turned the living room of their stately house in Center City into a small auditorium, complete with a second floor balcony. At the presentation, I was horrified to hear that the United States was supporting the government of El Salvador and that the government's military was implicated in "death squads" that murdered thousands of innocent Salvadoran civilians and had allegedly committed the rape and murder of four American nuns. How horrible! If this were true—and I wasn't sure yet—few Americans knew about it, nor understood that our tax dollars were being used to support a regime that used "death squads" to repress its own people.

Soon after seeing the slide show, one of the La Terrasse waiters introduced me to his friend David Funkhouser, an Episcopal priest and founder of the Central American Organizing Project, which educated people about the political realities in Central America. David was hosting a group of Salvadoran political refugees marching from New York City to Washington DC to protest the US support of their repressive government. They were staying at a church just up the street from the restaurant and had no money for expenses. David asked if we would contribute food from the restaurant. Since La Terrasse did not open until lunch, I suggested that the group of twenty Salvadorans come for a hot breakfast. If David would cook, I would serve the meals.

When the Salvadorans arrived in bandanas, straw hats, and black boots, I couldn't help but think what a contrast they were to our usual clientele. They were refugees in a political conflict in which my country—I was clear about this now—supported the opposing side.

After a hearty breakfast and good-bye hugs, the travelers formed a brigade out on Sansom Street, with the lead marchers holding a wide banner across the front calling for the United States to end its involvement in El Salvador. They waved good-bye and marched down Sansom Street, continuing their long journey to Washington DC.

Though we looked so different and spoke a different language, I was surprised to feel such a strong connection to the Salvadorans and their cause. The word that came into my mind to describe the feeling was "solidarity." I had always associated that word with socialism or even communism, but I was beginning to understand that what was often labeled as communist was actually simply a strong sense of community around common values. The traditional indigenous preference for communal activities did not mean they were communist, as some politicians in both countries suggested. In fact, they were struggling for democracy.

This volunteer breakfast solved a problem that had bedeviled me for some time: With all the work it took to run a small business, how could there be time to volunteer for all the other things I cared about? Some people did volunteer work in the evenings and weekends, but in the restaurant business there was no downtime. The answer was clear: Address the issues I care about through the business.

I immediately put this concept to use and held my first social change event for my customers—a reception for Charlie Clements, a medical doctor who was working in war-torn El Salvador. As a graduate of the Air Force Academy who had flown many missions in the Vietnam War, he had decided the war was immoral and had refused to fly missions supporting the invasion of Cambodia. As a newly trained physician, he saw that the villages he served in El Salvador were being bombed by some of the same aircraft he had previously flown in Vietnam. Dr. Clements had a message of peace and nonviolence I wanted my customers to hear.

My evening at the Millers provided a model for me. Observing how they utilized their living room as a gathering place for a presentation showed me how it could be done at La Terrasse. Years later, I would follow the Miller model more fully when I began educational programs at the White Dog Café to discuss the issues of the day and hear stories that demonstrated our interconnection with others at home and abroad.

In one form or another, in the years to come, I found that I could address all the issues I cared about *through my business*. It was here that I had the focus of time, space, resources, and people, and could use them effectively. I was excited to explore the many possibilities of this unique combination of good food with social activism.

Around this time, after many years of continued legal struggle and growing public support to "save the block," our community group finally won a settlement that spared the 3400 block of Sansom Street from the wrecking ball. Though we were disappointed to have lost the Walnut Street buildings, we were overjoyed to save Sansom Street. As part of the settlement, Neil and I, along with other members of the Sansom Committee, were each given the opportunity to purchase and restore one of the houses we had fought so long to save. At the same time, the university gained development rights for the Walnut Street side, where it demolished the houses—which, though in disrepair, had been far grander than those on Sansom Street—to build in their place a shopping center with offices and rooms full of computers above. The new shops and offices emptied out at 5:00 or 6:00 p.m., a few of the fast-food places stayed open until 10:00, but after that the Walnut Street side of the block was dead. The only signs of twenty-four-hour occupancy were the enormous air-conditioning and heating units on the roof, which roared their gray noise 24/7. Conversely, the Sansom Street side of the block remains to this day full of life day and night—cared for, watched over, and utilized by the shopkeepers and residents. Jane Jacobs would be proud.

After the settlement, the residents and businesses of Sansom Street enjoyed good relations with a new administration at the University of Pennsylvania and with the administrations that followed. Eventually our block, with its array of unique locally owned shops and restaurants with homes above, was held up by the university as a model of vibrant city living where they often brought visiting dignitaries and entertained prospective students and faculty.

Participating in the Sansom Committee showed me the power of working in a group aligned around a shared vision. Each member contributed his or her own unique talent, connection, or resource to the cause. A La Terrasse busboy working his way through Penn Law School had become an assistant to our lawyer. A regular customer with an advertising agency had designed our "Save the Block" buttons and T-shirts. And we all had fun working together. In the years to come, this experience, collaborating as a team around a shared vision, gave me insight into my role as a leader in the local living economy movement.

When I completed the purchase of my house at 3420 Sansom Street in the early 1980s, I had the idea of using my storefront space as a way to build business for La Terrasse by starting a coffee shop there and then moving the business up the street when the house next to La Terrasse became available for the restaurant's expansion. To a large extent, the only times La Terrasse was not already busy were at breakfast and the teatime lull between lunch and dinner. A coffee shop would fill those gaps. This was long before Starbucks and the coffee phenomena reached our neighborhood, but I could see that the university community would benefit by a charming coffee shop with delicious fresh muffins, and I liked the idea of having a nonalcoholic alternative to the bar scene.

I was overjoyed that the block fight was over and that we were taking title to the houses. Everything seemed to be going my way. I had a flourishing restaurant business with plans to expand and had finished my third Synapse publication, *Philadelphia Resource Guide*, updated from the more 1960s name of *Whole City Catalog*. In my personal life, I had two great kids, Grace, now four years old, and Lawrence, two years old. Neil, my architect husband, was able to buy the house next to mine (where sculptor Robert Engman once had his studio before moving out of the city) with plans to connect the upper floors to create a larger home for our family of four.

But there was hard news just around the corner. Elliot had changed his plans and decided to move back to Philadelphia to run the restaurant himself. Now with a successful business model that was making money, he planned to turn La Terrasse into a national chain. *A chain, of all things!* He was already using our profits to hire an old friend who was helping him find a location for the second La Terrasse in Cambridge, Massachusetts. As for me, Elliot no longer saw the need for me to run the restaurant, much less to continue as a business partner and put stock in my name as he had promised. The temporary job that had turned into a ten-year-long commitment, during which time I increased sales from $200,000 to $2,000,000 annually with a healthy profit, was suddenly over. I had forgone raises and bonuses as part of the path to partnership—the one I had failed to get in writing. When it came time to formalize the partnership, Elliot's offer to me was startling: The muffin and coffee business I had just started as part of La Terrasse would be mine. *Proprietress of a muffin shop? Give me a break!*

I was in shock at the thought of losing my stake in La Terrasse. My first reaction was to fight Elliot's decision, claiming my rightful position as co-owner, but when I picked up the phone to talk with a lawyer no sound would come out of my mouth. It was so against my nature to fight someone who had been my ally for so long that I was totally speechless. I could not find the words nor the temperament. This made me realize that my role in life was not as a fighter, but as a builder. It was better for me to walk away and use my energy to start building again.

In thinking it over, I saw it made no sense to be partners with someone who did not value my worth. I had been there before. Hard as it was, I understood that Elliot needed to work with someone who shared his vision for business, and I was far from that. My dedication to one particular community and my awakening interest in using the business for social activism conflicted with Elliot's goals to build a national chain. He was attracted to the corporate image he saw as a hallmark of success, and he described me as more like an "Earth Mother," something I would have taken as a compliment had he not meant it in a derogatory way.

At first, losing my role in the business I had run on my own for ten years felt as though I had lost my vehicle for expressing who I was and what I cared most about. La Terrasse had become my art form, my voice. It was as though somehow the business was who I was. But just as I had left Free People's Store looking for the person named Judy Wicks whom I had lost in a marriage, I needed to regain my own identity once more. It was time to move on again, realizing that what I wanted most was having the freedom to express who I was through my work—through my very own business.

But where would the money come from to start over again? I had not taken a commensurate salary while at La Terrasse, expecting stock in return for my efforts, so I had little savings. Remembering that my former husband and business partner, Richard Hayne, had promised to pay me my share when Free People's Store was sold, I thought I would ask for his help. True, the business had not been sold; but it no longer appeared that selling it was part of the plan. The store had continued to grow under Dick's leadership. In 1975, after I had been gone for a couple of years, Dick had moved the store up the street to a bigger and better location at the very edge of the campus and changed the name to Urban Outfitters. The business had opened a second location in Cambridge and started a wholesale brand called Free People. The enterprise hadn't yet made Dick the billionaire that it one day would, but it was doing remarkably well. Surely, I assumed, he would see it as fair that at this point he offer me some compensation for my role in starting the business.

I recall Dick smiling from behind his big desk and, with a friendly tone, replying that while both of us knew we had created the store together, no one else would. He also declared that he didn't remember making any such agreement about compensation and didn't believe he owed me a thing. After hearing of my experience at La Terrasse, he offered his advice: Stop allowing men to take advantage of you and start looking out after your own interests; that's the way the business world works.

Somehow, I was not surprised. It had been my choice to leave the business and marriage, and now it was clearer than ever that it had been the right thing to do. I did not begrudge Dick his response. He was being true to his own way of thinking, a way that had served him well. Though I knew Dick to be a very caring person, when it came to business he knew how to play hardball. This time, unlike the softball team I wanted to join when we were both ten years old, it was not a game I wanted to play.

Despite the shock and disappointment of losing La Terrasse, I had much to be grateful for, and I wanted to leave without bad feelings or regret. After all, if it had not been for Elliot, there would have been no La Terrasse, and the block would likely have been torn down. And I had met the father of my children at La Terrasse and so many of my good friends. I learned how to run a restaurant, but I also had learned that I could operate a business out of love. I had found that even when working in a for-profit business, I could know that I was doing good, allowing me to wake up in the morning with joy in my heart and excitement for the day ahead.

And it was La Terrasse that first brought me to Sansom Street looking for a waitress job so long ago. Here on this block I had found my place in the world. It was here that I wanted to be, and I would nurture and care for this neighborhood and continue building a warm and lively community in which to live, work, and raise my family. So I said goodbye to La Terrasse and turned my full attention down the street to the tiny muffin and coffee take-out shop I had recently started on the first floor of my house. Set up in the front corner, it was no bigger than my childhood forts. Despite my lack of resources, I vowed that I would turn it into one of Philadelphia's most successful restaurants. In time it became just that, as well as a full-throated expression of my social activism. From my life's most traumatic heartbreak bloomed my greatest love—the White Dog Café.

The character of a third place is determined most of all by its regular clientele and is marked by a playful mood. . . . They are the heart of a community's social vitality, the grassroots of democracy. . . .

—Ray Oldenburg, in *The Great Good Place: Cafes, Coffee Shops, Bookstores, Bars, Hair Salons, and Other Hangouts at the Heart of a Community*

❦ 5 ❦
The Blooming of the White Dog Café

WHEN I IMAGINED what the White Dog Café would look like, the first vision that came to mind was blue-and-white checkered café-style curtains hanging in the two front windows. The checkered fabric stood for old-fashioned hospitality—homey and unpretentious. Everything else would be built around those curtains.

At the time, I had not heard of sustainability, or fair trade, or even the concept of a socially responsible business. I just wanted a warm and friendly place for my friends and neighbors to gather for an enjoyable time, good conversation, and the kind of food I myself liked to eat. After my many years in a French restaurant with a menu rich in heavy cream sauces and imported ingredients, I was ready for a change. And I knew the change I longed for most. I wanted to serve up the food I enjoyed as a child—like Mom's marinated beef shish kebabs skewered with fresh vegetables from the family garden, which Dad grilled over charcoal, and for dessert—Nana's fresh strawberry pie. And I could not wait to put on the menu my childhood favorites—root beer floats and hot fudge sundaes—and order them whenever I wanted.

I had never been to the trend-setting restaurants of California, nor heard of the food revolutionary Alice Waters, who was leading the charge at her Chez Panisse restaurant in Berkeley, founded in 1971, to change American cuisine from the traditional meat and potatoes and highly processed foods to creative dishes that featured the natural flavors of fresh local ingredients. But as the White Dog emerged and grew, I was lucky to catch the wave of interest Alice inspired in a new American cuisine that was about to sweep the country. The White Dog Café would be among the first restaurants in Philadelphia, and perhaps in the country, to feature a cuisine that highlighted farm-fresh ingredients. But that came later. First we had to have a kitchen and some tables and chairs.

Actually, first we had to sell some muffins.

I had started the muffin shop just before leaving La Terrasse. We had opened our doors as the students and faculty from the University of Pennsylvania were returning from winter break in January 1983. During the coming months, the Penn Law School across the street provided a steady flow of students eager for a good cup of coffee and a morning muffin, freshly made in the La Terrasse kitchen just up the street.

Now, though, the muffin shop loomed much larger in my life, and turning my full attention to growing it, I looked for ways to expand the menu to attract a lunch crowd. But the food had to be something I could manage myself, since I had no money to hire a cook, and I only knew how to make two things—bread and soup from my Eskimo village days. So bread and soup it was.

I crowded two used refrigerators into my second-floor home kitchen to hold ingredients and began cooking in the evenings upstairs, while two-year-old Lawrence and four-year-old Grace tugged at my skirt for attention. Starting a restaurant with young children was obviously not my plan, but some things just happen that way. My most stressful challenge was not the usual business angst of inadequate capital or managing employees, but rather the constant pull between caring for the kids and tending to a business that needed so much of my time and energy. During the day, Neil was at his architecture office and Grace and Lawrence attended a nearby nursery school, but evenings and weekends I had to juggle work with care of the kids. They survived, though Grace still has a huge scar on her thigh where she cut herself when accidently sitting on the saw blade of a commercial grade aluminum foil dispenser left on a kitchen stool. Makes me scream "Ouch!" just to think about it.

With my bread- and soup-making, I was breaking my junior high school vow never to cook, but in only a month or so I could afford to hire a real cook to relieve me and expand the menu to include sandwiches and homemade desserts. We were still a take-out operation, but it was a definite step forward. I bought a brand new commercial range, figuring we would eventually move it downstairs after we were able to get a loan to install a professional kitchen in the basements of our two row houses. It was 1984, not long after Neil and I had bought our side-by-side row homes. The basements were still dark, dank, dirt-floored cellars. When spring brought good weather, we built a brick patio that spanned the fronts of both our houses and was bordered along the sidewalk with a green privet hedge. It was soon full of customers who seated themselves to enjoy soup and sandwiches, or just a good cup of coffee; the first outdoor café on Sansom Street, adding to the lively street life.

In my office at La Terrasse, I had worked at an old-fashioned rolltop desk next to a large antique oak dining table that served as a conference table. I had sat through many a situation at that table during my ten years as manager—hiring, firing, promoting, advising, cajoling, as well as holding our weekly manager meetings when we gathered to make plans, resolve problems, and celebrate our successes. And as the traumatized former busboy had reminded me, at times breast-feeding and tending to young babies as I worked.

Full of memories, my conference table and desk came along with me to 3420 Sansom Street, where I created an office on the first floor behind the muffin take-out shop. Before leaving La Terrasse, I had begun plans to continue the publishing at Synapse with the help of researcher and writer Wendy Born, who had worked on the *Philadelphia Resource Guide* and now shared my new office. Though we had just started research on a guide for working mothers on balancing work and home life (something we both saw the need for from our own busy lives), our plan soon changed.

One day at lunchtime, I noticed that the line for take-out stretched out the front door and down the steps. I asked Wendy if she had ever been a waitress. She had. "Good," I said, "me too. So let's open the door and invite that line of customers into our office to sit at the big oak table, and you and I will wait on them."

The customers had a merry time chatting around the table while eating homemade soup and sandwiches and were back the next day with their friends. Yikes, we needed more tables. I shoved our desks back into the corners and brought down the round oak table with four chairs from our home kitchen upstairs, along with an assortment of small tables—end tables, corner tables, anything I could find—and odd chairs, which immediately filled up with eager customers.

All of a sudden, White Dog Café was a sit-down restaurant with table service. I moved our office up to the house, which was becoming barren with so much furniture moved downstairs, and hired a waitress. I asked Wendy if she would move from research work to become café manager, overseeing daily operations, while I focused on building the business. I had no money to offer her a salary, so I suggested 5 percent of White Dog stock per year until we could afford to pay her from cash flow. She accepted and over the next three years she would receive a total of 15 percent of White Dog stock, an agreement that ended well for both of us. During the seven years Wendy worked at the White Dog, she provided grace and stability in a whirlwind time of rapid growth and change.

Of course, with all of our time and energy needed to build the White Dog, there was no time for our publishing work. Without sadness, I closed down Synapse, the nonprofit that had been a vehicle for serving my community for over ten years. It would not be long before I discovered that the very same desire for community building, social change, and information sharing that drove my publishing work would take a bright new form in the lively educational programs that became a signature feature of the White Dog.

Meanwhile, the big oak conference table I had brought from my old office became known as Table 20, and the round oak kitchen table from upstairs became Table 24. They remained in the exact same places in our first dining room for twenty-five years.

For décor, just as I did with my forts, I used what I had, hanging family photographs of people with their dogs on the cream-colored wall behind Table 20. One picture showed my grandmother Grace shaking hands with her little dog Tricksy. In the frame, I put her business card from her bed-and-breakfast in Florida, which read: "House of the Seven Gables—A good night's rest for every guest, Grace Scott, Proprietress." I was told that Grandma had once slept in the bathtub so that she could give up her bed to a weary soldier on his way home from the nearby naval base during World War II. Photos of Neil's family pictured his mother with her big white standard poodle and his great-grandfather with a shaggy black dog next to a covered wagon.

Over the years, I added photos of customers with their dogs and a few celebrities with *their* dogs, including Gertrude Stein with her big poodle and Eleanor Roosevelt with her little black Scottie. Above the photos, I installed a long shelf the length of the room that was soon crowded with framed pictures of customers with their dogs and a wide assortment of white dog figures that customers often contributed to the collection. On other walls, I began a gallery of antique prints, including one Neil and I had found in England on our honeymoon, not knowing at the time it would one day be hanging in the White Dog Café—not knowing there would even be a café—showing a little girl feeding a cookie to a large dog.

Now that we were providing table service, we needed real plates—as well as bowls, coffee cups, glasses, and utensils. And what about washing them? With all the cooking going on in my tiny home kitchen, there was certainly no room for dishwashing, so I installed a regulation three-bowl sink in the corner of the dining room where the dishwasher merrily conversed with the customers, who passed him their dirty plates as they finished each course.

It was an exciting day when Neil broke a doorway through the wall of the café that separated our two houses. Looking through the hole into the empty space, I thought, *Wow, a whole new room! Quick, we need more seats!* All I had left in the house was the living room furniture, which seemed a bit odd for a restaurant, but I pictured making a funky place for students to sip coffee and eat muffins while reading their books. I set up the coffee lounge with two sofas, a coffee table, assorted stuffed chairs, some paintings for the walls, a potted palm, and a big brass birdcage with two parakeets. No wonder that when people walked into the café for the first time, they would say, "My, Judy, it's so nice and homey in here—I feel like I'm in your house." One friend, taken aback by my unconventional furnishing, exclaimed, "Gee, Judy, you sure have a lot of nerve asking your customers to sit on old living room furniture." Little did we suspect that furnishing coffee shops with used sofas and coffee tables would soon become a hip trend. But for me, it was simply all I had.

What we needed most now were hot platters to begin building a dinner business. Too impatient to wait until we could afford putting exhaust ducts for a commercial kitchen up through our three-level house, I improvised again by setting up a charcoal grill in the backyard (shades of my father) and our first hot food service was born. A few used restaurant tables covered with blue-and-white checkered tablecloths that matched the front windows, along with our family's backyard picnic table, provided a couple of dozen outdoor seats. Neil enclosed the backyard with a white picket fence and built an arbor overhead, whimsically carving the ends of the two white-painted support beams at the top of the arbor into the shape of dog heads, which stuck out like maiden heads above the back-gate entrance. We planted big urns of wisteria that grew up the white arbor and placed pots of red geraniums on the blue-and-white checkered tables. That summer the backyard was our most popular dining area, except when an occasional rat would scurry across the yard. Since there was no way to prevent this, we would just laugh and say, "There goes another bunny!"

On the menu that summer of 1984 we offered four hot platters from the grill, which included two old family favorites—my mother's recipe for Betty's Beef Kebab and my brother's marinated chicken dish, Brother John's Chicken—along with a fish of the day and a vegetarian platter of grilled fresh vegetables with hummus. After making flyers with my drawings of white dogs to advertise the café, and with no money to post an ad or hire someone to hand out the flyers, I recruited five-year-old Grace and three-year-old Lawrence to help with our first advertising campaign. Once we finished passing out all the flyers on the nearby university campus, we raced home and peeked into the backyard to see if we had brought in any customers.

In these early days, you won't be surprised to hear that the White Dog was a funny kind of place: Not only was the food cooked outside and the dishes washed in the dining room, but the customers were sent upstairs to our living quarters when they asked for the restroom, waving to Grace and Lawrence playing on the floor as they made their way to the family bathroom. During the week, I would go to sleep before the café closed so I could get up early to take the kids to nursery school. At the end of the night, the last server would deposit the receipts under my pillow as I lay sleeping—the only safe place to hide the money. For years after, I had dreams of people leaving money under my pillow!

Fortunately, Neil was good humored about our unique lifestyle and the kids likely saw this as normal home life, with the restaurant as an extension of our home and the employees as our extended family. It wasn't long before Grace learned to use the intercom to order hot fudge sundaes from the kitchen to be delivered right to her bedroom. Who cared if we didn't have much privacy, or furniture either. Though our family's picnic table was commandeered to seat customers in the backyard, Lawrence's best friend Evan celebrated his fifth birthday in our outdoor dining room, which could now seat 30 kids. There was fun to be had for all ages.

When fall brought cooler temperatures, Neil and I enclosed the whole backyard with clear plastic over the arbor and down the sides, and constructed a chimney for the grill. We made it through the fall with many gallons of kerosene for the heaters, but by December only the chef, wearing a parka and boots, remained outside. I pleaded with him to hold on until the end of the year. I just had to celebrate New Year's Eve at the White Dog Café. The chef agreed and designed a festive New Year's Eve menu featuring beef roasted over charcoal, and we spread the word about our very first New Year's Eve dinner.

The night of the thirty-first the indoor dining room, decorated with streamers and balloons, filled up with thirtysome customers wearing party hats and blowing toy horns, including Neil and me at Table 20 with ten close friends who had all been customers or fellow employees from La Terrasse. Among them were Sam Little, a fellow Sansom Committee member, and his wife, Francie; Sandy Cadwalader, a fellow LaTerrasse alum; and Ollie Cherniahivsky and Mary Davis, whom I had met in the La Terrasse bar. The next year, Mary, along with June, the mother of Lawrence's friend Evan, established the tradition of dancing on the bar at midnight. All of these friends became regular customers at White Dog, and we enjoyed many more New Year's Eve parties together over the years. Table 20 and I had already gone through a lot together, and that New Year's party began a new era of gathering with friends and family, as well as staff during the off-hours, to celebrate special occasions, while Grandma Grace looked on with approval from her photo on the wall along with her little dog Tricksy.

People from other parts of my life in Philadelphia showed up that first New Year's Eve, too, including Bob Brecht, who had served on the board of Synapse, and his wife Susan; and next to them Ed Schwartz, the director of the Institute for the Study of Civic Values, whom I had met while researching for the *Whole City Catalog*, with his wife, Jane, and young daughter Ruth. Remarkably, Ed, Jane, and Ruth would spend every New Year's Eve at the White Dog for the next twenty-five years, watching our progress along the way, as Ruth grew old enough to dance on the bar with our daughter Grace.

From our house upstairs, I brought down the last piece of furniture still left in the living room—a piano. And Gertrude, wonderful Gertrude, filled the room with her joyful music for the first New Year's Eve at the White Dog Café on December 31, 1984.

The next day the chef left. I did not have the nerve to advertise for a new one and then show the way to our kitchen—an outdoor charcoal grill in January. Against my strong desire to keep going no matter what, I was forced to close the café and wait until spring or a loan, whichever came first.

It turned out that the White Dog's first New Year's Eve party would be the last one we shared with Gertrude. Her health was declining. With no family to care for her, she had asked me to take charge of her affairs. After she was found wandering the halls of her apartment building, knocking on doors at odd times of the night, the landlord called to tell me she must find a new place to live. After some research and visits to a number of sadly depressing warehouses for the elderly, I finally moved Gertrude from her apartment to a comfortable and cheery senior residence.

At the time of her record release, Gertrude had told a reporter, "I want to play 'til the last day I'm on Earth. I can't imagine living and not playing. I want to do it 'til the end. Then if I go . . . Goodbye! It's been fun! I've had a good time! Oooh! I've had a wonderful time, dear." I just had to make sure Gertrude could keep playing as long as she was able, so I talked the administrators at the senior residence into allowing Gertrude's piano to move in along with her. I suggested placing it near the dining room, imagining the residents gathering around the piano before or after meals while Gertrude played old-fashioned favorites. Instead, the piano was put in a small auditorium, a little-used room that was not very convenient.

Accepting this, I arranged for Gertrude to have a concert for the other residents, but as the date grew near, I could see that her strength was ebbing. My friend Jim Smith, a tenor banjo player who had recently begun playing at the White Dog, agreed to do a duet with Gertrude to help keep up the momentum. On the night of the concert, Jim and I got Gertrude to the piano—and an empty room. When no one else showed up, we went around to the rooms helping the elderly residents get to the concert, hobbling on walkers and canes or pushed in wheelchairs. We finally built up an audience of about ten people and Gertrude began to play but was soon falling asleep at the keyboard. While Jim kept the music going, I ran to Gertrude's room for her record player and a copy of *Gertrude Live at La Terrasse*. Back at the "concert," I put the record on full blast and Gertrude nodded her head and smiled while still sitting at the piano, likely dreaming that she was actually playing. When the record ended, the audience, who had also been dozing, clapped appreciatively and Gertrude took her bow before Jim and I helped everyone back to their rooms.

Gertrude died within a year at age eighty. She had often told me that she wished she could afford to yell out to a crowded room, "Drinks on me!" At her memorial service in Center City Philadelphia, I served her favorite cocktail, piña colada, to her friends and fans, telling them, "This one's on Gertrude!" A few weeks later, when I was in despair that we couldn't continue without more working capital, money suddenly appeared—a surprise $30,000 inheritance left by Gertrude, more than enough to cover her bar tab of piña coladas.

Gertrude wasn't our only benefactor. Though family members made loans totaling over $100,000, and I was able to get a $50,000 low-interest loan from a city agency that directed money toward minority- and woman-owned businesses, it wasn't enough. The business was growing and was able to make the monthly mortgage payment and provide all our meals, and though I was not yet drawing a salary, Neil's income covered other living expenses. But renovations were stalled until we could come up with enough capital to move ahead.

In early 1985, while we waited for warmer weather to reopen outside or the funds to build an indoor kitchen, we had a small miracle. A friend of mine, Sally Thompson, loaned me $75,000, unsecured and interest free, from the sale of her beach house in Cape May Point, New Jersey. Now we had enough to install a small indoor kitchen. That beach house was the place of many good times, beginning with what Sally described as the summer her "closet blew in" and her "leg blew off." The first referred to a stormy night when the wind blew down the wall of Sally's clothes closet, causing her to be late for the party where we first met. The second referred to an afternoon soon after when I drove her to the hospital after she accidently shot her leg with a miniature cannon filled with gunpowder.

I was very appreciative of Sally's friendship and her trust in me to succeed in my business and pay back such a large sum of money. We used Sally's loan to remove the wall between the two houses and install a beautiful horseshoe-shaped oak bar across the front section of both houses, where the take-out counter and coffee lounge had been. Behind the bar we added a real kitchen complete with a commercial exhaust system rising three stories through our house to the roof. No more charcoal grill in the backyard. Eventually, this kitchen would serve only the bar crowd, but it was all we needed for now as we waited for financing to install the main kitchen downstairs.

Also from Sally's beach house came two lovely Victorian, white, marble-topped tables that became Table 23 in the first dining room and eventually—about six years later—Table 94 in our eighth and final dining room, the piano parlor, after we expanded the restaurant into a third row house, where the table remains to this day next to the piano. With our first indoor kitchen in place, we could reopen with a roof over the chef's head. I was excited to expand our menu beyond family recipes and develop the all-American theme. I began collecting cookbooks of regional recipes from around the country, from southwest Tex-Mex cuisine to New Orleans Cajun to nearby Lancaster County Amish cooking, searching for what American cuisine was really about. I was not a professional cook, but I knew what I enjoyed eating. Most of all I was committed to finding fresh local produce like Mom used in her flavorful home cooking—something I didn't appreciate until I went off to college and experienced the bland food I found in the school cafeteria and the nearby American-style restaurants, serving dull platters of meat, potatoes, and overcooked vegetables. It would be later that I gradually recognized all the many other reasons why local food is best, but with the memories of farm-fresh food I had experienced in my childhood, I started off simply liking the taste. What I wanted for the White Dog Café was a style of food that highlighted the natural flavors of fresh local food—though finding the right chef would not be easy.

I also wanted an all-American wine list and an all-American beer list, too. When I first tasted California wines back in the 1970s, they could not compare to European wines, especially the great French, Italian, and Portuguese wines Pasquale had introduced me to at La Terrasse. But California wines had remarkably improved over the previous ten years, and I found they stood up favorably to the European wines, at least for my taste, and I wanted to stick to my all-American theme. Better, I decided, to have a depth of knowledge in American wines than attempt to select wines from around the world.

The same thing was happening with beer—a big change was underway, and American beers were no longer just the tasteless watery varieties that could not compare with beers from Germany and Belgium. The first new American beer I ever tasted—amber colored and full flavored—was Anchor Steam, brewed in San Francisco. I found it delicious and wanted it for my White Dog customers.

But not yet. At the time we installed the bar, we still had not been approved for a license to sell alcoholic beverages, a lengthy process in the state of Pennsylvania. For many months our beautiful new oak bar was used only for counter service during breakfast, lunch, and dinner with white paper placemats set at each bar stool. Big sugar shakers and ketchup bottles gave the feel of an old-fashioned diner, and homemade muffins (yes, we still sold those muffins) were displayed in several round pedestal pastry stands with clear plastic covers. On the shelves of the back bar, meant to eventually hold liquor bottles, we lined up a selection of breakfast cereal boxes. At night, we offered the same menu as for lunch—soup, sandwiches, salads, and a few special platters. Behind the bar we installed an ice-cream freezer and served a large selection of nonalcoholic drinks, including milkshakes, yogurt smoothies, and my favorite—root beer floats.

Our new little kitchen at the bar was so small that prep work still had to be done upstairs in the house, and it was a feat for our early chefs, Bob Fox and then David Spungen, to cook for as many as fifty customers at a time from such a small space, but little by little we were progressing. Commanding the kitchen for breakfast and lunch was none other than Yvonne, the fiery former soap-opera-watching lunch chef at La Terrasse who had terrified me during my waitress days and whose soap-opera watching I'd had to end as a manager. Yvonne found the open kitchen behind the bar at the White Dog provided a stage for her gift of gab and cheeky humor. A fan club of customers lined up along the counter every morning as she cooked and served their breakfasts, delivering hot plates right to the white paper placemats. Yvonne's familiar cackle and the clatter of her omelet pans hitting the stove once again rang in my ears. We were creating our own soap opera. And Yvonne made a great barbeque sauce for the short ribs we added to the lunch menu. Now we were really cooking!

But I still had to wait until the main kitchen was installed before I could start to look for the chef of my dreams who could develop an American cuisine that would put us on the culinary map. We couldn't do that until we got a loan from the bank. And that in turn depended on having a liquor license to show we had the capacity to do the volume of business needed to pay back the loan.

Finally, in the summer of 1985, our long-awaited liquor license arrived and we moved aside the cornflakes to make way for the Jack Daniels. I was ready to build a bar crowd, but not just any crowd. The most obvious bar customers in our neighborhood were students, but I did not want to hang out in a bar full of twentysomethings—just a few of them. To make the bar an interesting place for good conversation, I wanted an intergenerational clientele, where professors and neighbors from the surrounding communities—thirtysomethings to seventysomethings—would sit next to the twentysomethings and everyone would get to know each other and share ideas.

Just as I had done at La Terrasse, I used music as a way to groom the crowd, so rather than playing current top hits, I hired a duet called the Swing Set (including Jim Smith, who had befriended Gertrude) that featured songs from the 1940s. When not featuring live music, we played tapes (of course this was before the time of iPods and satellite systems) that I made up from my favorite long-playing records—music from the 1930s to 1960s. There were not many students who liked that kind of music, but just enough to build an interesting crowd of mixed ages who enjoyed a good conversation.

Along with the music, I was finally able to begin serving the new American beers I was longing for. Customers were surprised when they came into the bar and ordered a popular beer like Heineken to be told that we didn't carry the brand.

Then how about a Löwenbräu? Nope.

Well then, I'll take a Michelob. Not that either.

Then just give me a Bud. Sorry, but how about one of these beers?

Handing over our beer list (mighty short at the time), the bartender explained that the White Dog carried only beers from small independent breweries (later called craft or microbreweries) that brewed beer in small batches. We were the first restaurant in Philadelphia, and among the first on the whole East Coast, to serve Anchor Steam, the San Francisco microbrew. Back in 1985 most people had not heard of these small breweries, knowing only the flavorless beer made by large corporations that dominated the market with pervasive advertising campaigns.

I soon discovered that, unlike wine, beer is best when fresh and without the preservatives needed for long-distance shipping—just like local food. So I upped the ante. Not only did I want flavorful all-American beer, I became determined to have beer that was local, fresh, and made without preservatives. I carried all the locally brewed beers I could find, but at the time none were brewed in Philadelphia, and only a few were brewed within the state—including Yuengling, the oldest brewery in America, only forty miles north of Philadelphia; and Rolling Rock, brewed in the same town in western Pennsylvania where I went to Girl Scout camp.

But I still could not find local beer as good as California's Anchor Steam. So I was thrilled to hear in 1987 that an excellent new brewery had opened just sixty miles to the west in Adamstown. It was not only the first new brewery in Pennsylvania since Prohibition, but it was owned by a woman! I immediately called up the owner, Carol Stoudt, and asked about ordering her beer. At first Carol thought sixty miles was too far for her beer to travel (she was into local, too), but I convinced her to sell to me, and she drove into town with a keg strapped into her passenger seat with the seat belt. We laughed about that years later when Carol was celebrating the twentieth anniversary of Stoudt's Brewery after winning many a gold medal at the Great American Beer Festival. It wasn't long before Stoudt's began brewing our private label beer in twenty-two-ounce bottles. I named it "Leg Lifter Lager" and designed a label featuring my drawing of a white dog lifting his leg on a red fire hydrant!

As microbrews became popular, more breweries popped up in and around Philadelphia and adjoining states, so it wasn't long before we were able to have a beer list offering only regionally brewed beers. Back in the late 1980s and early 1990s, this was a rarity. Our customers soon took pride in drinking local brews with their fresh, full flavor and becoming knowledgeable of the various styles that the local breweries were developing. In later years, we were very excited when a local company began distilling gin and vodka right in Philadelphia. I never thought I'd see the day when martinis would be included in buy-local campaigns.

With the increased profits from the liquor license, the bank finally felt comfortable loaning us money by increasing the amount of our mortgage, which became our main source of capital for the rest of the renovations and expansion. (Investing in real estate in one's own community and making improvements to increase its value is a great way to invest, and turned out to be a key to my long-term financial sustainability.) Now with the funds from our new increased mortgage, we were ready to take a huge step forward to increase our seating capacity and give ourselves the cooking facilities of a "real" restaurant. We bid fond farewell to our charming backyard (and to the not-so-charming "bunnies") and built a new addition, designed by Neil, with two levels of dining rooms, which enabled us to seat an additional eighty people comfortably in all weather conditions.

The carved white beams from the arbor were reused to build the permanent roof of the addition, and the white dog heads still jut out from under the roof today. To replicate the rich, warm, woody feel of the dining room I admired while vacationing with my family at the historic Mohonk Mountain House in New Paltz, New York, the ceiling and wainscoting of the new dining room as well as the renovated original dining room and bar were done in wood. Along the wall facing south we installed large windows with hinges at the top that allowed them to swing inward and be held up on hooks from the ceiling so that the room, which we called "the porch," was open-air in good weather, keeping a bit of our old backyard feel.

Near the ceiling of the porch dining room was a small window that opened to the deck off our family's home above. When he was about six years old, Lawrence, fascinated by the little window, threw a cherry tomato down into the dining room that accidently hit a customer on the cheek. Lawrence was mortified when the maître d' made him come down to offer an apology.

How to deal with the outdoor space between the back sections of the two row houses was a design challenge, and Neil brilliantly turned the space into central halls in the basement and first floors of the restaurant and the second and third floors in our home above. What had been windows facing the outdoor light court became doorways leading into these central halls, allowing restaurant traffic to flow from the hall into the dining rooms to each side and into the large porch dining room addition in the rear. In order to keep the natural light flowing, Neil built an atrium at the top of the space and constructed the hallway floors with glass blocks to allow the natural sunlight, cheery and bright, to flow down through the center of our house and into the core of the restaurant at the first floor level.

From Neil's work, I learned about passive solar design: The glass on the south-facing walls of our buildings allowed the sun to warm the rooms in the winter. Two fast-growing London planetrees Neil planted on the south side provided shade in the summer, while in winter, when the leaves had fallen, the sun streamed through lace-covered windows, creating a warm and cozy feeling for customers gathered around antique oak tables decorated with fresh flower arrangements in old-fashioned dog-shaped vases or nestled at tables for two covered with our trademark blue-and-white checkered tablecloths. Throughout the dining rooms were antique prints of dogs, dogs, and dogs, and I constantly kept an eye out for more as the restaurant grew in size.

While this was going on, we also began work downstairs. We removed the wall between the two basements and poured concrete over the dirt floor to create a large space for a fully equipped central kitchen. Next to the kitchen, we installed four public restrooms—it was time to stop sending our customers to the family bathroom.

Though they were unisex, I labeled the first pair POINTERS and SETTERS, painting the SETTERS bathroom as the bedroom of a white poodle primping herself at her dressing table with a bottle of perfume labeled ESSENCE OF DEAD SQUIRREL. The POINTERS depicted an outdoor scene of a dog lifting his leg on a tree where a group of ladybugs struggled to move their picnic out of the way. The next two bathrooms were labeled DEMOCRATS and REPUBLICANS, with the DEMOCRATS decorated with political messages that we changed over time, including at one point a portrait of Ken Starr, who had investigated President Clinton, with a message painted above the toilet: HE'S WATCHING YOU. The REPUBLICANS bathroom was designed as a cat litter box, with litter glued to the walls and a large cat exiting. I once found a Japanese tourist standing before the doors greatly perplexed as to which of the four was appropriate for him to use.

When our big new shiny kitchen was finished it was equipped with a line of stoves to turn out hot items; a cold line for preparing salads, cold appetizers, and desserts; a bake shop for making homemade bread, pastries, and ice cream; along with a dishwashing room, a prep area, a pantry, and several walk-in refrigerators. Finally, we were the "real" restaurant I had dreamed of, and the customers who had grown to appreciate us back when the dish-washer was in the dining room, the grill in the backyard, and the restroom in our home, stayed and multiplied.

It wasn't until I tasted food cooked by chef Aliza Green that I understood exactly what I wanted for the White Dog Café. Hers was a fresh new approach to American cuisine—one that showcased local ingredients, rather than obscuring them with heavy sauces. Aliza's food was the best I had ever tasted—flavor-ful, beautifully presented, and downright delicious, yet simple. Inspired by her travels and time spent living abroad where she shopped in local markets and cooked at home, Aliza understood the importance of quality ingredients used in season.

While she was the chef at several Philadelphia restaurants in the 1970s, she used fresh herbs and house-made soup bases when most chefs still relied on processed foods. During a trip to visit the Chez Panisse kitchen in Berkeley, California, Aliza was offered a job by Alice Waters, an important influence and role model for Aliza. Luckily for Philadelphia, Aliza turned down the job. But the trip validated her culinary point of view and kept her on the path of fresh, local, unprocessed, vegetable-centric, simple food—a style that was becoming known as New American Cuisine, made popular by Alice.

Once I tasted Aliza's food I could not imagine any other chef in Philadelphia at the White Dog. Not only was her food unforget-table, but also Aliza had started to buy from local farmers—the underlying principle I wanted for the White Dog Café. She knew that local fresh food didn't spring up for the asking. It came from a small group of dedicated local farmers who said no to pesticides and grew everything organically. Though I knew Aliza was the right chef for us, at that time in 1986, she was working as the executive chef at a posh restaurant in Center City Philadelphia. How could I convince her to leave a swank environment and come out to the university community in West Philly to work in an unknown restaurant?

When I heard that Aliza was pregnant with her first child, I had an idea. I offered her the position of executive chef along with a private room near the kitchen (a dining room I would forgo for the time being) to be a nursery and a place for a babysitter, so that her child would be nearby for breast-feeding and nurturing while Aliza continued her career. It was an offer she couldn't refuse.

Aliza developed a style of cooking at the White Dog that she called *Cuisine Mongrel* (like a mixed breed dog, but pronounced with the accent on the second syllable to give it some class) because of the mixture of influences she incorporated into her cuisine, reflecting the diversity of American culture. Customers from all over town made their way out to the White Dog Café to try Aliza's *Cuisine Mongrel*.

Aliza brought along to the White Dog the farmers she had begun to work with and introduced me to Judy and Mark Dornstreich of Branch Creek Farm, who grow extraordinary organic microgreens, specialty vegetables, and edible flowers on their five-acre farm with three greenhouses for growing right through the winter. Establishing their farm to the north of Philadelphia near Perkasie in 1979, Judy and Mark were pioneers in the organic food movement and the first in our region to supply the restaurants of Philadelphia with fresh local produce. Though they first balked at the idea of following Aliza to out-of-the-way West Philadelphia, before long the White Dog was buying in such quantities that the distance didn't matter.

The Dornstreichs may be the most unusual farmers you will ever meet, having moved from life as Ivy League–educated Jewish professionals in New York City to rural farm life in Bucks County. Inspiration for the move came first from living with indigenous farmers in New Guinea, where Mark was working on his PhD in ecological anthropology. This experience was followed by a spiritual journey to an ashram in India, inspired by Judy, to study with a swami, during which time Mark announced simply, "I want to grow vegetables." And grow vegetables he did, becoming known for his innovation in cultivating exceptional organic food for more than thirty years.

Both Judy and Mark are deeply thoughtful about their work. Mark once noted that farmers must have both traditional female and male qualities to succeed—both nurturing and efficiency, each in the right balance. "Too much efficiency can end up in mediocrity," Mark explained, "but not enough efficiency will end up in bankruptcy, no matter how much nurturing the plants receive."

Getting to know Judy and Mark, visiting their home, and feeling their intimate relationship with the land had the effect on me of seeing in local, fresh food more than a wonderful meal. It was a way of connecting with the land and to life itself.

Another early supplier of organic fruits and vegetables was Green Meadow Farm in Lancaster County, run by Glenn and Karen Brendle and later their son Ian. Farmer Glenn, as he is known, also built a business of picking up produce, eggs, and meat from his Amish neighbors—who of course do not drive—and selling them in the city. An engineer by training, Glenn developed a system on his farm to convert used fry oil, which he picked up from his restaurant customers, into heating oil. He succeeded in powering everything on the farm with that reclaimed vegetable oil—from heating the greenhouses and the farmhouse to running the tractor, truck, and car. Glenn's system was one inventive step in reducing carbon, as well as lowering the cost of energy. "My customers have got to see this," I thought, and brought a group to visit the farm on one of our many community tours.

Glenn turned out to be a storehouse of knowledge about Lancaster County, and one day when I happened to mention that I had ancestors who had settled in the area as pioneers, Glenn surprised me by knowing all about them. In his vegetable-oil-powered car, Glenn took me to visit the cemetery where my foremother, Madame Ferree, a French Huguenot who had bought land from William Penn after fleeing religious persecution in France, was buried a few years after she and her offspring founded the town of Paradise in 1712 not far from Green Meadow Farm.

It seemed appropriate—and somehow right—that much of the food at the White Dog was sourced from the same area that my ancestors first farmed three hundred years ago. When my daughter Grace, home from college and about twenty-four, took up farming for a summer with Glenn and Karen, I was happy to think that a descendant of Madame Ferree's was back farming the land once again.

With the business doing well, I got to the point where I was no longer simply keeping my head just above water, and I began looking for ways to express and celebrate the values and people I cared about. As luck would have it, I had the opportunity to start with Martin Luther King, Jr., a man who had long been my greatest hero.

In January of 1986, after years of debate, the first federal holiday honoring Martin Luther King, Jr., went into effect, and I decided that for the next Martin Luther King Day in January of 1987 the White Dog would hold a dinner in his honor. When I told my mother about the idea of celebrating Martin Luther King Day with an event at the White Dog, her response surprised me: "But Judy, that's a black people's holiday." If my mother, whom I saw as an inclusive, open-minded person, felt this way, then I imagined that a lot of people likely saw the King national holiday as a "black holiday." That made me want to do the event all the more with the hope that people of many races would come together on this day to honor a man whose dream was for us all to love one another—and to be further inspired toward achieving that dream.

The White Dog dinner in honor of Martin Luther King, Jr., in 1987 became the first of many special events. The large dining room on the porch held fifty people, and with the windows of the adjoining rooms open we could hold a total of eighty people—all able to hear a speaker. I asked a prominent African American minister, Leonard Smalls, who had been a civil rights activist, to do a blessing. Three gospel singers and a keyboard player added to the festivities, and we began the evening with *Lift Every Voice and Sing*, sometimes referred to as "The African American National Anthem," and those who did not know it by heart followed the words I had printed out in our program. I invited Mayor Wilson Goode, the first black mayor of Philadelphia, to come, and he accepted along with his wife. The kitchen developed a Southern-style menu that we served family style, with everyone grouped around tables of four to ten people. The mayor enjoyed the food but declared that our black-eyed peas did not measure up to his mother's, and the following year—our Martin Luther King Day memorial dinner became an annual event—he came back, as he did every year while he was mayor, bringing a big dish of Southern-style black-eyed peas cooked by his mother.

A few years later, orator Rose Samuel Evans joined the program and recited King's speeches from memory to the delight of our customers; about half of them were European American, nearly half were African American, and a few were Asian and Latino. King would have been pleased. After dinner we had a moving group discussion about how King's work had influenced our lives, and ended by standing, joining hands, and singing "We Shall Overcome," reminding us that there is still work to be done, as we ended an evening full of hope and inspiration.

For twenty-two years we held that memorial dinner with a similar program every January, along with an opportunity for customers to do community service projects during the day. Though we developed many more special dinners that also became annual traditions, our Martin Luther King Day dinner was always my favorite, and I took the occasion to listen again to his stirring speeches on tape or video.

In 1987, after a year as our head chef, Aliza, with plans for a second child, left the White Dog and began work at home on a successful career as a food writer and cookbook author. (At this writing, she has published ten outstanding cookbooks.) Aliza's under-chef, Kevin Klause, whom she had brought with her to the White Dog, took over as executive chef, building with his own great talent and unique flair on what Aliza had started.

The first time I met Kevin, I was working at my desk when I looked up to see a figure dressed all in black, with a long cape and bowler hat. I felt as though a magician had entered the room. I soon learned that Kevin performed his magic in the kitchen. Also committed to local ingredients, Kevin soon became known for his ability to juggle orders from many different farmers, creating dishes from the variety of fruits and vegetables brought to him at our backdoor as they came into season and learning to use all the parts when buying a whole farm animal. Kevin's roommate and fellow graduate of the Culinary Institute of America, James Barrett, became our pastry chef and bread baker extraordinaire. Kevin and James made an excellent team, and over the coming years they would lead the White Dog toward culinary acclaim.

Though our first reason for buying from local farmers back in 1986 was because fresh-picked food tastes better, we came to understand that local food transcends culinary value. Fresh food is actually better for you, and this became part of the White Dog's commitment to fresh and local. When fruits and vegetables are grown commercially for long distance shipping they are bred for long shelf life as well as uniformity of size for ease in packing. What gets bred out is the taste and the nutritional value. We all know those flavorless, bland, mealy textured tomatoes and peaches that come from stores carrying the same fruits and vegetables year-round. When not eaten in season, fruits and vegetables are shipped long distance, using lots of carbon and not even tasting that good when they finally arrive. Even though during the winter the White Dog did buy from organic farms in California or in the South to augment a menu based on local greenhouse-grown and cold-storage fruits and vegetables, we cooked as much as possible in season. Not only did the food taste better, not only was it healthier—at the White Dog anticipation for the arrival of seasonal flavors was fun.

On a blackboard in the hallway, we would list the foods coming from local farms. When the first fruits and vegetables came into season after the long winter of eating cold-storage apples, squash, and potatoes, writing on the board in big letters Hooray, rhubarb is here! was cause for celebration. Kevin put duck with rhubarb sauce on the menu, and James added rhubarb pie to the dessert menu, and sometimes we even had rhubarb ice cream. Next would come asparagus season, then strawberries in late May and June—and before long the blackboard would be crowded with cherries, plums, blueberries, peaches, beans, squash, tomatoes, corn, and more and more until the whole blackboard was full of the delicious seasonal harvest of local farms.

When we bought from local farmers, they became part of the White Dog's extended family and part of the local food community. Knowing these people and their farms meant knowing exactly where our food came from and how it was produced. This information became more and more important over the years with the increasing number of national food recalls for tainted meat, spinach, and even lettuce. We were able to assure our customers that we knew where our food came from and that it was raised in a safe and sustainable way.

Over the years, I continued to recognize more reasons why buying from local farmers was a good thing—from keeping our dollars circulating in the local economy to giving local farmers a guaranteed market for responsibly produced goods. Perhaps most important among the reasons was that developing our local food system provided food security for our region, decreasing our dependency on long supply chains and high-carbon, long distance shipping.

The White Dog loved to celebrate—as you may have gathered by now—and as the years went by, I felt that we had more and more to celebrate. So I began developing many special events highlighting our outstanding food and our unusual selections of American wine and local beer. In 1987, we began an annual tradition of holding beer dinners to educate our customers about the qualities of fresh local beer. Kevin developed a special menu that paired each course with a different beer. Maybe that does not seem unusual today, but back then holding a special dinner that featured beer, especially local beer, was unique. For the first few years we started off with a reception in my home upstairs, where a station was set up for each of three or more brewers to meet the customers and offer a sampling of one of their beers paired with an hors d'oeuvre. The customers enjoyed the opportunity to mingle with others and get to know the brewmasters, who also spoke during the dinner as each course was served.

Customers were intrigued with the idea of visiting our home above the restaurant, gradually refurnished after losing its furniture to the restaurant in the early days. After all, anyone who had ventured into the hallways had likely looked up through the translucent glass-block floors to see shapes moving around above them, including little dog and cat paws pressed against the glass. One night while cleaning up after one of the parties in the house, a group of servers and I, in a fit of hysteria, decided to each sit down on a glass block—exposing our derrieres to those below, which prompted my sister-in-law to quip, "Judy has now shown her customers her bottom line!"

Beer dinners were only the start. The same year, in celebration of the fall harvest, we held our first annual Farmers Sunday Supper where each course featured a different farm or local producer who spoke about their farm or business and product. In November, we started an annual wine dinner I named the Post-Crush Invitational featuring winemakers from small California vineyards on our wine list, such as Frog's Leap and Bonny Doon, who visited us just after the busy grape crushing season. These annual dinners became a White Dog hallmark and a way for our customers to meet and learn from the farmers, winemakers, brewers, cheese makers, fisherman, and chocolatiers who produced the food and drink we all enjoyed.

Some events at the White Dog were just for fun. I'm a party girl—I admit it. For me, fun was an important part of the business, and I made sure to make it a big part of life at the White Dog and the community that developed around it. We celebrated in the street with the Dance of the Ripe Tomatoes, Rum & Reggae night, and Noche Latina with dancing to live bands under colored lights strung along the street. With so many outdoor parties, I bought our own tents and stored them in a warehouse full of props, including palm trees, huge stuffed tomatoes my mom helped me make out of red satin bed sheets with green felt faces, and a Bastille that we reassembled each year.

For twenty-five years, I continued the Bastille Day celebration I had developed at La Terrasse, for a day calling the White Dog "Café Chein Blanc." After a French dinner served under tent-top came our annual reenactment of the storming of the Bastille, in which two groups of customers played roles. Inside the eight-by-four-foot Bastille that towered about twelve feet tall, painted to look like a stone fortress, we locked up customers dressed as white French poodles wearing red berets. Just as the audience finished singing "La Marseillaise," sparklers held high, another group of customers that we dressed up as French revolutionaries stormed the Bastille with plastic axes and swords, waving the French flag as they released all the "poodles." Then the revolutionaries and poodles joined in the cancan to kick off a night of dancing to a mixture of American and French music, using some of the same songs I first played so long ago at La Terrasse.

Another La Terrasse event that I brought with me to the White Dog was our New Year's Day Pajama Party Brunch. One year when I was pregnant and tired from being up late the night before, I decided to take the liberty to go to La Terrasse in my pajamas. That made me realize that most people likely feel the same way on New Year's morning after being up late partying the night before.

The next year I sent out an invitation that said, "Don't get dressed. Just take two aspirin and pad on over in your slippers and robe to our New Year's Day Pajama Party Brunch." I had to convince my family and friends to be the first and even bought my father new pajamas so he would not have any excuses. Over time, and after I moved the idea to the White Dog, it became a famous event, and hundreds of people showed up at White Dog in their pajamas and were entertained by a banjo player playing songs like "Oh Dem Golden Slippers," and other favorites of the Mummers Parade, a Philadelphia New Year's Day tradition. As people arrived in their pajamas and robes, I took pictures, and posted my growing collection of photos on the wall each New Year's Day for customers to enjoy. There was a whole series I took over many years of a family of six who each time came wearing a new set of matching flannel pajamas made by the grandmother. I remember a college student coming in with his girlfriend to point out a picture showing him in his pajamas holding his teddy bear, a photo I took when he was four.

On the eve of the Fourth of July, we had the Liberty and Justice for All Ball, and on a stage in the street outside the restaurant I presented a skit called *The Birth of the Nation*. First came a Revolutionary War soldier with his drum, then a midwife with her lantern, and then I came out dressed as a pregnant colonial woman—with a clown face, a little colonial cap, and a sign on my back that said GEORGE WASHINGTON SLEPT HERE. I got into a big bed in the street, and my midwife delivered twins—a white woman and a black woman each dressed in red, white, and blue, one holding a sign saying JUSTICE, the other a sign saying LIBERTY. They hopped onto the stage and did a tap dance to "Yankee Doodle Dandy." Then we wheeled out the Statue of Liberty covered in pale green, which was often my daughter Grace or my cousin Debbie because they're tall. We lit our sparklers and sang "God Bless America." It was very patriotic!

A customer once gave me a book by Barbara Ehrenreich, *Dancing in the Streets*, which talks about the importance of "collective joy" and how it is often missing in our modern industrialized, materialistic society. We've come to think that a good time means spending a lot of money and burning a lot of carbon traveling to distant places to be entertained. But we can have more fun with our friends and neighbors right in our own communities. In my hometown of Ingomar, the annual community holiday party was thrown by the local grocery store. That's another often overlooked but hugely important role played by local businesses—hosting events that bring collective joy to the community.

I also closed the restaurant a few times a year to hold parties just for White Dog staff—a summer picnic and our holiday party where we took turns dressing up as Mr. Santa and Harriet Hanukkah to pass out funny gifts. But our most important annual staff gathering was the Anniversary Howl, where we "howled" about what we had accomplished during the year. In a restaurant, a lot of the staff—the majority of servers, bartenders, busboys, cooks—are either in school or they play in a band or make art, and what they do in the restaurant is not necessarily what they consider to be their real job. For a while this really frustrated me. I wanted everyone to be as committed to their career in the restaurant business as I was, until I finally realized that I was never going to get there and that I actually enjoyed the diversity of interests. So I started our Anniversary Howl to celebrate not only what we had accomplished as a workplace community but also what we had accomplished as individuals. People brought in their artwork, played the clarinet, performed break dancing, or read poetry so that we all got to know each other a little bit better.

For my part, I gave a "State of the Dog" address, reporting how we did in meeting our mission of service over the year and posting the good press we had received and awards we had won. I showed charts put together by our long-time financial officer Deirdre MacDermott, which showed our sales, expenses, and the year's profit. And then how that profit was used for such things as buying new equipment, paying down debt, and sharing profits with staff. In good years, we gave 10 percent of the profit to the staff in bonuses I handed out that night, plus 5 percent to Kevin who became a 5 percent stockholder. At the beginning 10 percent, and later 20 percent, went to contributions to nonprofit organizations that we listed on the wall at the Howl.

I recognized employees who had volunteered at community service events during the year, participated in the employer-matched charitable giving program, or contributed to (or were recipients of) the Sunshine Fund—a stash made up of voluntary contributions drawn from paychecks, usually one dollar per week and matched by the business, that provided emergency handouts to employees going through hard times such as an accident, fire, or illness. All these were ways that the staff joined in our mission of service. It was exciting to me when a dishwasher became a philanthropist by contributing a dollar a week in our charitable giving program, which when matched by the company became an annual contribution of $104 to the charity he chose.

Next I presented the Silver Bone Awards—sterling lapel pins in the shape of dog bones—in celebration of five-year anniversaries, and other thank you gifts for ten-, fifteen-, and twenty-year anniversaries. Best employee awards—such as the Greyhound Award for the fastest and the Rin Tin Tin Award for coming to the rescue—were chosen by the staff and announced like the Academy Awards in sealed envelopes. Platters of food were put out by the kitchen, and after the informational part of the meeting was finished, the bartenders brought out beer and wine. The Howl always ended with a concert by the White Dog Band, made up of singers, guitar players, drummers, and any other type of musician we had in our ranks. The Howl was one of the happiest times of the year at the White Dog—a night of meaning and merriment when we served not our customers, but each other.

In the meantime the business was growing—but in a new way. We opened a retail store next door. As a contrast to White Dog,

I called it the Black Cat. In April 1989 we expanded the business into the first floors of our third and fourth houses to make space for a good-sized store where we sold unique gifts and crafts. I saw this as a companion business to the White Dog that would add to the liveliness of our block.

Customers enjoyed strolling down the hallway between the Dog and the Cat to explore the gift shop before or after a meal, roaming through the store's seven rooms, each of which was designed as a room in a house—kitchen, dining room, living room, bedroom, bathroom, study, and porch. Everything, including the furniture, was for sale, from the glassware and ceramics in the dining room, to birdhouses and rocking chairs on the porch, to books and stationery in the desk of the study, to underwear and socks in the dresser drawers in the bedroom, to soaps and lotions in the bathroom and a bathtub full of squeaky rubber frogs (one of our best sellers!).

I used the skills and knowledge I had gained starting Free People's Store but added a feature of selling socially responsible products to express my evolving social consciousness. I saw that the customers we were cultivating at the White Dog enjoyed finding gifts that had meaning—boxes made by Brazilian street children out of invasive vines that needed to be cut down, soup mixes packaged by homeless women suffering from domestic abuse, picture frames made in Thailand by former prostitutes, and jewelry made from recycled Mardi Gras ball gowns and old television parts assembled by homeless and disabled workers in New Orleans.

An enthusiastic young man right out of design school, Eric Tucker, who had excellent taste in merchandizing and a good sense of humor, began as a salesperson almost from the day the Black Cat opened and soon became the manager. In the early days, Eric and I did the buying together, including antique furniture from auctions. After we sweated and laughed our way through many a day of loading and unloading furniture together, we developed our pretend business of Tucker and Wicks Moving Company, which kept us amused. Eventually Eric did all the buying as well as managing and stayed for twenty years, helping to make the Black Cat a special place in its own right despite its more famous doggy neighbor. The Black Cat added a whole new dimension to the experience of visiting the White Dog, as well as an additional $500,000 in annual sales.

In a couple of years, we expanded the White Dog again, cutting more doorways through the walls to add yet another house. We were now up to five row houses connected at the first floor level with a hallway running right through the middle of all of them. We moved the Black Cat into the fourth and fifth houses and expanded the White Dog into the third house where the Black Cat had started, creating a piano room—I just had to have a good place for a piano—with a small bar and increasing the seating to two hundred people. We had come so far from our muffin start that it was hard to imagine those humble beginnings.

When I started the White Dog Café, I did not have a grand plan—nor the capital upfront to carry out such a plan. In hindsight, I'm glad I didn't, because I would have missed all the fun. Of course there came a point when I put pen to paper and wrote out a business plan to figure out how much capital I needed and how I planned to be profitable and pay it back. But that came after I had the opportunity to move forward intuitively without knowing for sure where I was going. Without a plan to follow and the burden of a huge loan to pay off, I grew in a gradual organic way through a lot of trial and error, learning by doing. With little thought beyond the next day, I took many small spontaneous steps that advanced the business, gradually feeling my way into something new.

By 1993, our tenth birthday year, we were recognized by *Condé Nast Traveler* as "one of the country's Top 50 restaurants worth traveling to visit." That same year, *Inc.* magazine chose us as one of the best small companies to work for in America. Several years into the twenty-first century, between the White Dog and the Black Cat, we employed over one hundred full and part-time people, could seat more than two hundred customers, and grossed five million dollars annually. More than could fit under my pillow!

I had accomplished what I had set out to do—turn the business I had raised from a tiny muffin shop into one of Philadelphia's most successful—and most interesting—restaurants. In so many ways, I did not do this alone. And I celebrated our recognition and ten year success with another party, of course, by taking our management team of twelve out to dinner at Le Bec Fin, the fanciest restaurant in town, where we toasted with champagne and even smoked cigars! Three cheers—three barks—for the White Dog Café!

If God Invited You to a Party

If God invited you to a party and said,
"Everyone in the ballroom tonight will be my special guest."
How would you then treat them when you arrived?
Indeed, indeed!
And Hafiz knows that there is no one in this world
that is not standing upon His jeweled dance floor.

—Hafiz (c. 1320–1389)

❧ 6 ❧

A Table for Six Billion: Finding an International Perspective

EVEN AS THE WHITE DOG was making its mark in the culinary world, and we were having our parties and celebrations, I was eager to take up where I had left off at La Terrasse when I was just beginning to explore the unique combination of good food and social activism. I didn't want my career just to be about throwing a great party every night—much as I enjoyed that.

Of course, I wanted the White Dog to be a place of celebration where our customers could eat, drink, and be merry, and not be forced to face the world's problems. But I also wanted to address my concerns about all the pain and suffering in the world. How could I do that while showing my customers a good time? That was my challenge.

I had learned at La Terrasse that I couldn't address my social concerns during my time off: there was none. I needed to do it through the business itself. But how could I make it happen? How could I run my restaurant and try to make the world a better place at the same time?

Impulsively, perhaps, I picked the most difficult issue to begin with—foreign policy—but that's what was most on my mind in 1987 and I have always followed my passion. From the time I served breakfast to the Salvadoran refugees at La Terrasse years earlier, I had a growing interest in the events unfolding in Central America. I was dismayed by how few Americans seemed to care about the suffering of the Salvadoran people under a repressive regime that was supported by our own country. Nor was there much interest in the neighboring country, Nicaragua, where the Reagan administration was attempting to overthrow the democratically elected government. Nicaragua? El Salvador? Most people didn't know the difference, as I barely did. It was particularly bothersome that my own generation, the children of the sixties, who protested the Vietnam War, seemed to care nothing about misguided US policies in Central America. It made me ponder, was it only because we were the ones being drafted and killed in Vietnam that we worked to end that war, or did we actually care about peace and justice?

Around this time, I had a dream in which I walked into a restaurant and asked for a table, and not just a table for two or four people. "Table for five billion, please!" I declared. To me, the dream's meaning was clear. I was envisioning a world where everyone had a place at the table—economically and politically—and everyone everywhere had enough to eat. Believing, as I still do, that such a future is possible, I began thinking about ways I could do my part to bring it into being. Meeting the Salvadorans in person had sealed my commitment to their cause, so I began to think about how I could create opportunities for others to experience—firsthand—the effects of American foreign policy on other people, and then to take responsibility for demanding change if we found our country was not inviting all people to sit at the table. But how could I involve my customers? Did it make sense for a restaurant to be engaged in foreign policy?

An idea began to take shape. There were international sister cities programs—right? Then how about *sister restaurants?* Why couldn't the White Dog establish sister relationships with restaurants in other countries where we had questionable foreign policy and build people-to-people friendships, raising consciousness among our customers about our interconnection with other peoples.

I asked my friend David Funkhouser from the Central American Organizing Project, who had brought me together with the Salvadorans, if he would find me sister restaurants in El Salvador and Nicaragua. When he suggested that I come along on a study tour he was leading to Nicaragua, I thought, *Who me? I have a business to run! I don't go anywhere but upstairs to my house and downstairs to my restaurant. Sometimes I never go off the block for weeks at a time. Besides, there's a war going on down there. And I don't speak the language. I couldn't even understand if someone yelled "Duck!" in Spanish.*

But I couldn't stop wondering if it was true what President Reagan was saying—that the Sandinistas ruling Nicaragua were communists and the Contras (as in counterrevolutionaries) were the "freedom fighters." I really didn't know. I felt that I had heard this story before. As a teenager, I was fooled by my government into supporting the Vietnam War, and it took me years to find the truth. If we were being fooled again, I wanted to know.

So, despite my protests, I soon found myself checking on my life insurance policy and will, calling my parents to say good-bye, and then boarding a plane for Nicaragua where I would meet up with David. I was still apprehensive, but Nicaragua quickly washed away my worries. Rather than feeling threatened and vulnerable as a foreigner in a strange land, I had a comfortable sense of belonging, as though both the history and the future of our countries were inextricably linked, and that our presence in Nicaragua as US citizens seeking friendship and understanding was as important to our own country as to theirs.

David had made sure to arrange interviews that covered the political spectrum in Nicaragua, so we would hear the arguments for and against the Sandinista government. The Contra supporters we interviewed in Managua told us that all the businesses in the country were now owned by the state in this communist country, and I was beginning to worry because I did not want a sister restaurant that was state owned. Eventually, I chose a sister restaurant called Selva Negra located up in the mountains in a tropical forest near the town of Matagalpa. Despite the Contras' claims, the businesses we encountered were, thankfully, privately owned—including our sister restaurant and their family-owned organic coffee plantation.

Though the food we had at Selva Negra was very simple— platters of rice, beans, fried plantains, and a small portion of meat—the coffee was outstanding. At the end of the trip, the proprietor of Selva Negra gave me a necklace with a white dog he had carved from wood. On the back it said in Spanish: SISTER RESTAURANTS FOR PEACE AND FRIENDSHIP. I was happy about the successful connection but saddened by what I heard from him and many others whom we met on the trip. The Sandinistas were not perfect, but they were not communist and were looked up to by most of the people we met for the improvements they were making in education and health care to benefit a population ignored by the corrupt Somoza dictatorship, a dynasty of a father and two sons that had ruled Nicaragua ruthlessly from 1937 until the Sandinista revolution in 1979.

The Sandinistas had successfully overthrown the US-backed dictator, but now the Reagan administration was supplying arms to the Contras, who were responsible for the deaths of many Nicaraguan civilians and were bent on destroying the improvements made under the Sandinistas by targeting health care clinics and killing doctors and teachers. These were, I learned, the forces our government supported, if not directly with our tax dollars then indirectly by using the profits of arms sales to Iran, an underhanded deal to circumvent a congressional ban on US assistance to the Contras for the purpose of overthrowing the Nicaraguan government. This secret arrangement was just becoming known as the Iran-Contra affair.

On the trip home, I was sitting alone in the Miami airport waiting to change planes, when I suddenly burst out crying—much like the time I unleashed a flood of tears after chasing a black youth back in my Free People's Store days. Was I sad about what was happening to the Nicaraguans I had encountered? The mother I met next to a demolished schoolhouse where her nine-year-old son had recently been killed by a US-supplied missile? Or the older woman I sat next to on a bus whose grown daughter, a social worker, had been kidnapped by the Contras to be used as a "mule" to carry their supplies and cook their meals? These were terribly sad stories, but there was something more. I was crying as though someone close to me had died.

Then it came to me. I had still been carrying a bit of the John Philip Sousa patriotism I had been raised with, holding out hope that the Vietnam War had been an aberration, a misstep in history not to be repeated. Now my idealism had vanished. I could see clearly that, rather than spreading democracy, the US government was using force, this time through surrogates, to achieve domination of countries in the developing world. Ultimately, all this suffering was about securing a continued supply of natural resources and cheap labor in developing countries for US corporations. If Vietnam had made me question whether the country I loved was lost, Nicaragua had convinced me that, sadly, it was.

Though I had read about the history of US involvement and CIA coups in Guatemala, Chile, Iran, and other countries as well as Vietnam, none of this had really come together for me until I experienced it firsthand in Nicaragua. Now I wanted to do something. I felt a responsibility to tell others what I had seen and heard there.

So began the White Dog's international sister program, in which we would bring customers and staff to countries at odds with US government policies—a program I came to call (after a jump in population) "Table for Six Billion, Please!" I returned to Nicaragua two more times, in 1988 and 1989, bringing groups of twentysome White Dog customers on study tours led by David. One was an intergenerational tour, which included then-ten-year-old Grace—who led me on a midnight adventure to find a sea turtle—and a youth group from Harlem that was making a documentary. Our sister restaurant, Selva Negra, appreciated our visits that brought customers to enjoy their food and hear their stories about supporting the Sandinistas during the revolution as well as their approval of Sandinista government policies that were building a more democratic society in Nicaragua.

On returning home from that first trip to Nicaragua, I was appalled to see the poor coverage of the Nicaraguan conflict in the US media. Citizens were not being told the truth about the damage the Contras were doing with our tax dollars. The mainstream press seemed intent on giving equal credibility to both sides of the argument—those who saw Reagan's Contras as "freedom fighters" and those who saw them as terrorists. We were a democratic society. Wasn't the media supposed to inform citizens so that they could make wise political decisions? Yet what I saw with my own eyes and heard with my own ears I could not find in the mainstream news. It was then that I began to understand how important independent media was, and how it offered an alternative to a mass media overly influenced by corporate interests. I was determined to do whatever I could not only to support independent media and investigative reporting, but also to bring the stories of what we had learned on our study tours to our own community.

I began building a mailing list (before we had e-mail) of customer addresses to announce our trips and other events. After our international sister restaurant trips, I organized talks at the White Dog to report back to our customers, using slide shows. This was the beginning of what became a series called "Table Talks: Serving Food with Thought."

One Table Talk topic led to another, and one activity led to another, and in almost no time I had a White Dog calendar full of weekly events—dinner and breakfast talks, a storytelling series, youth and senior programs, community tours, and more international tours. Almost without trying, I discovered how to bring together my business and my desire to make the world a better place. I would think to myself, *My customers have got to hear about this issue* or *My customers just have to come here and see this*—be it an inner city garden in Philadelphia or the conflict in the highlands of Mexico. Together, I believed, we could further the awareness of our interconnectedness and our sense of community, local and international. Maybe the times were with me, but my customers were soon as eager and committed as I was.

Our Table Talks and activities addressed local concerns as well as societal ones. For the broad public issues, I developed relationships with speakers around the country, and our topics ranged from creating a sustainable future with Lester Brown, the well-known environmental analyst; to strengthening independent media with Amy Goodman, the progressive journalist from *Democracy Now!*; to ending the war on drugs and its human rights violations with Ethan Nadelmann, executive director of the Drug Policy Alliance.

Through many programs on food and farming, we cultivated an awareness among our customers about the importance of local food systems both with tours to the farms who supplied the White Dog and through Table Talks with authors such as Frances Moore Lappé (whose first book, *Diet for a Small Planet*, we carried at Free People's Store in 1970); Michael Pollan, author of *Omnivore's Dilemma*; Eric Schlosser, author of *Fast Food Nation*; and Dan Imhoff, author of *Food Fight: The Citizen's Guide to a Food and Farm Bill*. All of these authors helped fuel the surge of the local food movement around the country. Ethicist Peter Singer, best known for authoring *Animal Liberation* in 1975, spoke at the White Dog several times over the years and wrote about us in his book *The Ethics of What We Eat: Why Our Food Choices Matter*, noting our commitment to serving only humanely and pasture-raised animal products.

Crowds for our Table Talks would often overflow the White Dog's largest seating area (around eighty seats by the early 1990s) and fill the Law School auditorium across the street, which held two hundred people. Books by our speakers were featured at the Black Cat next door, with book signings following the talks. Scheduled for times when business was slow, Table Talks, which were offered as a fixed-price hot breakfast or three-course dinner with speaker and discussion, increased our sales while increasing knowledge, consciousness, and citizen engagement.

Sometimes a new project sprung from these talks. During a breakfast-time series of Table Talks focusing on inner-city youth, a speaker pointed out that there were playgrounds in low-income communities with broken or missing swings, sending a message to children that nobody cared. So we initiated the Philadelphia Swing Project and succeeded in raising money to buy and install dozens of new swings around the city.

It was during the Swing Project that I met a volunteer, Sue Ellen Klein, whom I invited to join me at the White Dog in a position I created for her as the Director of Community Programs. I made room for Sue Ellen in my own office, and we became the best of friends over the twelve years we worked side by side on program development. She began our program "Storytelling: Real Stories by Real People," during which customers were brought together in a more personal way than at Table Talks through sharing their life stories. Often the speakers were people who did not have much opportunity to be heard—a recent immigrant from Central America explained the challenges of US immigration laws, two men in love told of their struggle to be married and adopt a child, an exoffender described life in prison and the challenges of finding a job once released, which morphed into a series of its own called "Tales from Jails." Criminal justice was also a subject at Table Talks, bringing to light the racist nature of the prison-industrial complex, which profits from the growing number of incarcerated people in the United States, the largest jailer in the world.

Soon after a local children's rights activist, Shelly Yanoff, delivered a Table Talk describing Marian Wright Edelman's program on child poverty, we launched our own Child Watch tours that took our customers to witness, firsthand, the lives of inner-city children. Held at least once a year in partnership with Shelly's organization, Philadelphia Citizens for Children and Youth, each tour had a different focus—child health care, education, recreation, or juvenile justice—showing both the conditions that needed to be improved and the successes that needed to be replicated.

On Saturday mornings, we added a different kind of talk program—"Saturday Rap," talks by and for teens—to generate discussion and inspire student activism among diverse groups of young people. To our surprise, it was an immediate success in a way we hadn't anticipated. The speaker at the first program was Eric Braxton, a recent high school graduate who was starting what he called the Philadelphia Student Union. Its mission was to build the power of young people so that they could speak up and demand a high-quality education in the Philadelphia public school system. When Eric asked the attending teenagers if they were interested in meeting every Saturday morning to help build this new organization, to my surprise most of them raised their hands. *How many young people are really willing to give up their Saturday mornings?* What surprised me even more was that the next Saturday and for many weeks following, they continued to show up.

To house our expanding youth programs, Sue Ellen and I founded a nonprofit affiliate of the White Dog, which we named Urban Retrievers—this became the institutional home for the Philadelphia Student Union. The organization became so successful that we soon turned our nonprofit corporation over to them. Today the Philadelphia Student Union is still going strong, offering leadership training to young people so they can address the problems in their communities, speak with policy makers in Philadelphia, and give students a voice in the state capital—where they lobby for public school funding.

We cared about the elderly also. My efforts to find adequate housing for Gertrude had been an eye-opener to the issues of aging in America, a problem that seemed often overlooked. I was inspired to feature seniors in our storytelling series and to include a project to help elderly shut-ins in our monthly community service day program. And I realized that it worked both ways when I heard the story of a college student who enjoyed this community service program because she missed her grandparents back home in China. We launched a "Take a Senior to Lunch" promotion that halved a customer's bill for Saturday lunch if they were accompanied by a senior. If customers did not have an elderly friend to bring along, we suggested they contact Little Brothers—Friends of the Elderly, a service organization that would match them with a senior who wanted the opportunity to get out more often, as Gertrude so loved to do.

That first Nicaraguan trip had unleashed a torrent of activism, but it also had another effect on me that I never anticipated: it made me more aware that there were parts of Philadelphia where people did not speak English. Being in Philadelphia's barrio was almost like visiting another country. There were plenty of cultural misunderstandings and the need for community building right here in Philadelphia, and so in 1990 the Philadelphia Sister Restaurant Program was born, through which the White Dog developed sister relationships with restaurants in ghettoized neighborhoods of Philadelphia and nearby Camden. After dining at minority-owned restaurants, groups of White Dog customers attended cultural events in the neighborhood, such as a play at Freedom Theatre, one of America's oldest African American theatres.

Just after we announced our first Philadelphia Sister Restaurant event—an evening in the barrio—a front-page article in the *Philadelphia Inquirer* called attention to the problem of drug trafficking in what they called "the Badlands." A map showing the high-trafficking areas had a black dot right on the corner where our sister restaurant was located. Would any of our customers dare come with me now? We quickly organized a Table Talk called "The Good People of the Badlands," demonstrating all the positive things that were happening in the neighborhood. Our evening in the Badlands was sold out! In fact, we ran two consecutive groups that evening so that everyone had a chance to see the art exhibit at the Puerto Rican cultural center, have dinner, and go salsa dancing. White Dog customers from the suburbs and other parts of the city found that enjoying diverse cultural life right in our own city was one good way to make life interesting—and was a lot easier than being a tourist in a faraway country.

But, as usual, I wanted to do more than eat, drink, and have fun. So I began running community tours into neighborhoods to meet local activists, combining meals with visits to inner-city community gardens, affordable housing sites, projects at prisons, and examples of sustainable living in green building and renewable energy.

Our first and most popular community tour was inspired when I was driving through an unfamiliar neighborhood in 1990 and came upon a gigantic mural picturing a family tending a garden. The mural occupied an entire side of a three-story house in an otherwise bleak neighborhood. I heard myself thinking my now common refrain, *My customers have got to see this!* And our mural tour was soon underway.

Beginning with muffins and coffee at the café, we took our customers on a two-hour tour by motorized trolley to see the work of the Philadelphia Mural Arts Program—murals done by local artists in cooperation with community groups that, under the spirited leadership of director Jane Golden, eventually made Philadelphia the wall mural capital of the world. Our annual tours of community wall murals, both by trolley and bicycle, sold out every year for twenty years.

That same year, we began annual tours of Philadelphia's prize-winning community gardens. Customers from the suburbs would compare gardening techniques with inner-city gardeners and then all would enjoy lunch together back at the White Dog.

We also began our annual "Native American Thanksgiving Dinner"—that, too, had a twenty-year run. The dinner recognized and gave thanks for the many foods in our diet that were originally cultivated by the first people of the Americas. Each year we invited a Native American leader to speak about issues of concern to Native American people today and share indigenous wisdom from their own culture, something I feel is very important in learning to live sustainably in today's world. Among the most memorable guests was John Mohawk, who brought some corn for us to try from his Iroquois White Corn Project (then in Victor, New York) and spoke eloquently about the indigenous peoples' relationship with nature. Each year we always invited elders and leaders from the Lenape tribe, the original inhabitants of our own region, who gave a blessing and welcomed the guest speaker from the visiting tribe.

Our calendar kept growing. Soon it was full of one or more special events a week—biking adventures, Rollerbladers Over Forty (I thought that was old at the time!), community service days, African American Heritage Tour, our annual Freedom Seder, and more. All of our tours and talks involved a meal at the White Dog, and we welcomed people who came alone and sat them with others at tables that mostly held four to eight customers. Bringing people together who share a concern for the same issues and a desire to learn, as well as sharing a delicious meal together, created a special feel of community at these gatherings and initiated many a new friendship.

This was especially true on our international sister restaurant trips when groups of twenty White Dog customers would bond during a one- to two-week study tour. These became so popular that we did one or more trips every year. After sharing meals with the Sandinistas, the Zapatistas, the Cubans, former Viet Cong, and the Soviets, we nicknamed our international program "Eating with the Enemy," and realized clearly that we achieve world peace through dialogue and understanding rather than by military and economic domination.

To keep our customers posted on what was happening at the restaurant, we began publishing a quarterly newsletter, *Tales from the White Dog Café*, a much longer and more elaborate version of the one I had begun publishing at La Terrasse. Eventually more than twenty thousand customers signed up to receive it. In the days before e-mail, it was expensive to print and mail so many, but I looked forward to the opportunity to write to my customers, often acting as a sort of citizen journalist in telling the tales of our trips to countries with cultures and systems so different from our own or publishing pieces on the issues we addressed in our Table Talks. In an essay about our study tour to the Netherlands called *Pass the Marijuana, Please!* I told the story of how our group of customers learned about the benefits of Dutch drug policy compared to the failed US war on drugs and were intrigued with our Dutch sister restaurant where marijuana was served along with salads and sandwiches!

People who came to the White Dog were not only hungry for delicious, ethically sourced food, they were also hungry for community, for being part of something bigger than themselves, and learning. "Food, fun, and social activism" became the White Dog motto. And we were not always preaching to the choir. Though you could easily dine at the White Dog without attending an event or getting involved with the many issues we addressed, the fact that we were a successful and popular business and served delicious food caused unlikely people to give our educational programs a try. These are some of the ways I was able to lure innocent customers into social activism!

But customers also introduced me to new ideas and led me to interesting places. It was a customer on one of the Nicaraguan trips, Bill Rieser, who suggested that we find our second sister restaurant in Vietnam, a country suffering from an economic war with the United States through an embargo still in effect fifteen years after the end of the Vietnam War—or as the Vietnamese call it, the American War.

So I set out to find a sister restaurant there, joining a tour led by Don Luce, who became another hero to me. First traveling to Vietnam as an agriculture specialist introducing sweet potatoes to the Vietnamese diet, Don was swept into the war in the 1960s by his students who supported the Viet Cong against the Americans. It was Don who led journalists and a US congressman to expose the notorious "tiger cages" in a South Vietnamese prison, resulting in photographs in *Life* magazine that helped turn public opinion against the war.

During the three trips I took to Vietnam guided by Don, I was fascinated to see how the Vietnamese were experimenting with combining the best of capitalism with the best of socialism. At one point during the first trip, a Vietnamese government representative described the recent opening of the economy to allow free enterprise. "We are not communist or socialist," he explained, "we are a country trying to find its identity. We knew capitalism only during the oppression of colonialism, but on the other hand, we do not want dependency on the state. By opening the economy, we have released the creative energy of the people."

When I returned the following year with a group of White Dog customers, I could see the huge difference made in only one year by the release of "creative energy." I could feel the entrepreneurial vitality in the air, and new businesses were springing up every-where. The first floors of the houses along the streets in Hanoi had transformed into stores and cafés with lights strung along the sidewalks where only the year before it had been dark.

Not all the changes were good. During the war Hanoi had maintained its traditional culture while Saigon had been inter-nationalized by the Americans. Now I could see that, just as the old guard had feared, the same unwanted elements that plagued Saigon were coming to Hanoi—materialism, classism, pollution, prostitution, AIDS, alcoholism, and crime. The old Hanoi, with its dignified, quiet streets and demure women in traditional dress, was disappearing. Just a year ago, the six-lane-wide boulevards had been filled only with thousands of bicycles, silently spinning by, miraculously weaving in and out of crowded intersections with no need for stop signs or lights. On my return in 1991, I was shocked by the dramatic change. The quietly streaming streets had been invaded by a stampede of roaring motorcycles and honking, smoking cars spewing clouds of exhaust.

Returning to Vietnam four years later in 1995 with another group of customers and employees, I found that even more eco-nomic and cultural change had come to this small country. But this time I was not altogether surprised, because in the previous year President Clinton had lifted the embargo that had been crippling the Vietnamese economy. While living in the Eskimo village, I had seen how exposure to globalization could pull people away from their unique local cultures and economies and thrust them helter-skelter into modern life. Since those days in the village, I had been pondering if there could be a way to preserve culture and protect fragile ecosystems, while still incorporating modern conveniences. It was partly this question that encouraged me to set out for another destination suffering from a US embargo, not only to witness the harm done, but also to experience a society that was largely isolated from American culture: Cuba.

On our first White Dog sister restaurant trip to Cuba, we had the good fortune to have as our guide Medea Benjamin, cofounder of Global Exchange, a human-rights organization based in San Francisco that conducts "reality tours" around the world. Having spent time living in Cuba, Medea had expertise and many contacts that provided our group an insider's view of Cuban society.

Although Medea was taken aback when chef Kevin and I beat her and her Cuban dance partner in a contest for being the sexiest dance couple at a Havana nightclub (it was much more comic than sexy), we became fast friends and enjoyed many future times together as fellow activists (as well as dancers). In support of Code Pink, a women's peace group Medea cofounded with Jodie Evans, I brought several busloads of peace activists dressed in pink from the White Dog to join Medea and Jodie in anti-war demonstrations in Washington DC. When a young American peacemaker, Rachel Corrie, was killed in Palestine by an Israeli bulldozer in 2003, Medea was the first person I thought to call. We quickly organized a joint White Dog/Code Pink group trip to the Occupied Territories to recognize the life and work of the slain activist and gain firsthand knowledge of the issues dividing Palestinians and Israelis, while I looked for possible sister restaurants in both Israel and Palestine.

When our first group of White Dog customers arrived with Medea in Cuba in 1993, the embargo had been in force for more than thirty years and had clearly impoverished the island. But it was hard to distinguish how much of Cuba's floundering economy was due to the embargo and how much to the economic policies of the Castro regime. I found it fascinating how the Cubans, like the Vietnamese, were experimenting with a new system that hoped to blend the best of socialism and capitalism. I was impressed with their healthcare and education systems, their care for the young and old, their exuberant art and music, and their renowned community-gardens. I returned to Cuba three more times, drawn to the island, like many other visitors from around the world, to witness a country that has achieved food sovereignty—the ability to feed itself and the right of people everywhere to create a healthy, fair, and culturally appropriate local food system.

After the collapse of their major trading partner, the Soviet Union, and the tightening of the US embargo, Cuba had very little access to oil and fossil-fuel-based fertilizers and pesticides, as well as imported food and medicine, and endured a harrowing time of widespread hunger. Out of necessity Cuba directed the energy of its people toward sustainable agriculture, based on organics rather than fossil-fuel products. Turning swords into plowshares, many soldiers began new careers as farmers. Our group visited high schools where students were taught skills in self-reliance, including growing and cooking food, growing and using medicinal herbs, sewing clothes, making shoes, and even growing grapes to make wine for celebrating their graduation.

Planting organic gardens most everyplace imaginable in and around Havana was part of the nation's food-sovereignty strategy—a remarkable achievement and a model for other countries in these times of climate change and the need to end dependency on fossil fuels and long-distance shipping. We ran three sister restaurant tours to study the community gardens. On one trip, Mark Dornstreich, a farmer supplying the White Dog, marveled at the advanced organic techniques used by Cuban farmers.

Our tours, which included customers and White Dog staff from our kitchen, bar, dining room, and office, also examined the lives of Cuban children. We observed the stark difference between young Americans, who lived in a world of advertisements, and young Cubans, who lived in a nation where the government prohibits commercial advertising on billboards, television, radio, and newspapers. Our group found the young people we met, both informally and in arranged visits, to have greater self-confidence and a freshness and authenticity we often found lacking among many American young people. Young Cubans also weren't overly concerned with appearance or self-conscious about their bodies. Could that be because our children and youth are continually bombarded with images of models and stars, and advertising that makes them feel they have to be beautiful to be loved?

These were the positive effects of a government that did not want to open the doors to advertising that glamorizes wasteful consumerism and self-image based on appearance and wealth. That's not to say Cuba is an idyllic country. I did not support the lack of free enterprise and the heavy hand of the central government (that I recently heard is stifling the growth of the food system they so carefully built, causing the need for some imported food). On the other hand, I did understand why the government is proceeding with great caution in opening their economy, so as not to damage their remarkable culture and its refreshing all-for-one and one-for-all society.

I found it curious that the United States has had economic embargos to cripple the economies of two countries that are experimenting with new economic systems, trying to find the blend of socialism and capitalism that could create a sustainable way forward. There is so much the United States could learn from Cuba and Vietnam, and they from us. What was the United States really afraid of? Was the idea of successful economic systems not dominated by large US corporations viewed as a threat, rather than a way for us to learn and evolve to a better system ourselves?

Though most people think of civil rights and peace when they think of Martin Luther King, Jr., the quote from my hero that I hang in my office is about our economic system:

> Truth is found neither in traditional capitalism nor in classical communism. Each represents a partial truth. Capitalism fails to see the truth in collectivism. Communism fails to see the truth in individualism. Capitalism fails to realize that life is social. Communism fails to realize that life is personal. The good and just society is neither the thesis of capitalism nor the antithesis of communism, but a socially conscious democracy, which reconciles the truths of individualism and collectivism.

Of all the countries where I could eat with our enemies, I had no interest in visiting the epicenter of communism—the Soviet Union. The Soviets seemed as stubborn and entrenched in communism as we did in capitalism. That is, until President Mikhail Gorbachev initiated his reforms with perestroika and announced in 1987 that restaurants would be the first privately owned businesses. I just had to go. By having a Soviet sister restaurant, we would have a front-row seat during this historic time of change, and I welcomed the chance to assist in the fledgling free-enterprise movement.

A Philadelphia friend, Krista Bard, was organizing the first culinary tour of the Soviet Union in 1988, the perfect opportunity to identify a restaurant to be a sister to the White Dog. I knew almost nothing about the Soviet Union and had the false idea that the Soviet people opposed our consumer society and lived frugal lives voluntarily as good communists. I was shocked when we arrived in Russia and I learned that the people there wanted material goodies as much as Americans did, but simply couldn't afford them. In one home I saw a china cupboard displaying the wrappers from perfume bottles and other consumer goods and learned it was a common practice—a way of revering material things. Here I thought I was visiting a society that had risen above consumerism!

Our delegation of about twenty was comprised of national food and wine writers and several restaurateurs—including, to my delight, my culinary heroine Alice Waters. The red carpet was rolled out for our group as we visited the best state owned restaurants as well as the new privately owned ones that were more to our liking. I remember the surprise of our Soviet hosts when they asked Alice what she liked best after a huge meal with all the trimmings at a fancy state run restaurant. Under the crystal chandeliers and next to the ice carving that sat amid a lavish display of delicacies, Alice, petite in stature and with a girlish demureness that camouflaged a powerhouse of energy and passion, held up a plain pale cookie and gave it her highest praise for its flavor, coarse texture, and simplicity. Though the Russian meal was delicious, it was not the extravagancies that Alice wanted to encourage, but simple preparations with natural ingredients.

While observing the Soviet world, it occurred to me that the better-run state owned restaurants in the USSR were quite similar to the restaurants in corporate hotel chains in the United States, and their massive state run farms not unlike our industrial mega-mono-crop farms. Through the lens of food—from farming to cooking—I began to see that communism and corporate capitalism were two sides of the same coin, with power concentrated in the state on one side and in large corporations on the other—with the treat of totalitarianism on both sides of the coin. The choice for a better society was not between a life controlled by big government or big corporations, as many around the world and at home seemed to argue. Rather, we could build a new economy based on smallness, made up of many unique small independent businesses and decentralized small diverse farms. This is where democracy begins! And it is also the most delicious way to organize an economic system.

After eating in restaurants in a number of the Soviet republics, I ended up choosing a restaurant called Stiklai (The Glassblower) in Vilnius, Lithuania, to be our Soviet sister restaurant. It had great food and engaging owners—and also was the first private business in the republic of Lithuania and the second in the whole USSR.

In 1989, the three owners of Stiklai—Romas Zakarevicius, and Ana and Aleksandras Ciupij—and four of their staff traveled to Philadelphia, for most of them the first trip out of the USSR, made possible by our invitation. At the White Dog they cooked a traditional Lithuanian dinner for our customers and told stories of what it was like to run a private business in a communist country—the challenges of finding employees who were not afraid to quit their secure state jobs and the troubles finding ingredients in a bureaucratic centralized farming system.

In 1990, we were planning a trip to Vilnius where we would reciprocate by cooking an American dinner in Lithuania, but as I was organizing a delegation of customers and staff to make the trip our plans were interrupted by a change sweeping the USSR Lithuania had announced its desire to secede from the Soviet Union, and suddenly the Lithuanian airports were closed down and the roads into the country blockaded. We could not take responsibility for a large group, so we called off the tour—but went ourselves. Somehow our White Dog delegation of three—chef Kevin, pastry chef James, and myself—would get to Lithuania, determined as we were to present an American dinner in the Soviet Union as planned.

Though the Lithuanian airports remained closed, as soon as the road blockades were lifted, we made our move. After flying to Finland and then to Latvia, we were greeted at the Riga airport by our sister restaurant friends and piled into a van along with a translator and a good supply of Lithuanian sparkling wine. During the drive across the border, we learned of the exciting prospects for a free Lithuania and also of the concern for what the Soviets might do next.

The next morning we were surprised to find a photo of our arrival on the front page of the Vilnius newspaper. Our American dinner in Lithuania was an important occasion and would be broadcast on television. Kevin and James created a menu that reflected the cultural diversity of the United States—from tacos to spring rolls to fried chicken and greens, and of course apple pie for dessert—and described the cultural significance of each course to the guests and television audience.

Our hosts were disappointed when the governor of Lithuania, who had planned to attend the dinner, was called instead to a meeting with President Gorbachev in Moscow. But this led to a more exciting evening than any of us had anticipated. Toward the end of the dinner, the cameraman who had been in Moscow to film the meeting burst into the room, bringing the news: He had heard Gorbachev promise that he would not prevent Lithuania from seceding from the Soviet Union. The road to independence was clear! "To a free Lithuania!" the toasts began, and the champagne flowed. We were happily surprised when suddenly we no longer had a Soviet sister restaurant—we had a Lithuanian one.

The next day our sister restaurant hosts were eager to show us what they had learned from their trip to the White Dog with a dinner they cooked for us in our honor. Under the highly conformist Soviet system, creativity was not encouraged. A chef was expected to prepare a dish just as it had been done by the chefs for generations before. The real challenge was in finding the ingredients to replicate a classic dish in a country with many shortages. While working with Kevin in Philadelphia, the Stiklai staff learned that our approach to cooking was just the opposite. Rather than starting with a standard recipe, Kevin looked first at what fresh ingredients were available from the farms that day and created a dish around them. Our culinary exchange brought the Lithuanians a new way of thinking that depended as much on innovation as on traditional culinary skills.

Sitting down with our Lithuanian friends for a meal at Stiklai, we were served a salad that seemed unremarkable at first glance, until the translator explained that in the Soviet Union, all salads were shredded like coleslaw, while this one featured whole leaves—a revolutionary concept here and one they had learned when visiting the White Dog.

Next our hosts proudly served a new entrée they had just created based on seasonal ingredients. The name of the dish— "Chicken Judy." What could be a higher honor? Cuisine perestroika had arrived.

"Goodbye," said the fox [to the prince]. "And now here is my secret, a very simple secret: it is only with the heart that one can see rightly; what is essential is invisible to the eye."

—Antoine de Saint-Exupéry in *The Little Prince*

❧ 7 ❧

Living above the Shop: Lessons of Place and Community

IN THE BEGINNING, living above the shop was pretty much a necessity for me, and not a philosophy. How could I possibly have managed to raise two young children while starting a new business, especially a restaurant, if we hadn't lived upstairs? There were other advantages. My commute was free and took only a minute. (Nowadays, I think about the carbon I saved, too.) We only had one mortgage to pay, one property to look after, one community to belong to. And on top of all that, living above a restaurant, I didn't have to cook.

But there was a larger benefit for me, one that helped me make the right decisions and choices in running the White Dog. By living in the same neighborhood where I worked, I saw most every day the people and place affected by my business decisions.

So it came naturally to me to make decisions in the best interests of all those around me. This did not mean that profit was not an important factor; I had come a long way from my early Free People's Store days when I saw profit as a dirty word. I now understood that without profit, a business could not exist, but I also understood that profit was not the only factor I needed to consider, nor was it more important than the well-being of all the people involved in the business.

Beginning with my first White Dog decision—what color the curtains would be—I saw how decision making, both large and small, was my most important function as a business owner. The freedom to make those decisions—expressing my own values and creativity, and to gain or lose by them—was the reason I most wanted to run my own company. But I saw quickly I wasn't just deciding things for myself. What my customers would like—and would appreciate—became the basis for so many decisions that followed the curtains. When I chose a lamp. Or music. Or when I tasted a new dish our chef had created, I would say to myself, *My customers are going to love this!* Sometimes I thought of a certain customer. Sometimes I thought of everyone in general—a collective sea of humanity that I hoped to make happy.

Soon enough, living above the shop helped me appreciate that customers weren't the only ones affected by my decisions. There were other stakeholders to keep in mind. So when I made a decision, I would say to myself, *How will this affect my employees, my suppliers, my whole community, as well as my customers?* It was in this way that I began to build a community of shared values around the White Dog that grew wider and wider from our block on Sansom Street, throughout our region, and even to international relationships.

The prevailing advice about the relation between work life and home life is that people should keep a clear physical separation between them, relying instead on commutes from one to the other. I found there were a lot of advantages and important consequences to intertwining the two—not necessarily living above the shop, but living in the same community—and unfortunate consequences of not doing so. I came to see that physically separating home life from the workplace often leads to the compartmentalization of values. Business schools often teach students, "Leave your values at home when you go to work." This means: practice the Golden Rule at home with family and friends, but at work, *gold rules*. No wonder many people feel empty and unhappy. Work is where we focus the majority of our time and energy, and if we want fulfilling lives, it makes sense that our workplace be aligned with our personal values.

You can see that, in my case, leaving my values at home was impossible since home and work were in the same place, and that's really the point. When we live and do business in the same community, reconnecting home life and work life, we are more likely to run businesses in the best interest of the community we care about, using the very same values in business decisions that we teach our children—do unto others as you would have them do unto you.

I developed a deep sense of place from living and working in the same community, just like the shopkeepers back in my hometown of Ingomar and the feeling I briefly experienced living "behind the shop" at Free People's Store. Like the old time family farm, family inn, or family-run store, work and family life were integrated for us—a way of life that seems to have vanished with the coming of the suburbs, which compartmentalized work and family and required long distance commuting, primarily by car. Here on Sansom Street, Jane Jacobs's vision of vibrant urban living had become our reality.

The total separation between home life and work life, perhaps beginning with industrialization, means that children often don't understand what their parents do for a living. I've always admired the Ms. Foundation for Women's "Take Our Daughters and Sons to Work," the program that addresses the division between work, home, and school life by encouraging parents to bring their

The early years: Judy with her first beagle, Peppy, in Ingomar, and with Augie in Chefornak, Alaska, as a VISTA volunteer. Below: Eskimo women catch prizes tossed into the air at a seal party, a ritual that epitomized the Eskimo culture of sharing that influenced Judy's views on community and social enterprise.

A handpainted sign and shelves made from packing crates adorn the original Free People's Store, opened by Judy and Dick Hayne in 1970 in Philadelpia. Below: Judy, Elliot Cook, and Pasquale Iocca sample wine at La Terrasse.

Judy opened The White Dog Café in 1983, in a row house she helped save from demolition. Below: Yvonne Lighty, the restaurant's first chef, and Gertrude Redheffer, the jazz pianist that played at La Terrasse.

Clockwise from top: Zapatistas in Chiapas approve the entry of the fair-trade coffee delegation; Judy in front of the Mut Vitz coffee cooperative along with fellow travelers Bill Harris and Hal Taussig and local growers; indigenous women from Chiapas's largely nonviolent rebellion against the Mexican government; Judy and chef Kevin Klause with head busboy on trip to visit White Dog's sister restaurant in Vietnam.

Activism was key to the White Dog mission. Above: Judy with protesters she organized to speak out on the need to label food with GMOs. Below: one of the Wicky Wacky Woods gatherings that brought together like-minded business people and helped launch some key groups in the local living economy movement, including BALLE, which she cofounded in 2001.

What began as a muffin counter grew into a 250-seat restaurant through which Judy helped build the local food system, bring community together for Table Talks and events, partner with restaurants around the world to explore different economic models, and help create a resilient local economy in her Philadelphia neighborhood.

child to see and experience their parent's workplace. For me, the story took a different turn. On my first day back to work just one week after Grace was born, I closed up La Terrasse at the end of the night and went home. As I was crawling into bed, I had the strange feeling that I was forgetting something. *The baby!* I had left Grace in the restaurant! I ran up the street, unlocked the door, and found her still sleeping soundly in her basket on the piano. My problem wasn't bringing my daughter to work—it was remembering to bring her home.

Living and working in the same community not only gave me a stronger sense of place but also an uncommon business outlook. As time went on, I came to see that my decisions around purchasing, waste reduction, or energy use at the White Dog had consequences to the natural environment. There were also consequences to the quality of the human-made environment. I came to ask if my decisions added or subtracted from the unique character of my block on Sansom Street and the quality of life in the wider community in which I lived and worked.

In large companies, there is usually a very long distance between the decision makers and those they affect. CEOs or boards of directors may never experience or feel the effects of their decisions on people and places. In fact, the law points them in another direction, requiring publically traded companies to make decisions in the best financial interest *of their stockholders*, often at the expense of other stakeholders—the people involved in the business or living in the community. This separation encourages the disconnection of moral values from making a profit and creates a divided "us" and "them" world.

As a small business owner who lived in the world in which I saw the effects of my decisions, I gradually found that I was more likely to make decisions from the heart, not just from the head, and that these decisions were more likely to be in the best interest of others, and ultimately in my own best interest as well.

I didn't learn this all at once. It took me a while to get a grip on Carl Jung's observation, "The longest journey we have to take is from the head to the heart." But it became clear to me that most of my important business decisions that involved change were inspired by the heart—and implemented by connecting my head and heart.

My decision to pay what is called a living wage is one example. I was attending a conference on responsible businesses when I first heard about the idea of paying a living wage—which means a voluntary commitment by business owners to pay their employees not the unlivable federal minimum wage, which at the time was $5.15 an hour, but rather what actual living expenses cost. At first, I had a typical businessperson's knee-jerk reaction—no one was going to tell me how much to pay my staff. Then I thought it was a nice idea, but that it just could not work in the labor-intensive restaurant business with its many low-wage earners. I mean, how could I pay all my dishwashers and prep people a starting wage of $8.00 an hour, the living wage in Philadelphia at that time? Anyway, I thought, we never paid that pitiful $5.15. People were already making a minimum of $6.50 or $7.00 as dishwashers, and others were already making $8.00 or more an hour. That was that, or so I thought.

But then one day I was in the kitchen—most likely getting a piece of pie out of the refrigerator for my dessert—and I happened to look over at three young entry-level workers lined up prepping vegetables. They all looked up at me at once, and I had a sudden realization, saying to myself, *What am I thinking? Of course I want Tyron, Greg, and Thomas to make a living, to be able to pay their rent and buy their food and clothing.* I gathered together the six or seven employees who were not already making the $8.00 living wage, along with their supervisors, and talked about what a living wage is, how we wanted to pay that, and what they had to do—including showing up for work and being on time. We went through a process by which they were given incremental raises, and by the end of that year, 1999, everyone was making $8.00 an hour, which became our starting wage (that increased over time as the living wage went up).

Or consider another example of a decision inspired by the heart. I had heard about renewable energy and how important it was, especially as the problem of climate change was becoming more obvious. Global warming and the resulting change in climate had already been a focus in White Dog Table Talks. And I had read that since electricity had been recently deregulated in Pennsylvania, utility customers could choose wind-generated electricity. I knew about this intellectually, yet I had not taken action to select a renewable energy option—not until the summer of 1999 when we had a severe drought in Pennsylvania.

In early August, I drove up to the Pocono Mountains north of Philadelphia. I had purchased a small cottage there a couple of years before—something inspired by a visit to my mother back in Ingomar after my dad had passed away. After living in the city for more than twenty-five years, I had suddenly realized how much I missed the woods of my childhood. Our family life had changed. Neil and I had divorced in 1993, after fifteen years of marriage, and Grace was away in college. Lawrence and I were enjoying our life together on Sansom Street, especially our movie and pizza nights, but I felt the need to get away from the hustle and bustle of city life.

Returning to the natural world was like falling into a welcome-back-home embrace from Mother Earth herself. I felt like I was seeing the world for the first time—the extraordinary beauty of sunlight on green leaves, the tiny blue flowers along the lakeshore, the smell of the pines. Life in the woods is so intoxicating. I fell in love with nature all over again. Escaping the intensity of the restaurant business, I began spending much of my free time in the Poconos. Sometimes Lawrence came along and took up trout fishing in the Wicks men family tradition, but often I spent time alone in the woods with my dogs, just as I had as a child. I never feel lonely when in nature, where I have found a profound sense of belonging to the world.

On the way up to the woods during the 1999 drought, I could see that all the cornfields were either brown or, where farmers had lost their whole crop, already plowed under. When I reached my little piece of paradise in the woods, I saw the effects of the drought there, too. My favorite creek was just dust on the rocks. I walked up Fern Hill to find that all the ferns, which usually were tall, green, and waving in the breeze, were flattened like shredded brown tissue paper. Except for the crackling of breaking stems and crushed leaves as I walked, the woods were eerily silent; I couldn't even hear the birds chirping. The danger of fire was all around me. Suddenly it came to me—I was seeing the natural environment under great stress. It was almost as though the woods were speaking to me. *This is what it's going to be like with climate change. Parts of the world are going to perish by drought and fire, other parts by storms and floods.* And then I went over to a big oak tree and wrapped my arms around it as I promised to do my part in stopping global warming. I had become, literally, a shameless tree hugger.

When I got back to the White Dog, I went to the office and said, "You know, we've got to get more information about our electricity choices and get signed up for renewable energy." I wanted to start addressing climate change, and through a local nonprofit called the Energy Cooperative Association of Pennsylvania, we purchased as much wind-generated energy as was available to us. Once the energy producer increased its capacity by building additional wind turbines in our region, we were able to purchase all of our electricity from wind-generated sources. In 2002 the White Dog was recognized by the US Department of Energy for becoming the first business in Pennsylvania to buy 100 percent of our electricity from wind power, reducing our environmental impact by about 432,000 pounds of carbon dioxide a year.

I also looked for other ways of lowering the amount of carbon I burned at work or home. As soon as I heard about hybrid cars, I bought one in 2003. To cut down on burning natural gas, I installed several banks of solar tubes on our roof for preheating the water to wash all those dishes in the restaurant. I also removed two big hot water tanks that kept water hot 24/7, and replaced them with on-demand heaters that only heated water as needed. Before my experience in the drought-stricken woods, I had known in my head what I should do, but I had to be moved by my heart, by my love of nature, to finally take action in all of these ways.

A third example of acting from the heart had to do with the White Dog's relationship with its community, particularly its teenagers. One day, with the White Dog approaching its tenth anniversary, I was stopped at a red light next to West Philadelphia High School, watching the students coming out of the school. They were all African American and living in a part of town where chances to get ahead were often hard to come by. I thought about how this was our own public high school that my own children would have attended if they hadn't been sent to private Quaker schools.

Who are these kids? I asked myself. I really wanted to know and to have relationships with the children growing up in my community. I met with the high school principal and discovered that there happened to be a special program at the school for students interested in the hospitality business, and there was a need for workplace experience.

In 1992, I began a mentoring program for high school students that went on in various forms for a period of more than fifteen years. During the school year, students spent time interning in the kitchen, dining room, and office of the White Dog Café. We also took them on many field trips—to Branch Creek Farm, for example, to see where food really comes from; to eat meals at African American–owned restaurants that were part of our sister restaurant program, to learn from successful businesspeople in their neighborhoods; and sometimes, just for fun, to go ice skating, on a picnic, or to a movie. Culminating each school year, we put together an event called the "Hip Hop," an intergenerational dinner-dance held outdoors in which the students, with the help of our staff, planned the menu, chose the music, designed publicity, hung decorations, cooked the food, sat and served the customers, and cleaned up.

One year at the Hip Hop, after I tried unsuccessfully to keep up with the dancing, I was standing on the sidelines when a student from our first class of mentees arrived with his girlfriend.

He was now in community college and had come back to visit. I was so glad to see him looking so good, and as I watched him walk toward me I could feel my eyes well up. I remembered the question I had asked myself years before while first watching the students coming out of the high school—*Who are these kids?* Now I had the answer. They are our children.

In each of these examples—paying a living wage, signing up for renewable energy, and starting a mentoring program—I was motivated to make positive decisions by connecting with my heart. Having firsthand, real-life experience with people and places in my own community helped me to do that. But it was not the only factor. After all, there are plenty of examples of acting locally with a closed heart and on the other hand, making compassionate decisions that affect people and places far away. It's really about that journey Jung spoke of—the one from the head to the heart. In the business world, that's often a difficult journey. So many messages tell us, *Don't be a softy. Success comes by keeping a stiff upper lip.* This is a lesson boys are traditionally taught from a young age, and women adopt in order to compete successfully in business.

As a child growing up in the 1950s, before the time when girls were directed toward careers outside the home, I had refused to participate in doll playing, cooking, and sewing, which was meant to prepare girls for a life of service as mothers and wives. *A life of service, while the guys get to do all the cool stuff? No way!* But now as an adult, I found myself embracing the feminine qualities I had once rejected—the qualities of the heart—actually making them part of my business philosophy and even my definition of the very purpose of business.

Since my coming of age during the 1960s, I had questioned the role of business in our society and then, at La Terrasse, had seen that business was not about money, but about relationships. With my own restaurant, I wanted a mission statement that recognized this.

What was the mission of the White Dog Café? The satisfaction and pleasure of our customers gave me part of the answer. Gradually, I came to believe that the purpose of business is to serve. Yes, serve—the very thing I had rejected in my adolescent days as unimportant . . . and not cool. And it was not just about serving our customers. The White Dog would be a "full service" restaurant in more ways than one: we would serve our customers, serve one another as fellow employees, serve our community, and serve our natural world.

Because I didn't view profit as part of our mission, but rather a tool to better serve our mission, I did not make decisions based only on short-term profit. After being inspired by walks in the woods to purchase renewable energy, I discovered that it would cost the business about seven thousand dollars more a year. If our mission had been to maximize profits, I would not have been able to justify the decision to make the change to renewable energy. But because our mission included serving nature, this was an opportunity too good to pass up. At the same time, we were serving another part of our mission—our community—by putting less coal-burning pollutants into the air and creating less hazardous nuclear waste.

By being an early adopter of renewable energy, we helped make the cost go down in the long run. As the first business in our state to buy 100 percent renewable, we received a lot of press and several awards. Our customers and community were appreciative of our choice, and I can't help but think that sales increased more than enough to cover the difference in cost.

There were often hard choices to make—trade-offs to consider—between our several business stakeholders. At the end of the year, once I saw how much we made in profits, I would decide what changes we could afford to make in the coming year to better serve our four-part mission. Should I increase benefits to better serve the employees? Install a solar hot water system to better serve nature? Make larger contributions to worthy causes in our community? Each year I tried to do something more in each area. Employee benefits far exceeded industry standards—including paid holidays and vacations, contributions to their retirement funds and health insurance coverage, as well as opportunities for travel, education, and loans. Even the tipped employees, traditionally excluded from any benefits at all, received all these benefits after a certain length of employment, which eventually was after one year. To maintain a fair distribution of resources, I kept the wage gap between our highest and lowest salaries capped at a ratio of 5:1—meaning the managers, including myself, did not draw a salary more than five times that of the lowest-paid dishwasher. So when we had the resources to raise salaries at the top, I made sure we raised the entry-level pay rate as well. A key factor in my own financial security was owning the real estate that housed my business. My rental income allowed me to be more generous with benefits for the staff, which I continually increased over the years.

Being a socially responsible business, I came to see, was a continual journey rather than a state of perfection. There were so many things I wanted to do that would advance our mission of service, but we couldn't afford them all. This was especially true in the early years when we were hanging on by a thread. Not only were we not able to pay a living wage back then, or pay me at all, but also I once had to ask all the employees to accept a pay decrease to the minimum wage of just over $5.00 an hour in order to get through the slow summer months. Luckily, they stuck with me. Maybe some felt that the mission of the White Dog was their mission, too.

Around the time I was contemplating the purpose of business, I was asked to speak to a group of young professionals as part of a panel on philanthropy and volunteerism. The process of preparing for the talk and listening to the other speakers helped me think through my ideas and deepened my business philosophy of service.

The first speaker, a well-respected conservative city council representative, told the group that he would share with them the good advice that had been passed on to him by his father and, earlier, by his grandfather to his father: "Before you can do good," he advised the eager listeners, "you must do well."

What? Could he really be saying that one cannot do good and do well at the same time? But rather must make a lot of money before contributing to the common good? As I listened to the philosophy of Philadelphia's respected gentry and traditional philanthropists, I realized that I was about to give just the opposite advice.

I had not thought of myself as a philanthropist. Though I represented an example of a small businessperson who contributed to the community, I didn't feel that I gave away enough money to be considered an actual philanthropist. So in preparation for the panel, I had looked up *philanthropy* in the dictionary. Surprisingly, it was defined as "the effort to increase the well-being of mankind." This made me realize that making money by any means and then donating the excess change to charity did not truly fit the definition. Do we improperly measure philanthropy by how much money we give away at the end of the year or our careers, rather than considering how we earned that money in the first place? I remembered a recent conversation with an acquaintance who worked for the foundation of a major corporation. In despair she confided that all the money given by her foundation could not begin to make up for the environmental damage and social inequity caused by the corporation in the process of making that money in the first place.

Looking out at the youthful audience and thinking that most had come with an earnest desire to learn how to do the right thing, I wondered how many felt forced to compromise their own values in order to do well in their business careers. Were they getting the idea that they had to make a choice between doing the right thing and making enough money to live on? I wanted to make sure that they understood the concept of "doing well while doing good." It was my turn to speak:

Well, I must say that my advice to you is quite different. I don't believe you need to separate doing good from doing well, but can actually do well *while* doing good. In fact, I believe that the separation of making a profit from doing good has caused most of the problems in the world. And really, it's the combination of making a profit with doing good that provides perhaps the most effective way to create a peaceful and healthy world where *everyone* can profit. When we have livelihoods that do good in the world, we can be a philanthropist every day of the year.

I'm not sure what effect I had on the audience. Perhaps I caused some bewilderment. But this little talk gave me a clarity that strengthened my own understanding of the purpose of business and the true meaning of philanthropy. From then on, I expected not only my charitable dollars to do good, but also asked what good I could do with every dollar I spent in the daily course of business. What I gave away as charitable contributions to nonprofits was insignificant compared to the dollars I spent on day-to-day business expenses. What effect did those dollars have on our community and environment? I saw this as the real force for change and examined every dollar spent to consider the effect it had.

To illustrate this concept to my staff for presentation at the annual Anniversary Howl, I drew a picture of a giant watering can with dollar signs flowing into the can to represent the dollars customers spent at the White Dog. The dollar signs representing the paying of business expenses flowed out of the watering can through a sprinkle head, which distributed the flow in many directions. By spreading money broadly across the community, the business was nurturing and growing what we cared most about—our dollars were helping to grow local farms, local breweries and bakeries, renewable energy companies, sustainable fisheries, fair trade importers, a green office supplier, an eco-friendly soap manufacturer, local musicians, living wages and benefits for employees, as well as nonprofits working for social justice, local arts and culture, and environmental sustainability. Seeking a larger impact, I constantly asked myself questions: *Is there a better alternative to the current supplier—a minority-owned supplier, a more local supplier, or one that was more eco-friendly? Could I encourage a current supplier to become more green? In our day-to-day business, how could White Dog dollars have the most meaningful impact toward greater prosperity for all?*

Perhaps the young people I spoke to that day on the panel about philanthropy and volunteerism did not fully comprehend my message of doing good while doing well. But there was one young person who got it—my daughter Grace. Some years later, when I took Grace to a business conference where we listened to a lecture by a renowned philanthropist and financier, I was shocked when I saw her in line to ask a question. She was only sixteen at the time— what in the world would her question be? I was a little apprehensive until I heard her speak: "I admire all the wonderful work you do in supporting many important causes, but how can you justify earning part of your fortune by manufacturing land mines?"

The financier's answer reflected the same philosophy as the city council person who had spoken before me on the panel—the ends justified the means. But Grace had made her point, and made it well. I was a proud mama!

In our society, and especially in the business world, success is measured by continual material growth. There is no end to this pursuit of growth, because there is never enough. Most business schools teach "grow or die" as a truism. In my own career I was often asked, "How many units do you have?" or "Why don't you start a White Dog in another city?" At first I questioned my own ability and courage to go further—to build a national chain of White Dogs. But eventually I realized that if I were to grow a chain of restaurants, I might make more money, but I would be spreading myself thin over more than one place and would lose what was most important to me—the deep and authentic relationships I had with my customers, employees, neighbors, and suppliers. I made a conscious decision to remain a community-based business deeply rooted in the community where I lived and raised my children, because that's what made me happy.

I don't mean to say that growing physically is always a bad idea. In fact, I discovered several ways to reinvent growth.

Instead of starting another White Dog in someone else's community, another way to grow was to look at what businesses my own community needed. Instead of another White Dog—a Black Cat! Our retail store not only offered our customers a convenient and friendly place to find carefully selected socially responsible gifts, but it added more character and vitality to our block. Open seven days a week until 9:00 p.m., and 11:00 p.m. on weekends, the Black Cat brought more foot traffic and liveliness to the street day and night, increasing the number of visitors to our block—and, in effect, to our community. Many of our products were locally made by potters, woodworkers, jewelry makers, and soap and candle makers. There were also fair-trade crafts, often from our sister restaurant connections. By the cash register, we sold fair-trade chocolate bars as a way of letting people know that the cocoa beans used in most chocolate are harvested by slaves in West Africa. We also specialized in products made from recycled materials such as bottle caps, gum wrappers, rubber tires, watch parts, electric wire, and many other supplies that would have ended up in the trash heap. Tags for the merchandise said LOCALLY MADE or FAIRLY TRADED or MADE FROM RECYCLED MATERIALS.

By our tenth anniversary in 1993 when we celebrated our success in growing to two hundred seats, I realized that my business was as big as I wanted it to be. We had reached a financially viable size, so I stopped growing the White Dog physically and focused on growing it deeper—strengthening relationships with all those involved with the business. You might say that rather than making business decisions to maximize profits, I made decisions to maximize relationships. And in the long run, I believe this was also the reason for our financial sustainability.

I had come to realize that we could measure our success in other ways than growing physically. We could grow by increasing our knowledge, expanding our consciousness, deepening our relationships, developing our creativity, building community, and enhancing our natural environment. All this while also increasing our own happiness and well-being, and having more fun. In the words of the Earth Charter, the document developed by members of the United Nations Educational, Scientific, and Cultural Organization (UNESCO) to help guide sustainable development, "After basic needs are met, it's about being more, not having more."

One nonphysical way I found to grow was to spread our model, rather than our brand. Instead of starting White Dog Cafés in other people's communities, I taught our model through writing and speaking, helping entrepreneurs in other parts of the country start businesses based on ours. Many restaurants were inspired by the White Dog to serve local food and beer, to have a retail companion business, or even to have a nonprofit affiliate—and some even adopted the idea of offering educational programs. One noteworthy example is Busboys and Poets, a restaurant in Washington DC that I greatly admire for their extensive programming on progressive issues, which went far beyond what I was able to do at the White Dog. It meant a lot to me to learn from the owner, Andy Shallal, that the White Dog had been his model for launching the restaurant's educational programs.

Sticking to our mission of service to nature, as well as customers, community, and employees, another way to grow was to continually build our green business model. We recognized this growth by having an annual Green Dog Day with a breakfast talk to demonstrate to our customers new practices initiated over the past year, such as a compost project that supplied compost to inner city school gardens or installing the solar hot water system.

Each year, our goal was to enact at least one new green practice to be announced on Green Dog Day. In 2008 we stopped selling bottled water since it not only creates waste from plastic bottles and packaging and emits carbon in long distance shipping, but it also threatens water security in other communities where bottling companies often drain aquifers. In spite of the price tag, bottled water is less likely to be pure because it is held to lower standards of water quality than public water systems. By being the first restaurant in Philadelphia to stop selling bottled water, we helped educate customers and again became a model for other businesses. These improvements were all about increasing energy efficiency and reducing our environmental footprint, rather than reducing labor costs and the number of jobs we were able to provide.

Through our many educational programs and sustainable practices, I was engaged in all these alternative ways to grow at the White Dog Café and Black Cat—and in helping my customers, as well as interested staff, grow with me. Financial sustainability was an important factor in serving all of our stakeholders from suppliers to investors, but ultimately we measured our success not simply by profits and continued material growth but by the continued growth of happiness and well-being of our customers, employees, community, and natural world.

I felt as though I had reinvented growth in a way that worked for me, and worked for the planet and the people around me, too.

The time of the lone wolf is over. Gather yourselves!
Banish the word struggle from your attitude and
your vocabulary. All that we do now must be
done in a sacred manner and in celebration.
We are the ones we've been waiting for.

—Hopi Elder's Prophesy

❧ 8 ❧
Basta! We Have Had Enough: Coffee and the World Revolution

I WAS HAPPY in my above-the-shop life. Like my childhood forts, I created my own world, building a different kind of business that truly expressed my values and ideas, as well as my sense of fun. In a way, my business was my ministry—spreading the gospel of food, fun, and social activism.

But I was a maverick, largely working in isolation from most other businesspeople. I even thought my unconventional approach to business might be a sign of madness! There were also times when I felt discouraged to think that as hard as I was trying to provide a model for doing good through business, I was only one small company and could not make a significant difference in the world.

That all changed when I met Ben Cohen of Ben & Jerry's ice cream company. You might say that Ben discovered me.

One night in the late fall of 1992, my cousin Debbie and her friend Alice brought a college friend of Alice's to the White Dog. The college friend was Ben, who had just been speaking at the nearby university. Ben and I immediately found that we had much to talk about, and a longtime friendship began. Ben didn't think I was crazy, at least no crazier than he was. He affirmed my work. He appreciated the sister restaurant project and the Table Talk programs on peace and justice issues. He was the first to accuse me of using good food to lure innocent customers into social activism. He ought to know because he did the same thing. Like me, Ben also saw fun as an essential ingredient in our work to use business as a vehicle for social change.

Ben was a teacher to me, and an inspiration. He gave me business language for some of what I was already doing. Purchasing from local farmers and small growers in other countries was *alternative sourcing* and paying a fair price was called *fair trade*. The White Dog's mission of serving our employees, customers, community, and nature was like measuring success with, as Ben put it, a multiple bottom line. The concept of the multiple bottom line—that business success not be measured solely by the bottom line of profit—was first developed by Ben when he included "shared prosperity" in the mission of Ben & Jerry's. Figuring that people value what they measure, Ben used a double bottom line to measure the success of his company in both profit and social impact. As awareness about the natural environment grew, others made it a triple bottom line with the three Ps of people, planet, and profit, and sometimes the three Es of equity, ecology, and economics.

This triple bottom line became a widely used tool in the socially responsible business movement, which I knew nothing about until Ben clued me in. The aim of the movement was to change the way the world does business from a purely profit-driven model to using business as a vehicle for building a just and sustainable society. I had been doing this without realizing that a whole movement was devoted to it!

I was amazed how much Ben and I had in common in the way we thought about business. Of course, I was a very small businessperson compared to Ben & Jerry's, but nevertheless I felt as though I had met a soul mate, and that emboldened me to go even further in my work. I wasn't working alone anymore. Not only did Ben validate my work, but he told me that there were other businesspeople that shared our progressive values and introduced me to an entire community of like-minded, socially responsible businesspeople who belonged to an organization called Social Venture Network (SVN) and who gathered twice a year to learn from each other, hear inspiring speakers, and come up with new ideas for improving their business practices, starting new ventures, and advancing the movement.

Ben nominated me for membership in SVN and in the spring of 1993 invited me to attend my first meeting. At last, I had found "my people." Joyfully, I joined the ranks of the growing national movement for socially responsible business. With so many working together, I sensed there was real hope that the world would someday offer everyone a place at the Table for Six Billion. What a great party that will be!

In a few years, I was asked to join the board of directors of SVN. Before my first board meeting I was thinking about the organization and trying to find words to articulate what was at the heart of SVN that so attracted me. At the time, I was listening to a tape of Mohandas Gandhi's life. Having discovered that my hero Martin Luther King, Jr., was strongly influenced by Gandhi's work, I had bought the tape to see what I could learn.

It contained a story about someone asking Gandhi why he—as a spiritual man—was also engaged so deeply in economics and politics, which were not spiritual at all. Gandhi disagreed. He replied that it made perfect sense that he be involved in the three fields. Spirituality, economics, and politics were all interconnected, he explained. When I heard this, I knew I had exactly what I was looking for. I saw the work of SVN at the intersection of economics (or business), politics (in the broad sense of social change), and spirituality (which I interpret as the belief in the interconnection of all life). This is the place from which I acted in my own life and business, and why I was so attracted to SVN. I drew a picture of three intersecting circles, and marked them as BUSINESS, SOCIAL CHANGE, and SPIRITUALITY. In the center, where the three overlapped, I wrote SVN.

The morning of my first SVN board meeting, a three-day retreat, I was having breakfast in the dining hall and happened to sit with fellow board member Ram Dass, the spiritual teacher, whom I greatly admired. (We had carried his book *Be Here Now* in Free People's Store back in 1970.) I showed him the diagram of the three circles and explained that I wanted to share it with the board but was afraid that as a new board member it would be presumptuous. Ram Dass looked at the diagram and with a big grin said, "Be presumptuous!"

And so I was, and before the end of the retreat, the board had accepted this new way of describing the work of SVN—though the term *spirituality* was eventually changed to *community*, perhaps a more widely accepted term in the business world for defining life's interconnection. The experience helped me begin to see how much the ideas of Gandhi resonated with me and helped guide the way forward in the work that lay ahead at the intersection of economics, politics, and spirituality. Just as I had been celebrating King's birthday at the White Dog for many years, I began to hold "Happy Birthday, Gandhi" breakfast talks each year on October 2nd to explore Gandhi's work around nonviolent social change and to hear from like-minded activists.

It really wasn't until I engaged with SVN that my journey from a lone-ranger kind of businessperson to a business collaborator and convener began. Eventually, my life would be consumed by bringing together entrepreneurs to change the way business was conducted, revive local economies, and make a positive impact on the world. But my first collaborative project—a large step forward for an individualist like me—began in the highlands of Chiapas, the southernmost state of Mexico, in 1998.

Chiapas was not new territory for me. I initially had gone there in 1995 to find a Mexican restaurant to become part of our international sister restaurant project. I had wanted to learn more about the Zapatista rebellion and prodemocracy movement and then return to Chiapas with groups of our customers and staff to see for themselves. On this first trip I joined a Global Exchange "reality tour," as I had done on my first trip to Cuba. It seemed that wherever in the world there were important human rights struggles taking place, I would find Global Exchange's Medea Benjamin working tenaciously on the front line.

I brought along sixteen-year-old Grace, who had also accompanied me on the visit to our Nicaraguan sister restaurant six years earlier. We landed in the airport in Tuxtla Gutiérrez, the hot, flat, and dusty capital of Chiapas, and began the long ride up the mountains to Los Altos, the Mayan highlands, and the colonial city of San Cristóbal de las Casas, the strategic center of Zapatista influence. As our van drove several hours up and up the narrow, winding mountain roads, the scenery changed from arid plains to lush mountains and the temperature dropped dramatically. Along the roads we could see patches of corn grown by the local farmers, the ground often carved into the sharp incline as hillside terraces so that the dirt was level enough to plant seeds. It was here in Mexico, I explained to Grace, that corn was first cultivated. The Mayans call themselves the "People of Corn," and they see corn as a sacred food.

On the first evening in San Cristóbal we wandered among indigenous vendors who lined the cobblestone town square, or *zocalo*, and chose hand-woven woolen shawls to wrap around our shoulders in the surprisingly cool temperature for a summer night. At the *zocalo* we sat on a bench eating ears of roasted corn flavored with salt and lime, which we had bought right off the hot coals of a tiny street stand. I studied the front of the town hall, so staid and still, trying to imagine the scene here on New Year's Eve in 1994, when the Zapatistas had staged their uprising.

What courage and audacity it took for a ragtag band of indigenous farmers, some armed with only symbolic wooden guns, to don black ski masks and red bandanas and challenge the Mexican army by taking over the town halls in several cities in Chiapas, including this one in San Cristóbal, without firing a shot. Led by the charismatic *subcommandante* Marcos, the indigenous people had shouted "Ya basta! No mas!" which is roughly translated "Enough already!"—a phrase declaring war (a largely nonviolent one) against the Mexican government's seventy-year-old one-party-rule and making demands for democracy, justice, and land. Having endured five hundred years of oppression, broken promises, and exclusion from the democratic process, the indigenous people of Chiapas, one of Mexico's richest states in natural resources and one of its poorest in per capita income, had had enough.

It was no coincidence that the uprising had begun on January 1, 1994, the day that NAFTA—the North American Free Trade Agreement—went into effect. In order to comply with NAFTA requirements to deregulate government trade restrictions and allow direct foreign ownership of land and businesses, the Mexican government was forced to change their country's constitution. Article 27 of the Mexican Constitution was of particular importance to indigenous people. Won through the Mexican revolution of 1910 led by Emiliano Zapata, from whom the Zapatistas took their name, this article protected the community-owned ancestral farmlands of the indigenous people. With the NAFTA-required changes, these lands—and their rich supply of natural gas, oil, and other resources—were opened to ownership and exploitation by Mexican and foreign corporations.

There was also the issue of corn. NAFTA opened the Mexican market to cheap corn imported from the United States. Subsidies from the US government to corporate agribusiness allowed US-produced corn to be sold below the cost of production, which threatened to put out of business the local indigenous farmers, like those we had seen on the terraced hillsides on our journey up the mountains. Without the means of self-sufficiency, indigenous people would be forced off their land to take jobs in corporate plantations or factories called *maquiladoras*, or risk illegal immigration to the United States to seek work. Another danger was the importation of genetically modified (GM) corn, widely grown in the United States, that could easily pollute the ancient varieties of indigenous corn, doing irreparable harm to a food cultivated over thousands of years.

I was eager to learn more from the perspective of those living in Chiapas, and the next day Grace and I began our search for a Mexican sister restaurant. Taking the recommendation of our knowledgable Global Exchange guide Margaret O'Shea, whom Medea had suggested for our group, we walked for lunch to a restaurant and bakery called *Casa del Pan* (House of Bread). On entering, we were immediately struck by a large mural covering the back wall of the dining room—a collage of an Indian woman and child surrounded by large ears of corn, the sacred food of the Maya, and next to them the black ski-masked face of a Zapatista rebel. It looked to me like we had come to the right place!

After enjoying our enchiladas in mole sauce served with fresh mango juice, we met the welcoming owner, Kippy Nigh. I was surprised to find that she was originally North American but had been living in Mexico for over thirty years and now called it home. We ended up choosing Casa del Pan as our sister restaurant not only for its delicious vegetarian food made from fresh local organic vegetables and fruits, but because of Kippy's deep commitment to helping the indigenous people, whom she assisted in many ways—from job training to buying their crafts for her café shop to supporting a school and orphanage with a portion of her profits. Bridging the two worlds of Mexico and the United States, Kippy and her husband Ron Nigh, an anthropologist working on indigenous economic development projects, taught me a lot about the historic events taking place in Chiapas.

Kippy and Ron eventually traveled for a visit to Philadelphia where they shared their stories about life in Mexico with our customers at a special dinner, and a White Dog kitchen worker spent a month working at Casa del Pan as part of our exchange.

Through our sister restaurant program, I returned to Chiapas in 1996 and 1997, with Margaret as our guide each time, bringing twenty White Dog customers and staff—and on one trip included two high school students the White Dog was mentoring and my son Lawrence, then sixteen, who kept the video camera going throughout the trip, an interest that led him toward his future career in film. As usual, we did not bypass the hallmark of White Dog events—having fun—and we thoroughly enjoyed the Mexican food, culture, and nightlife with lots of dancing, as well as the beautiful natural environment. But we were also there for a serious purpose—to travel to the countryside and learn from indigenous leaders about the roots of their unrest and become aware of how US foreign policy affected the Mexican people.

It was a widely held belief in Chiapas that the guns, helicopters, and armored vehicles used to repress the indigenous people were supplied by the US government. When American activists questioned our government about the doubling of military aid to Mexico in the year following the Zapatista uprising, the officials had justified the arms sales as being needed to fight drug trafficking.

It was also widely known that more soldiers from Mexico than any other country were trained at the notorious School of the Americas (SOA, now the Western Hemisphere Institute for Security Cooperation) at Fort Benning, Georgia, nicknamed the "School of Assassins" because its graduates have been implicated in massacres and repression throughout Latin America.

Our customers knew something about the US Army SOA. At a Table Talk in the summer of 1997, as we listened in the comfort of the White Dog, we were appalled to hear from Roy Bourgeois—a Maryknoll priest, Vietnam vet, and founder of SOA Watch—that over two-thirds of the Salvadoran officers cited in a U.N. Truth Commission report on murder, rape, and torture during El Salvador's civil war were trained at this school, making me think back to my Salvadoran friends at the La Terrasse breakfast long ago.

Among those inspired by Father Roy that day was the White Dog's financial manager, Deirdre, who joined the board of SOA Watch to work on closing down the notorious school. That November we organized a delegation of customers and staff to Georgia, including Deirdre, Sue Ellen, and myself, to join thousands of other protestors at the gates of the school, demanding its closure. I was among those who committed civil disobedience by following Father Roy onto government property in defiance of the blaring bullhorns warning us to stop. I never felt more true to the ideals of truth and justice than when I was arrested at Fort Benning and locked up in the stockade for the day. While in the stockade I met another Philadelphian, Frank Corcoran, who was active in the local chapter of Vets for Peace. Under Deirdre's leadership, the White Dog led delegations to the annual protest for the next ten years, and we partnered with the veterans' group, whose members—particularly Frank, John Grant, and Bob Hennel—became our close friends and regulars at the White Dog bar. On Veterans Day, they participated along with other veterans in our storytelling series, sharing their experiences of war that led to their activism in the peace movement.

Soon after my act of disobedience at the School of the Americas, and just before Christmas in 1997, I received some extremely disturbing news from Chiapas. A coffee importer and roaster from Colorado, Kerry Appel, whom I had learned about from a friend, drove his Volkswagen bus from Denver to the village of Acteal in the highlands of Chiapas to pick up a year's supply of coffee beans from indigenous growers. He had made his annual journey to Acteal for three years, but that year he found the storehouse empty. The entire coffee harvest had been stolen. Worse, he learned that the day before his arrival, forty-five Mayans from the coffee-growing community had been killed in a massacre. The dead, mostly women and children, were all members of the pacifist group *Las Abejas*—which translates to The Bees—who had gathered at a chapel in Acteal to pray for peace. Terrified survivors told him the story of dozens of men wearing dark uniforms, armed with machetes and automatic weapons, attacking the villagers along with refugees who had just fled paramilitary violence in neighboring communities.

From a cybercafé in Chiapas, Kerry sent an e-mail to a list I belonged to of fair-trade advocates describing what he had witnessed and repeating the survivors' accounts of the Acteal massacre. Although I didn't know Kerry, as I sat at my desk in Philadelphia, I was deeply upset by his account of the tragedy.

Just a week before, I had been alerted by an e-mail from Kippy at our Mexican sister restaurant that violence against the indigenous people of Chiapas was increasing at an alarming rate. She described how hundreds of Mayans, who were supporters of the Zapatista indigenous rights movement, were being driven from their homes and farms by paramilitary forces believed to be armed by the Mexican army. It was growing cold in the highlands, and refugees who had fled their villages were hiding up in the mountains without adequate food and shelter during the chilly December nights. Fearing for their lives, Kippy urged me to find a way to help them. "Tell your government to intervene," she pleaded. "Find a way to stop the US from providing guns to the Mexican army. Do something, before it's too late."

The night I read Kippy's plea, I felt powerless to help and that we were worlds apart. Indeed, we were. It was the night of the annual White Dog Café staff holiday party. I had gone downstairs and into the bustling kitchen with tears in my eyes to share the disturbing news with chef Kevin. After listening sympathetically, Kevin provided his characteristically sardonic yet practical advice: "Go wash your face and put on a pretty dress." Yes, the show must go on, and as proprietress, I needed to be in good spirits for the holiday party that would soon begin.

But as I climbed back upstairs to change my clothes, I felt troubled. Though Kevin's advice was meant to be lighthearted and comforting, it captured the contradiction I was feeling. The comfort and affluence, and sometimes superficiality of our Christmas season—the overabundance of food and drink, the holiday outfits, the material gifts, really our whole way of life—was in such sharp contrast to the hardship and sacrifice of the indigenous peoples of Chiapas who were struggling for simple human rights. It was this difference in lifestyle, culture, and language that I had hoped to bridge through our international sister restaurant program, building people-to-people relationships. I wanted participants to realize that despite our different circumstances, the struggle for human rights was universal. Now I felt that the strength and effectiveness of this vision was being tested.

My discomfort had been building. Earlier in the year Amnesty International reported increasing numbers of human rights violations by the Mexican army and the paramilitary forces that the army allowed to operate with impunity. As the violence and oppression escalated, Kippy, along with many others, sensed something terrible was about to happen, and this is why she wrote to me on the night of the staff holiday party pleading for help. Now, just one week after she had written, Kerry was reporting on the tragedy at Acteal, which occurred only a few miles from Kippy's home in San Cristóbal. Her worst nightmare had come true.

I had to come up with some effective way to respond to the Acteal massacre—to not let it pass as though unnoticed. Though many peace activists were speaking out about the violence in Chiapas, no one seemed to be listening. Bringing our customers to bear witness to the indigenous struggle for democracy no longer felt like enough. Nor was it enough to get arrested for the cause. What could I do that would be heard? How could I make a difference?

A few days later, an idea came to me.

I realized the fact that Kerry had been in Chiapas as an American businessman made his story stand out. His perspective wasn't essentially that of a peace activist, but of a businessman in Mexico to conduct business who had concern for his suppliers—the people who grew the coffee. As a businessperson myself, I felt drawn to this perspective. So why not organize an alliance of other business owners who bought products from Mexico and send a delegation to Chiapas to investigate how the violence was affecting business and the lives of our trading partners? Perhaps then our voices would be heard.

With a plan now unfolding in my head, I looked through my directory of Social Venture Network (SVN) members for names of businesspeople who might possibly buy from Mexico and came across the name of Rick Stewart, founder and CEO of Frontier Natural Products Co-op, an importer of organic herbs, spices, and coffee from many countries, including Mexico. I hadn't met Rick, but as a fellow SVN member, I hoped he would join my alliance and make the trip to Chiapas.

As he later told the story, Rick had just landed at home in Iowa on a return flight from South America and was still on the plane calling in for messages from his cell phone when he picked up my voice mail. After hearing my plea, he turned to Jim Handley—Frontier's coffee buyer, who was sitting next to him on the plane—and said, "Sorry, Jim, I need you to turn around and head back to Mexico."

I was overjoyed when Rick responded to my call and told me he would send two representatives from his company—Jim, and Rob Stephen, Frontier's coffee plant manager. Although some of White Dog's coffee, our decaffeinated line, came from a cooperative in Mexico and we carried crafts from Chiapas in the Black Cat, I knew nothing about importing coffee. I could not have made the trip without representatives from Frontier, a company with thirty million dollars in sales and a lot of experience in coffee buying. Jim and Rob added the credibility and expertise I needed for a successful delegation.

New Harmony, the coffee roasting company in Philadelphia that supplied the White Dog, owned by my friend Myron

"Mickie" Simmons, who had been on our delegations to Nicaragua, was also willing to send a representative, Katie Rogers. Two more delegates, both Mexican representatives of companies in our alliance, would join our group in Chiapas. That made six of us, plus a guide/translator—enough for a delegation to represent the alliance.

I gave our alliance a name—Businesses for Ethical Trade and Human Rights in Chiapas, or BETHRIC, as we began to call ourselves. I knew I needed a lot more businesses as members to give BETHRIC a position from which to speak. Ben & Jerry's bought coffee from Mexico for their coffee ice cream, so I called Ben Cohen, and he signed up and also gave me the name of another coffee importer in Vermont, Dan Cox.

Explaining that BETHRIC was formed in response to the Acteal massacre, I called importers around the country who were known for paying fair prices for Mexican coffee and textiles. The list grew to fifteen companies. At that point, I made up a letterhead for BETHRIC and listed the names of the members down the side. In a matter of days, BETHRIC had become an impressive alliance of businesses committed to ethical trade, care for the environment, and improving human rights for our indigenous trading partners in Mexico.

Next, I turned to Global Exchange and my friend Medea Benjamin for help with the BETHRIC trip. Not only did Global Exchange provide our guide, Medea also helped me plan the media strategy and introduced me to a Mexican public relations firm that would arrange for our press conference in Mexico City. Global Exchange sent a press release to both the American and Mexican media, announcing our press conference at the conclusion of our fact-finding trip to Chiapas, when we would report the findings of our investigation.

It took only six weeks from the time I learned of the Acteal massacre to organize the trip. By mid-February 1998, the BETHRIC delegation had left for Chiapas. My idea was taking form. Now we needed to see if we could make a difference.

In San Cristóbal, our BETHRIC delegation and our guide, Amanda Brown, piled into a van with notebooks and cameras and drove into the countryside to the region of unrest. Our first stop was Union Majomut, an indigenous coffee cooperative that supplied coffee to BETHRIC member Equal Exchange. There we heard from cooperative representatives about how the government had once controlled the coffee production and had forced the growers to give up their traditional natural growing methods to buy and use chemicals. Frustrated with the low prices they received for their coffee, the growers formed the cooperative in 1983 and began to sell directly to fair-trade importers in the United States and Europe. The cooperative stopped using chemicals and went back to their traditional indigenous growing methods, now in demand by the expanding organic market abroad.

The cooperative leaders explained that the violence toward their members began almost six months before the Acteal massacre, in the late spring of 1997, when paramilitary forces began running growers off their land and stealing or destroying their coffee, corn, beans, and other vegetable crops. The violence escalated during coffee harvest time, and the cooperative's entire crop worth more than $750,000 was lost, its processing plant was shut down, and many of the growers were forced into refugee camps. Years of hard work on the part of the cooperative and its trading partners in the United States and Europe were in jeopardy.

The cooperative members we spoke with felt that the paramilitary used weapons belonging to the Mexican army, and were likely supplied by the United States, and that the violence was focused on destroying the productive base of the indigenous economy. Without cooperatives, which made it possible to organize direct exports to fair-trade importers, the coffee growers would have to go back to selling their coffee to large corporations through brokers called *coyotes*, who paid very little to the farmers. This was the prevailing system that many in powerful positions in Mexico and the United States had an interest in preserving.

The next stop on our fact-finding trip was a visit to a refugee camp, where we found thousands living under torn plastic sheets held up by thin poles. They were unable to make fires to cook or warm themselves because the firewood was damp from the winter rains. In conversations with refugees from many villages, we heard that the harassment of the workers and the damage to crops was not limited to a single cooperative but was pervasive throughout the region. To international visitors the soldiers around the camp appeared as though they were providing protection, but we learned otherwise from the refugees who felt threatened by the military.

From there we traveled to one of the Zapatista "communities of resistance" located in an indigenous autonomous zone. In February 1996, following a series of lengthy talks, the government had signed the San Andrés Accords with the Zapatista National Liberation Army (EZLN), which granted indigenous people the right to build autonomous communities within Mexico and establish self-governance structures. An oft-repeated quote by a Zapatista at those peace negotiations with the Mexican government is paraphrased this way: "Gentlemen, you don't seem to understand. I am a farmer. My father was a farmer and his father was a farmer as far back as we know. You don't seem to understand that we don't want your welfare handouts, your political positions are meaningless to us, and your factory jobs are what we oppose. We want our sons and daughters, and their sons and daughters to continue to be farmers on our own lands with our own languages and our own cultures and traditions. This is what we are fighting for and this is what we are willing to die for."

I had visited "communities of resistance" on White Dog trips in previous years and had been impressed to see how residents grew their own food, maintained their cultural identity, and developed their own governance system based on consensus. Long denied adequate health care and education by the Mexican government, the Zapatistas had set up medical clinics in every community and schools to teach children in their own language and customs. I saw this concept as a model for the rest of the world: When the dominant system is destroying what you cherish, then create your own community governed by a just and caring system and a local economy that is self-reliant in basic needs.

Though the peace accords had clearly upheld the legitimacy of these autonomous zones, we found the Mexican army camped just outside each village, and the residents told us that they were harassed daily by troops marching past their houses and by helicopters flying above. People were afraid to go out to the fields where they could be captured or raped. Occasionally someone was killed or beaten, or their animals were killed. Since the military arrived, the production of corn, beans, and coffee had declined. Clearly, the concept of self-reliant communities was a threat to the prevailing power structure. From the Zapatista point of view, the government wanted the indigenous people to become part of the industrial global economy—either selling their crops to the large corporations at low prices or leaving the land to work in factories where they provided cheap labor for export production, and of course buying their basic needs from the same system.

The most moving experience on our trip was visiting a women's weaving cooperative where a BETHRIC company, SERRV International, was arranging to purchase the cooperative's embroidery work for a US store. To reach the cooperative, we drove far into the mountains along dirt roads, and then walked along a narrow path that ribboned through fields of high grass along a mountainside. After a twenty-minute walk, we reached a small cluster of wooden shacks where a group of fifteen women were assembled to welcome us. The women were all dressed alike. Clean white blouses embroidered in red across the shoulders and chest were set off against black skirts, and the women's straight black hair was parted in the middle and neatly woven into two long braids reaching below their waists and entwined with bright colored ribbons.

The women greeted us with shy smiles and handshakes and invited us into one of the small buildings. Inside was a table in the center of the room with samples of their embroidery work and chairs for us along one side of the table. The women sat across from us on a wide bench along the wall, many of them nursing babies or holding young children. At the end of the table were two translators—a man to translate from the indigenous dialect to Spanish, and our guide, Amanda, translating from Spanish to English.

The women began by telling us that they were members of *Las Abejas* (The Bees), the same pacifist group as those killed at Acteal. *Las Abejas* was formed in 1992 to work for justice nonviolently. "Since the massacre," the women explained, "there is such great sadness in our hearts that we cannot weave." We learned that no work had been done in almost two months. Here, in this remote place where no one else could hear them, the women began to describe in hushed tones what had happened at Acteal. The rampage had gone on for four hours as the killers hunted down the women and children who had hidden in caves along the river or in the cornfields. Police were seen at the top of the hill, but they only stood by and did nothing to stop the massacre. The stories were heartbreaking, and as they spoke, the women began to cry. Then both the translators began to cry, and before long we were all crying, men and women alike.

Slowly each of the women took a turn speaking. They knew who the killers were, and even knew some by name. They were recognized as members of the Mexican ruling party, PRI, who were called PRIistas. Because they supported the government in power, they were allowed to go free. At the funeral in Acteal, the women had overheard PRIistas talking about how they were going to kill the rest of *Las Abejas*. The women were terrified that the killers would attack any time. They lived in constant fear. The PRIistas wanted the Zapatistas to take up arms, because they knew they would win an armed struggle, but *Las Abejas* continued to resist nonviolently.

Before we left, the women stamped our notebooks with their logo. It was a bumblebee breaking a chain with its stinger.

Back in San Cristóbal, I went to Casa del Pan to type out the statement of our BETHRIC delegation for the press conference we were holding the next day in Mexico City to report our findings. Through all our interviews we heard the same story: While Zapatista supporters uphold the peace accords and enforced nonviolence, well-armed and well-supplied paramilitary forces loyal to Mexico's ruling party were conducting a reign of terror and systematic attack on the indigenous economy, resulting in the loss of the region's coffee harvest, a disruption in craft and textile production, and the destruction of the Zapatistas' food supply.

In our statement we would be reporting, of course, on the plight of our indigenous trading partners, but something else was becoming clear to me. As I sat alone in the tiny office at Casa del Pan, not much bigger than a phone booth, the pieces of a larger view came into place—a vision that I would follow for the rest of my life.

I realized then that it was not only the indigenous economy that was jeopardized. What was really under attack was the global network of direct fair-trade connections between the people of the south and the north. What was under attack was the opportunity for community self-reliance and strong local economies. All this was a threat to a power structure that profited from a world population whose livelihoods were increasingly dependent on jobs in the offices, factories, and plantations of the corporate industrial economy.

Sitting alone in that little office, in February 1998, I came to the realization that the call of the Zapatistas for economic self-reliance and a connection to the land was the same call of the small farmers in my own country. In Chiapas, the powerful were using violence to force people off their land where they could be self-reliant; but the same thing was happening at home—not with government-supplied guns but with government-supplied policies such as the Farm Bill, which serve the interests of large corporations over locally owned farms and businesses. As in Mexico, family farms were being lost in rural communities at home, and many of the former farm owners were now workers on corporate factory farms—or driven from their communities altogether. Life in rural America was being destroyed. It was all part of the same global struggle. The Zapatistas' call for independence and local self-reliance was the call of threatened communities everywhere.

Throughout this trip I had begun to link what I had learned by buying from local farmers for the White Dog Café to the plight of farmers in Chiapas and to what I had learned in other sister restaurant travels to Central America and Southeast Asia. I had seen firsthand in all these places how communities and the environment around the world were suffering from the effects of corporate globalization. My thoughts were crystallizing. The Zapatista experience was nurturing the seeds of my own role in the global rebellion against corporate globalization. In the call of the Zapatistas, I discovered my own voice of protest and eventually my call for a new economy. This was my fight, too.

I added to our report, "We have come here in defense of the indigenous people with whom we trade, but we also come here to protect an economic system we believe in." *Yes, that was it, and an economy that worked in harmony with nature as the indigenous do.* "We share the indigenous respect for the natural environment and promote the use of organic farming methods critical to the health and well-being of consumers and future generations." *And this was all connected to what was happening in our own rural communities and on Main Street, USA.* "And like the indigenous communities, we believe in an international economy based on healthy local economies, buying from family farms and neighborhood businesses."

The next day, February 14, 1998, we four American delegates of BETHRIC flew to Mexico City to read our statement to the press. Taking a cab from the airport, we reached the press conference just in time. To our astonishment the room was full. Thirty or more reporters were set up with earphones for instantaneous translation. The public relations firm arranged by Medea had done an excellent job. We North American businesspeople sat at a table at the front of the room, and Jim Handley, Frontier's coffee buyer, and I read our statements before taking questions. Along with our findings, we asked that the Mexican government enforce the peace accords, provide security for the displaced people to return to their homes and businesses, compensate for the stolen crops, and disarm and disband the paramilitaries. Of the US government, we asked that it investigate whether US weapons ostensibly supplied for curtailing drug trafficking were actually being used to repress the indigenous people, and that it close the SOA, which trained so many human rights abusers.

At the end, I read aloud more of what I had written in the tiny restaurant office at Casa del Pan the night before:

> The struggle of the indigenous people in the highlands of Chiapas for self-determination and self-reliance is our fight, too. Their demand for the right to raise their children in communities free of fear and according to their own culture and values is one we share. It is the struggle to make a living wage when you work hard for it, and it is the fight to save family farms and neighborhood businesses. In essence this is a global struggle between those who are working to build a world economy built on business relationships which benefit all people and the forces of globalization based on exploitation of people and the environment that benefit only a few.

The next morning the front-page headlines in the English language paper in Mexico, *The News*, read "US Firms Call for Peace in Chiapas." The popular weekly Mexican magazine *Proceso*, the equivalent to our *Time* or *Newsweek*, also picked up our story. During the questions at the press conference, the reporter from *Proceso* expressed puzzlement about BETHRIC, asking if we were a business organization or a human rights organization. "Both," I had proudly replied. This was a new concept for the reporter, and likely the others in the room. BETHRIC was demonstrating a new way of doing business that provided an alternative to the status quo—a way of doing business that was beautiful.

The interest of the press showed that in one way we had succeeded. Our voice had been heard, and our story would likely be read by thousands of people. We had demonstrated that by working together we could use the voice of business to speak out against injustice. This felt very empowering. On the other hand, it was equally likely that we were not going to be heard by either government. It became clear that if we really wanted to change the economy to be more just, we would have to bring that change about ourselves, by building that economy from the bottom up. But what exactly did this mean? How did you go about building an economy from the ground up?

Back in Philadelphia, I began to feel that we had only scratched the surface of what businesses could do when we worked collaboratively. What was happening in Chiapas was not just a struggle for justice, but also a struggle for survival. How could BETHRIC help?

As far as Chiapas was concerned, the next step seemed obvious. Some coffee from indigenous groups in Chiapas was being exported to the United States, but there were no exports directly from the Zapatista communities—except for what Kerry Appel was able to load into his van. Why not take what he was doing to the next level and help put together a plan for shipping to the United States *a whole cargo container of coffee, 250 bags, grown by Zapatista communities?* This would help build an economic base for the prodemocracy movement and at the same time strengthen the connections between the indigenous growers and the network of fair-trade coffee roasters, coffee shops, and restaurants in the United States.

BETHRIC member Jonathan Rosenthal, president of Equal Exchange, a fair-trade importer in Boston, put me in touch with Monika Firl, a North American living in Chiapas who had a background in economic development. She also knew the territory and had good relationships with Zapatista leaders. Responding to Monika's inquiries on behalf of BETHRIC, the Zapatista leadership identified a cooperative ready to export.

Seven months later, in September 1998, I was back in Chiapas. This time Rick Stewart from Frontier was able to come on the trip, and he, Monika, and I set off to visit the coffee cooperative *Mut Vitz* (which translates as Hill of Birds), located in the highest parts of Los Altos in the Zapatista autonomous zone. There we met with the leaders of the cooperative and began a conversation that continued over the course of a year before the first shipment of coffee was ready to leave from Mut Vitz.

Our next step was to find investors and importers, and once again I looked to my community at SVN. After our return from Chiapas, Rick, Jonathan, and I—along with a few other SVN members—had established the Sustainable Trade Committee at SVN to see in what ways we might work together in general. Now we agreed that the Chiapas project was ideal.

The next BETHRIC trip to Chiapas, now in conjunction with the SVN Sustainable Trade Committee, was in February 1999. Rick and I returned to Chiapas with six more people: two potential investors from Philadelphia—Hal Taussig, a model social entrepreneur who ran a nonprofit development fund from the profits of his travel business, and Mort Sand, a retired executive; Rosario Castellon, a coffee buyer for Equal Exchange in Boston; Bill Harris, a BETHRIC member, owner of Cafe Campesino, a coffee roasting company, and founder of Cooperative Coffees, an importing cooperative of fair-trade, community-based coffee roasters around the country based in Atlanta, Georgia; and Joe Flood of Indigenous Designs in California, who was interested in looking at local textiles for his fair trade eco-fashion company.

On the way to Mut Vitz our caravan of vehicles navigated numerous roadblocks and searches of our vehicles by the Mexican army. During one search, when the *commandante* asked me to open the trunk, I looked in and, feigning surprise, playfully said in broken Spanish, "Caramba, I forgot our guns! I left them all in the hotel!" There was a shocked silence until the officer finally smiled and then began to laugh. Our guide, Monika, told me later that she thought for sure I was going to get us all deported.

At last our delegation made it to Mut Vitz, where we met with representatives of the cooperative to devise a plan. Mut Vitz produced enough high-quality coffee to make up a container for shipment to the United States, but they needed $40,000 in prefinancing funds in order to purchase the coffee from cooperative members, whose hand-to-mouth existence required payment at the time of harvest, or they would be forced to sell to *coyotes*. Rather than loaning money directly to Mut Vitz, the cooperative leader suggested that we loan it to the US importers to avoid the complicated exchange from dollars to pesos and then back to dollars on repayment.

The likely importers were Kerry Appel from Human Bean Company in Denver and Bill Harris of Cooperative Coffees in Atlanta, and they both agreed to purchase half a container. Though I had still not met Kerry, I felt I had come to know him through his work and e-mails and could trust him. I loaned $20,000 to Kerry, and Hal Taussig loaned Bill Harris the other $20,000. In addition, Mort, Hal, Rick, and I each pitched in $1,000 to pay for Mut Vitz's organic certification, which could take several years to obtain. Rick offered technical support from Frontier in helping them meet the standards for certification, and Rosario offered her expertise in assisting with the paperwork and process involved in making the shipment.

The highlight of the trip came when we were assembled at Mut Vitz finishing our plans in the meeting room and suddenly representatives of the Zapatista leadership arrived—in masks! Four men and two women wearing red bandanas or black ski masks over their faces entered the room and joined our group. We were awestruck to see real masked Zapatistas before our eyes (though I'm sure we had unknowingly seen many in our travels who were unmasked). They sat with us and through translators asked that we each introduce ourselves and explain why we had come to Chiapas, which gave us the opportunity to articulate our support for their democracy movement. It finally sunk in—we were doing business with the Zapatistas! After hearing so much about their courageous movement, it was an honor to be in their presence.

After the loans had been made to Kerry Appel and Bill Harris and the coffee purchased, the next step was for Mut Vitz to transport the coffee by truck to the port city of Veracruz, where it would be shipped to New Orleans, and then trucked to Kerry in Denver and Bill in Atlanta. There was some apprehension that the Mut Vitz truck could be ambushed by the paramilitaries on the trip out of Chiapas to the coast, so we were all relieved when we received word that the Mut Vitz drivers had made it to the port and that the cargo was safely on its way to New Orleans. Bill and Kerry sold their coffee to their customers, who were roasters around the country—including two roasters in Philadelphia, New Harmony and Fonseca Coffee, who would then sell to the White Dog Café. After Bill and Kerry were paid by their roasters, they repaid the money that Hal and I had loaned to them.

The next year, Hal, Rick, Bill, and I returned with several roasters from Bill's cooperative who wanted a direct relationship with their coffee growers. BETHRIC had become not only an effective business vehicle but also a community of friends from around the country who shared values and many a bottle of tequila while traveling together. On that BETHRIC trip the White Dog made a contribution to purchase fruit trees for the Mut Vitz coffee fields, which was a way to offset the carbon emissions from our long-distance travel. The fruit trees not only provided needed shade for the coffee plants, but also fresh fruit for the village and enhanced honey production, which was another enterprise at Mut Vitz we eventually supported.

Through Monika, who continued throughout our trips to provide good-humored expert guidance in working with Mut Vitz, we met a Mexican businessman who wanted to help Mut Vitz sell their coffee within Mexico—quite important since Mut Vitz did not want to be too dependent on exports. Hal and I made investments in this domestic coffee project and eventually saw that Mut Vitz coffee was even being sold in the airport in Mexico City as we passed through on one of our trips. Hal and I repeated the loans to Bill and Kerry for the second harvest, and by the third year our loans were no longer needed.

In 2001 and 2004, I traveled back to Chiapas to visit Mut Vitz, continuing to bring businesspeople who might develop trade relations. I also brought employees from the White Dog and Black Cat to connect with the people who grew the coffee we served in the café and to purchase embroidered coffee bags, weavings, and crafts from the indigenous women's cooperative, Women of Dignity, to sell in the Black Cat—where they were displayed on store shelves along with bags of locally roasted Mut Vitz organic, fair-trade coffee beans.

On our last trip in 2004, we learned that Mut Vitz had expanded from the annual one-container export we prefinanced back in 1999 to shipping fifteen containers of fair-trade coffee to the United States and Europe per year—and it was still growing. We visited Zapatista villages and saw the progress they were making to provide health care and education, and also training in organic farming, textile, and craft businesses.

We also learned that, unfortunately, the paramilitary violence still existed. Clearly, the Zapatista prodemocracy movement continued to be seen as a threat to the status quo of a corporate controlled global economy.

One day back at the White Dog, sipping my cup of Mut Vitz coffee, I tried to remember the long journey the coffee had taken to reach my cup. At last I felt that my efforts had made a real difference in the real world. With business as my vehicle, I had set out to bring some assistance to a beleaguered community with whom I felt a kinship in our mutual desire to build a just and sustainable world, and, working with like-minded partners, had succeeded. In a small way, we had built an economy from the ground up.

Some might think that such a small coffee enterprise could not be significant, but the idea of connecting many small businesses together can become a powerful force. BETHRIC had connected a network of communities working for self-reliance in the highlands of Chiapas with our network of small businesses building local self-reliance across the United States. It is this alignment of values, this connection of multiple networks of small producers and businesses, that has the power to change the world.

From my experiences in Chiapas and with small farmers at home, I began to envision an alternative to the corporate-based global economy—an economic system that was locally self-reliant in basic needs and interconnected globally by an intricate network of small-scale business relationships that were win-win and supportive, rather than exploitive of the local communities where products originated. I saw a way out of the current form of globalization and the ruin it brought.

Imagining this vision and the work ahead, I raised my cup of Mut Vitz coffee and toasted, "*Ya basta!* To the worldwide revolution against corporate tyranny!"

This was just a toast. But in a modest way, it foretold my future.

Let yourself be silently drawn by
the stronger pull of what you truly love.

—Rumi (1207–1273)

❧ 9 ❧

What I Learned from Animals: Building a Caring Economy

MY WORK IN CHIAPAS taught me that connecting networks of businesses with shared values was the way to begin building a new global economy. At home, too, we had been building a business network—a network of local farmers who supplied the White Dog Café. But after Chiapas I had been wondering: How could I make it grow stronger and faster? What was the key to bringing real change—an entire new economy—beginning with my own hometown?

Soon, and surprisingly, I would find my answer, which began in lessons I learned as a child—from my dogs. When my parents answered the constant pleadings of a nine-year-old with the gift of a beagle puppy, they likely were unaware that bringing an animal into my life provided me an even greater gift of building my capacity to care. Like many children, I loved my pets deeply. Their innocence and reliance on me showed me how important it was to take responsibility for the voiceless and vulnerable, beginning with animals under my care. And I learned what everyone who bonds with a pet knows—even though some believe otherwise: that nonhuman mammals do have emotions and can feel happiness and sadness. I have seen for myself the joy expressed by my dogs when I return home, or the glee when it is time for a walk in the woods. There is also the expression of guilt and even embarrassment on their faces when I discover they have sneaked a sausage off the table. Feelings of grief and despair are evident when a dog loses a close companion—both dog and human companions. Like all mammals, close relationships matter to dogs; perhaps they even matter most of all.

But unlike humans, it doesn't take much to make an animal happy. I think of my dogs snoozing in the sunshine on the porch, sniffing the breeze, going for a walk, chewing on a stick, or digging in the dirt. Yet too often, farm animals, while providing so much for humans, are routinely denied the most basic pleasures of being alive. Though a large part of the White Dog's business was to buy and sell the meat of farm animals, I was ignorant of this betrayal. Then, one day in the late 1990s when I was listening to a book on tape while driving, this all changed.

The book was John Robbins's *Diet for a New America*, and it reported on one of the worst examples of animal deprivation and cruelty—the industrial production of pork. The tape described the grotesque way mother pigs are kept in windowless barns, known as factory farms or concentrated animal feeding operations (CAFOs), which in one operation can hold tens of thousands of sows, all identical in size and fleshy color, locked in row after row of individual metal crates, each only as big as one pig. Unable to move at all, forward or backward, the sows stand in one place most every day of their miserable lives on a floor of cement and slated steel, a surface painful and crippling to their feet, legs, and joints.

In many of the CAFOs the fumes from the lagoons of manure languishing below the pigs are so intense that they suffer lung disease—a danger to the factory farm workers as well. The waste pools go on to pollute the groundwater in the surrounding rural communities, and the stench in the air is so powerful that nearby residents cannot sit outside and often develop headaches and other health problems.

The sows never experience sunshine or a breeze coming through. They never take a breath of fresh air through their sensitive nostrils. Highly intelligent, very social creatures who are as capable of friendship as dogs and cats, these pigs never have the opportunity to socialize with other animals, or sleep in big pig piles as they love to do, or root in the ground, build their nests, and raise and care for piglets. Simply put, they live without any pleasure at all in their life as a pig. The deprivation is so intense that most animals go insane and gnaw incessantly on the bars of their crates. The mother pigs are artificially inseminated, their babies are taken away prematurely, and then they are reinseminated—a process repeated over and over again until the mother is spent and useless.

When I arrived home, the book on tape was still playing, and I sat in the parked car continuing to listen until I could hear no more. I was stunned by what I learned. And outraged! Pigs are mammals. As my dogs are. As I am. When living creatures are treated like machines, the industrial system has reached a pinnacle of perversion. To me this is sacrilegious; it's a violation of nature to treat these mothers in this way, a disrespect of life itself. And it's a breach of our fiduciary duty to be good stewards of farm animals.

I was horrified to think that the pork we were serving at the White Dog was coming from this barbaric system. But that's where the vast majority of pork in our stores and restaurants comes from. At first I was frozen, not knowing what to do. I had no idea if it was possible to find humanely raised pork. If I stopped serving pork, would it hurt my business? If we found a humane source, could we afford it?

There is something about animal cruelty in our food system, and even cruelty toward humans, that makes people close down. They don't want to hear about it; they just want to eat well and get on with business. There had been times, I regret to say, when I had done that myself. But this time I could not bear the thought that we were participating in a system that was so cruel and immoral. The next day, I went into the kitchen and announced, "Take all the pork off the menu. Take off the bacon, the ham, and the pork chops. We cannot serve pork again until we find a humane source."

I did not know how long it would take. But I was ready to wait it out. To our surprise, what we wanted was close at hand. Our chef Kevin asked farmer Glenn Brendle, who was bringing in free-range chicken and eggs, if he knew a place that raised pigs in the traditional way, and he did. It wasn't long before he started bringing in a pig every week, and soon after that we were receiving two pigs a week—the whole pig too. Since most businesses order only the prime cuts, this is best for the farmer—but a creative challenge for the kitchen. Successful in developing a use for all the parts, Kevin added menu items like pulled pork sandwiches at the bar, pork belly appetizers at dinner, and sausage for Sunday brunches.

Meanwhile, I was on a tear and next discovered the plight of the cow. Cows are herbivores; they are supposed to eat grass. But partly because of the government subsidies to the commodity grain producers, it's cheaper (when external costs to the environment and human health are not counted) to take cows off grass and feed them grain in CAFO barns and filthy, crowded feedlots where the animals stand knee-deep in manure. Cows fed an unnatural diet of grain are continually sick and produce large quantities of methane, a greenhouse gas harmful to the environment. They also produce meat with a higher content of unhealthy fat, while grass-fed cows produce meat and milk with essential nutrients grain-fed cows lack. Many believe that grain-fed cows produce a dangerous strain of *E. coli* not found in grass-fed cows, one that has shown up in lettuce and spinach after being irrigated with water contaminated by factory farms.

Again, the solution came quickly. We heard that Bill Elkins, a retired medical scientist, and his wife Helen of Buck Run Farm raised Black Angus on grass out in Chester County, and we began ordering our beef from them—as with pigs, buying the whole cow, which Dr. Bill appreciated. While the prime cuts were served as steaks, the rest was made into ground beef, and Buck Run Farm angusburgers were thought by many to be the best hamburger in the city. The bartenders bragged that legendary Philly singer Patti LaBelle made stops to the bar just to devour a Buck Run grass-fed angusburger.

Dairy cows in the industrial system have it even worse than beef cattle. Like pigs, the mother cows are kept indoors confined in stalls and attached to often painful milking machines as though the cows themselves are only machines, cranking out milk until spent and hauled off to the slaughterhouse to be turned into hamburger. As with beef cattle, we looked for an alternate source and began to source our milk, yogurt, cheese, and other dairy products from grass-fed cows on small family farms.

The White Dog had long been buying only free-range chickens and cage-free eggs, often from some of the same diversified family farms that sold us organic fruits and vegetables. On these farms, hens engage in natural behaviors—foraging, scratching, stretching, preening, dust-bathing, perching, nesting. It was on these farms that I first appreciated the way hens walk: they do it with such dignity, comb-topped heads held regally atop long necks of layered feathers gliding so smoothly forward and backward with each graceful step of their slender legs and outstretched toes. Their tail feathers are always held proudly aloft as they walk up and down ramps and through little doors to reach their nests. This is a far cry from factory-farm operations where the birds live their entire lives crammed into tiny crowded wire cages, unable to walk or spread their wings. These free-range hens have yet another advantage: Their mobile henhouses are rotated around the field to provide fresh grounds for foraging—something that has a benefit for farmers as well, as their waste fertilizes the field for a new crop. On farms that integrate crops and farm animals, manure is a valuable fertilizer, while on factory farms housing thousands of animals in close confines, manure is a gigantic waste disposal problem.

GOOD MORNING, BEAUTIFUL BUSINESS

After much work on chef Kevin's part to find humane sources for all our animal products, I looked at our menus and thought, *At last! We've done it!* All of our meat, poultry, eggs, milk, yogurt, and cheese come from farmers who treat animals kindly. No product comes from the industrial system of factory farms. And we are the only restaurant in town that can make this claim. So this can be our market niche, a way to stand out in the marketplace. Our competitive advantage! Yes!

Then my transformational moment came. I thought I had done what I needed to do for animals, but I saw that I was not finished. I had to go further—and I said to myself: Judy, if you really do care about the pigs and other farm animals that are treated so cruelly; and if you care about the small farmers who are being driven out of business by factory farms; if you care about the environment that's being polluted by the concentration of waste and unhealthy practices; if you care about the workers in these ghastly slaughterhouses and factories; if you care about the rural communities that are being destroyed; if you care about the consumers who eat meat that's full of antibiotics and hormones, then rather than keep this as your competitive advantage, you will—yes, you will—share your knowledge with your competitors.

Up until this point I had always felt that my highest calling was to model socially responsible practices within my company, but it was no longer enough. After all, there is no such thing as one sustainable business, no matter how great our practices are; we can only be a part of a sustainable system. I had to move from a competitive mentality to one of cooperation in order to build that system—an entire local food system based on the values I upheld.

This was a huge step for me. As a businessperson, I was taught to be competitive and to want *my* restaurant to be the best. It shouldn't even have occurred to me to share what I knew with competitors. Perhaps living with the Eskimos, in a community based on cooperation and sharing, was now bearing fruit.

I was ready to roll. We needed to expand the small network of local farmers supplying the White Dog to a much larger network of farmers supplying as many restaurants and retail markets as possible. We could all be part of the same regional food system— one that was humane and healthy.

I asked farmer Glenn, who was now bringing us two pigs a week, if he would like to expand his business.

"Yes," he replied.

"What's holding you back?"

"I need thirty thousand dollars to buy a refrigerated truck so I can deliver to more restaurants." I loaned Glenn the thirty thousand dollars, and he bought the truck.

It took barely a day to see that there was much more work to be done than I could possibly handle alone in developing our network, and in encouraging both the supply of and demand for local farm products in our region. So, in the fall of 2000, I started a new project and hired Ann Karlen as the founding executive director of what we soon called Fair Food. With no more office space in the White Dog, I turned over a room in my home for the Fair Food office, where it remained for four years until we moved to larger quarters.

Ann's first job was to provide free consulting to the other chefs and restaurant owners in Philadelphia, connecting them to White Dog suppliers and teaching the chefs the importance of buying humanely raised pork and other family farm products. Ann put together a guide for chefs that listed the farms and their products and gradually expanded the network, discovering more family farmers who wanted to sell in the urban marketplace.

Soon, though, I realized that I needed not only to share my knowledge (and my house), but also my profits. The earlier duo of Free People's Store and Synapse had shown me how a for-profit and nonprofit could work hand in hand. So I formed a not-for-profit sister to the business that eventually became known as White Dog Community Enterprises, with a mission to build a just and sustainable local economy in our region. Luckily, Sue Ellen Klein, the director of community programs at the café, was willing to chair our board, which we began to build with colleagues who shared our vision—people like Tim Bowser, founder of the Pennsylvania Association for Sustainable Agriculture, and Antje Mattheus, who ran workshops on building a more inclusive and just society.

I increased White Dog's charitable giving from 10 to 20 percent of profits and through White Dog Community Enterprises we funded Fair Food and the Sustainable Business Network of Greater Philadelphia (SBN), which I founded the following year, as well as contributed to many other nonprofits in the community. Still, it was clear that much more funding was needed. Help, I soon discovered, was on the way.

Not long after I started Fair Food, a waiter told me that there was a customer in the dining room who wanted to see me. That's when I met Cathy Berry, who invited me to sit down at her table. Visiting from New Hampshire, Cathy told me that she had recently inherited money and wanted to do good things regarding local food.

Funny how things happen. Cathy had been in the audience a half dozen years earlier, in 1994, when I received my very first award, one that recognized outstanding businesswomen who demonstrate leadership on both business and social issues. The award was founded by Rosemarie Greco, the president of a major Philadelphia bank who had worked her way up from a position of secretary to be its first female president. When she became the first woman to chair the board of the Greater Philadelphia Chamber of Commerce, she saw that the prestigious annual award given by the chamber to recognize the outstanding businessperson of the year always went to a man. So Rosemarie started the Paradigm Award, which I received in its second year. My acceptance speech about local food inspired Cathy to become a White Dog customer on her frequent business trips to Philadelphia. After observing my work for several years, she offered her support just as our Food Fair program was starting, and a longtime partnership began. Cathy covered Ann Karlen's salary as executive director for the first three years, and Fair Food was off and running. It would not be the only support Cathy provided in the years ahead in helping to build a new economy in our region and beyond.

Over the years Ann would begin many projects at Fair Food: an annual *Philadelphia Local Food Guide* that lists a growing number of farm stands and Community Supported Agriculture programs (CSAs) as well as restaurants, caterers, institutions, and retail stores that buy local; an annual event to introduce chefs to farmers and their products; one program that helps farmers develop their products for the urban marketplace; another that connects institutions with medium-size farms to bring fresh local food to schools, hospitals, and senior centers—which too often serve government-subsidized processed foods full of fat and sugar and low in nutrition. Trying to get local food to institutions made Fair Food realize that there was a need for a local distribution program. White Dog Community Enterprises provided staff time, a financial contribution, and a no-interest loan to support our friends in the creation of the Common Market, which serves our region by picking up farm products, aggregating them at a central warehouse, and delivering them to larger buyers.

In 2002, I saw a notice online about something called a "Hog Summit" to be held in Iowa that would focus on sustainable hog farming. I had never been to Iowa, knew of no one else going, and had never heard of the Waterkeeper Alliance, the sponsoring organization. But I wanted to know more about the subject that had triggered so much for me and soon was on a plane to Iowa.

It turned out the summit was the hotbed for those passionate about humane farming, including one of our suppliers, Bill Niman of Niman Ranch who raised cattle on his ranch in California and contracted pig farmers in other parts of the country to raise animals under strict humane guidelines developed by Diane and Marlene Halverson of the Animal Welfare Institute, who were also at the summit. When the White Dog first made the commitment to buy only humanely raised animal products, we could not always find enough local supply—especially of bacon and pork chops, which we always needed more of—and ordered from Niman Ranch where we could trust the quality and humane standards. When faced with the choice between organic and local products, I choose local. But when it comes to meat, there is no compromise. I choose only humanely raised, even if not local, or I don't eat or serve meat at all.

At the Hog Summit I met pig farmer Paul Willis, who also manages Niman's network of pork suppliers. A most likeable man with a ready laugh and twinkling blue eyes in the tan weathered face of a lifelong farmer, Paul enjoys sharing a beer and talking about saving rural communities from the invasion of factory farms and about working to change public food policies. Paul is passionate about sustainable animal agriculture and loves his pigs.

This became very clear when I went on a tour of his nearby seven-hundred-acre pig farm in Thornton, Iowa, which showed me pig farming at its best. Driving through Iowa farm country on the way to Paul's farm, we first saw the worst—row after row of long, windowless buildings that had replaced the bucolic red barns and green pastures I once imagined. The sterile, lifeless landscape was a motionless dead zone bare of trees and with no people or animals in sight.

When we finally arrived at the Willis Free Range Pig Farm, home to some six hundred pigs, I saw the most beautiful sight. On a gently sloping green hill, I watched huge sows moving across the pasture followed by their families of little piglets—brown, tan, pink, white, black, and spotted—trotting behind their mothers in the warm spring sunshine. Peeking into the huts scattered around the pasture, I found piglets nestled with mother sows in straw beds. Pregnant sows were stretched out in the sun or busy gathering straw for their nests. Other pig families were cuddled in cozy straw-filled barns with free access to the outside, and goats and chickens ambled about the barnyard. Boars and sows mingled freely in large pens, while others foraged and explored the pastures, rolled in mud baths, or snoozed together in pig piles.

As Paul walked among his herd with noticeable care and affection, he explained that these heritage breed pigs, unlike those bred for confinement, have the body fat and hardiness needed to spend time outside even during the cold winter months. Surprisingly, I did not notice any offensive odors on my visit to this farm where the animals had plenty of room to roam. It was a joy to see such health and happiness for animals that provide so much humane nourishment, and to see that there is a profitable way to raise pigs that is humane and respectful—and smells just fine.

At the summit I learned even more about the dangers of industrial pork production, such as how the antibiotics fed daily to the pigs in the factories to speed growth and prevent illness in the crowded conditions are consumed by humans through the meat and through groundwater as well, gradually making the drugs ineffective in fighting serious illness in humans and producing superbugs that are causing life-threatening infections.

The highlight of the summit was the keynote address by Robert F. Kennedy, Jr., a passionate environmental attorney and president of the Waterkeeper Alliance, a nonprofit working to protect our waterways from industrial pollution. Kennedy explained how factory farms, designed to increase profits, cannot actually produce a pork chop or bacon cheaper than a family farmer unless they break environmental laws meant to protect our water and air. Factory farms profit by externalizing the true costs onto the public through sickness and degraded soil as well as contaminated water and air, and in the process they destroy both the economy and our democracy by concentrating power and money in the hands of the few giant corporations that control meat production in our country.

Factory farming provided me one horrific example of what was happening to our whole economy: Corporate power was being misused in the pursuit of profits. What belonged to all of us—fresh air, clean water, and more—was being destroyed so that ever more money could flow into the pockets of the powerful. Laws meant to protect our environment—indeed, our common wealth—were either being broken by corporations or being weakened by their lobbyists. And it was not only the environment and democracy that were at stake. As Kennedy went on to say, the institutionalized cruelty to the pigs was destroying our own humanity. Amen to that.

Back in Philadelphia, after having learned of the damage done by pig factories to rural communities in Iowa and North Carolina, I wanted to raise awareness of the danger in our own state and educate local pig farmers about how to raise pigs on pasture. I convened leaders from the Pennsylvania Association for Sustainable Agriculture, the Delaware Riverkeeper Network, Fair Food, and a few others to form a local group that agreed to bring the national Hog Summit to Gettysburg, Pennsylvania.

The following year I was thrilled when I saw that two local pig farmers, Paul and Ember Crivellaro of Countrytime Farm, had registered for the conference. Interested in selling their pork to White Dog, they had invited me to visit their pig farm in Berks County a few months earlier. But the conditions I had seen there had not met our standards. Though I was relieved that the sows were not confined in crates and were allowed to mingle freely with each other and the boar, the pigs were kept in the basement of a barn, a large room filled with shredded newspapers. I could see that the couple was very well-meaning and cared about their pigs, even bragging that their boar was so smart that he knew how to turn the barn lights off and on with his snout. I was hoping they would be open to allowing their pigs access to the outdoors, but they were at first skeptical that this could work.

After watching the presentation by Paul Willis at the Hog Summit in Gettysburg, Paul and Ember were convinced that this way of raising pigs was a possibility for them. But it took money to make the changes. I had heard that Campbell's Soup heiress Dorrance "Dodo" Hamilton had an interest in heritage-breed farm animals, and I appealed for her support of our program to assist area pig farmers to convert to outdoor farming with heritage-breed pigs. She kindly contributed fifty thousand dollars to White Dog Community Enterprises, from which we made grants to area pig farmers (including Ember and Paul) to help build fences and huts to convert to pasture farming, buy trucks for deliveries, or improve their herds with heritage breeds. I felt that we were beginning to make a difference, especially for the pigs!

After reading about factory farming as well as the environmental costs of eating meat, I realized how important it was to reduce meat consumption. Why eat meat every day, or even at all? At the White Dog we increased the number of vegetarian and vegan dishes on our menus to at least three entrées and numerous appetizers and began offering a dessert of homemade nondairy ice cream served with vegan cookies. We also began educational programs through farm dinners to make sure our meat-eating customers understood the importance of knowing how the animals were raised and demanding an ethical system.

I made changes in my own diet as well, vowing to eat meat only on special occasions, and only if I know that the animal was raised with kindness and respect in a natural setting with access to pastures—the same standard I hold for poultry, dairy, and eggs. I stopped drinking milk a long time ago (I find it peculiar for adult humans to drink milk meant for baby calves). I was appalled to learn that almost all dairy farms take the calves from their mothers at birth and, except for the female calves meant to replace their mothers, they are most likely sent to "veal factories" where the calves are confined in crates and fed a synthetic formula until time for slaughter. Since discovering this perversion, I have been searching for dairy farms that keep their calves with their mothers as nature intended.

One such place—and they are rare—is Hawthorne Valley Farm, a four-hundred-acre biodynamic farm in Ghent, New York, that is part of a community that follows the farming and educational principals of Rudolf Steiner, the Austrian philosopher and social reformer. Hawthorne Valley keeps calves with their mothers for the first fifteen weeks, yet the farm has been financially successful. So it is possible to do well by doing good in the dairy business. There is no reason but greed that humans cannot share milk with calves, rather than taking it all for ourselves. I have no doubt that most people would rather pay a little more for milk than have animals suffer so cruelly, especially if they heard the mournful cries of a cow for her newborn calf, and the calf for its mother.

Fair Food and White Dog were raising consciousness about the importance of eating only pastured meat in restaurants, but people couldn't go out to dinner every night. We needed a retail outlet so our customers could buy humanely raised meat and poultry to cook at home. Ann went to visit the butcher shops at the Reading Terminal, Philadelphia's historic central food market under the old Reading Railroad train terminal, asking them if they would carry humanely raised pastured meat from local farmers. The butchers had no interest, feeling that the meat was too expensive and that local was not of value to their customers. So the Fair Food Farmstand was born.

In 2005, Ann started out with a simple folding card table covered with a blue-and-white checkered cloth from the White Dog, set up in an aisle in the center court of the market where she sold frozen pasture-raised meat and fresh farm produce every Saturday. Over time Ann tenaciously built the business into a permanent stand with a prime location in the front of the market, open seven days a week, year-round. With the help of ten employees and fifteen volunteers, the business now does over $800,000 in annual sales, with products from ninety different sustainable local farms as well as local producers making such things as tofu, *seitan*, stone-ground flours, energy bars, and cheese and ice cream from pasture-raised cows.

As the Fair Food network grew, hundreds of local Philadelphia restaurants and institutions and many thousands of citizens were connected to hundreds of local farms and producers, helping to build a vibrant local food economy.

And all this began with compassion for pigs. Building a new global economy, I came to realize, rested on a simple quality: our capacity to care—followed by our willingness to do what is necessary to defend and nurture what it is that we truly care about. I had found the key I had been searching for that could bring real change to our economy. It was one I had known all along. Change begins in the heart of the entrepreneur. And, for that matter, the heart of the consumer as well. It's the power of love and compassion that can bring transformative change.

In applying farmer Mark Dornstreich's theory that successful farming is a balance between the masculine quality of efficiency with the feminine quality of nurturing, the factory farming of animals exemplifies an extreme case of imbalance. Industrial agriculture with its animal factories as well as large corporate plantations around the globe (and likewise, the entire industrial economy) is weighted toward masculine energy—a lot of efficiency and control, even domination, and little nurturing and partnership.

Our materialistic culture desensitizes consumers to the suffering that underlies the industrial economy and teaches business people to close our hearts and be guided by a false idea of what it means to be strong, a false idea of the masculine—not as protector, but as exploiter—where efficiency is gained by wringing every last penny from the land, from the farm animals, from the workers, from life itself.

Ultimately, industrial agriculture, though highly efficient and profitable, produces food that is inferior to the food produced by Mark and Judy Dornstreich and Paul Willis. Organic and humane farmers across the world master the correct balance of efficiency and nurturing to produce the most nutritious and delicious food in an economically sustainable way, while acting as good stewards of the land and farm animals.

When I made the decision to follow my heart and cooperate rather than compete, I felt as though I had finally come to the point of fully embracing my feminine energy, no longer competing to make it in a "man's world," but rather balancing my feminine and masculine qualities to build a new economy—one that is prosperous and strong, yet one where compassionate and loving relationships matter more than money.

Speak the truth. Speak it loud and often, calmly but
insistently. . . . Material accumulation is not the
purpose of human existence. All growth is not good. . . .
There is such a thing as enough.

—Donella Meadows

❧ 10 ☙

Pursuing Small Scale
on a Large Scale:
The Founding of BALLE

TWO EVENTS in the fall of 1999 signaled me, like a one-two punch, that it was time to expand the work I was doing around local economies to other communities around the nation and act on the vision for a new global economy I had developed while working in Chiapas.

The first was the Battle of Seattle, as it came to be called. All that fall, I had been hunkered down in my restaurant, oblivious to the fact that activists were organizing protests around the World Trade Organization meeting that was to be held in late November in Seattle. But my daughter—then a student at Prescott College, where she was majoring in globalization studies—clued me in. Grace was among the fifty thousand protestors who went to Seattle, and along with her fellow students was part of a "cell" to lock arms and block delegates from entering the WTO meeting. I was so impressed by how knowledgeable the young people were about the WTO—especially how its agreements among the world's largest transnational corporations, beginning with the General Agreement on Tariffs and Trade (GATT), were set up to override local legislation meant to protect workers and the natural environment. Free rein was given to corporations to cross borders where they could exploit natural resources and cheap labor and develop new markets. The North American Free Trade Agreement (NAFTA), which ignited the Zapatista uprising, is part of the same set of agreements. Contrary to what I heard reported in the mainstream news, the protestors did not come to oppose global trade, but rather to defend democracy and our environment from the power of corporations. They were there to say "no" to the trade agreements that overturned local legislation, "no" to sweatshop labor, and "no" to robbing future generations of natural resources for the sake of higher corporate profits today. Like the Zapatistas, the protestors were crying out, "*No mas!*" I was proud that my own daughter was among them.

When Grace finally made it home to Philadelphia, she gave me the shirt she had worn for four days in Seattle, where the street blockades had kept her from returning to her hotel room to change clothes. It may seem odd that I placed the shirt in a box and put it in the china cupboard along with family heirlooms, but it was a special keepsake to me, and it brought back memories of other treasures. As a child I remember discovering a mysterious trunk in my grandmother's attic. When I slowly opened the creaking lid of the trunk to peer inside, I found my father's navy officer uniform from World War II, spotless white with navy blue trim and a white cap to match with a shiny black brim. The uniform was cherished by my family, and just as precious to me was Grace's dirty shirt— the humble uniform of our contemporary fight for freedom in a nonviolent revolution against corporate power and greed.

When I looked at who was protesting in Seattle, I saw environmentalists, human rights workers, farmers, labor leaders, students, and teachers—but I could not find representatives of progressive business. Though the protests were against a global economy controlled by corporations, no one seemed to be articulating a new vision of what our economy should and could be. I asked myself, *How might we direct all this energy, especially that of the young, toward building a positive alternative—a new economy?*

Before I could answer that question, only days after Seattle came the second alarm in my one-two punch wake-up call: Ben & Jerry's announced the sale of their ice cream company to the Dutch conglomerate Unilever. It wasn't by choice. Jerry and Ben did not want to sell, but because the company is publicly traded, by law the board of directors had to make decisions in the best financial interests of their stockholders, and that meant selling to the highest bidder when an offer was made that was too good to refuse. I knew the sale was coming because of my friendship with Ben, who was in despair over the loss of the company that had long been his powerful vehicle for social change.

At first, I did not fully comprehend the significance of the sale beyond Ben's personal loss, but when it finally sunk in, I sat up in bed in the middle of the night: *My god, they've got Ben & Jerry's.* I just couldn't believe it. The company was the leader of our socially responsible business movement and had taught us so much. I learned about the living wage from Ben & Jerry's, and about committing to a fair ratio between the highest- and lowest-paid employee, and about the multiple bottom line. How could it be that such a cutting-edge company would become a cog in the wheel of a huge global conglomerate?

When I thought about it, I realized that other companies that were also models of social responsibility were being sold to transnationals, thereby adding to the concentration of ownership, wealth, and power—just the opposite of what our movement was founded to do. Odwalla Juice had been sold to Coca-Cola, Rhino Entertainment to Time Warner, Cascadian Farm to General Mills, and later others would follow suit. The majority of Stonyfield Farms was sold to Group Danone (makers of Dannon Yogurt). Tom's of Maine went to Colgate-Palmolive, The Body

Shop to L'Oréal, Honest Tea to Coca-Cola. With these respected companies as models, how many more businesses in our movement might view selling to a transnational corporation as the best exit strategy for their business? Clearly, we needed a new model.

At the time of the Ben & Jerry's sale, I was vice chair of Social Venture Network (SVN) and would be chair the following year, so I was thinking deeply about the movement for socially responsible business (SRB) and our mission to build a more just and sustainable economy through business. *What had the movement accomplished? What are the next steps?* These were the questions on my mind in 1999.

It was true that the SRB movement had accomplished much over the previous fifteen years or so, modeling many new environmentally and socially sustainable business practices. New SRB organizations had been spawned, many out of the SVN. Among these were Investors' Circle, which introduces investors to progressive companies seeking capital, Net Impact for business school students, and Business for Social Responsibility, which eventually came to focus on large corporations.

The SRB community had much to be proud of. Yet in spite of these successful efforts, conditions around the globe had gotten worse. In many areas, much worse.

The environmental crisis had deepened, with all natural systems in decline—our water and air more polluted, topsoil eroded and depleted, dead zones in our oceans, fisheries exhausted, and a rapidly growing list of species gone forever or nearing extinction. Humankind was clearly using up more natural resources than could be restored and polluting more than could be absorbed by nature. Around that time a speaker at the White Dog, Rosalie Bertell, who studied nuclear waste and toxic buildup, told us that the most likely prognosis for the human species was slow death by poisoning. And in a 1998 Table Talk, Ross Gelbspan, author of

The Heat Is On, warned us that, despite the misinformation spread by the fossil-fuel industry, accelerating climate change brought on by human-caused global warming was a threat to life on Earth as we know it. So, as much as we were trying, our SRB movement had not succeeded in changing the direction of our economy toward protecting and restoring our natural environment.

What about people? Had our society become more just? No, the social crisis had also deepened. Philadelphia-based investigative reporters Donald Barlett and James Steele, authors of the newspaper story series and subsequent book *America: What Went Wrong?*, raised the alarm at multiple White Dog Table Talks between 1992 and 1999, as they authored additional books based on their research. Wealth inequality was rising rapidly, they warned, making the United States the most unequal among industrialized countries—with a disappearing middle class and a top 1 percent rapidly controlling more wealth than the rest of us. The news was full of tragic stories of the decline in family farms forced out by industrial farms and development, and of businesses that had been in families for generations closing down as customers poured into chain stores, sending their dollars right out of the community into the coffers of transnational corporations. Our SRB movement, with our own consolidations, was only adding to the problem of increasing inequality.

And what about the political crisis? Large corporations were gaining ever-greater control of our government, with their lobbyists influencing legislation to tighten their grip on the economy and our lives. I already was well aware of how large corporations were gaining control of food supplies here and abroad. With the aid of government subsidies, they were also producing an abundance of cheap, unhealthy food that was causing an epidemic of obesity. But when I thought about it, I realized that large corporations were also controlling the clothes we wore, the energy we used, the culture we live by, and much of the news we heard.

They were even controlling the government that made our laws, since politicians of both parties were beholden to corporations and the most wealthy for their jobs. Then as now, attempts to pass effective campaign finance reform had failed and corporations had a stranglehold on our democracy. Even so, I don't think anyone then could have guessed how bad the situation would eventually become by 2010, when the US Supreme Court decision in *Citizens United* opened the floodgates of unlimited and anonymous contributions from corporations for political advertising. Under the concept that corporations have constitutional rights like people, the court ruled that their free speech right to express their political views could not be restricted by government.

With all these major environmental, social, and political trends going in the wrong direction, shouldn't we ask why? Shouldn't we be reevaluating our movement's strategy for creating a just and sustainable world through business?

Suddenly it became clear to me—our socially responsible business movement was using the old paradigm to measure success, *continuous growth*. Not only was continuous growth on a finite planet headed toward a disastrous conclusion, it was also increasing inequality and weakening democracy. While the movement talked about measuring success by the triple bottom line, people, planet, and profit were clearly not being valued equally. What mattered most was the continuous growth of businesses, sales, and profit.

As I realized this, I began to see what else had gone wrong. While focusing on growth, the SRB movement that I had been dedicated to for so many years was neglecting three issues that had become very important to me—appropriate scale, connection to place, and broad-based ownership. And in neglecting those issues, the movement had often lost sight of our direct participation in the environmental, social, and political fractures that were eating away at the quality of our lives.

Human-scale businesses foster close and meaningful relationships, but when companies grow too big to be purchased by a new owner within the community—employees, a family member, or a local entrepreneur—they are most likely bought up by a distant corporation. Then profits are drained from the community; local procurement of supplies and services typically decreases, as do contributions to local charities; and if the company is moved out of town, jobs and local tax payments are lost—ultimately decreasing community wealth and weakening the local economy.

As corporations grow beyond their own region, they often eliminate local businesses while spreading their brands across the country, getting larger and larger. They also burn more fossil fuels distributing goods increasing distances. But perhaps even more importantly, they make communities dependent on faraway corporations to deliver what they need to live.

My travels through the White Dog's international program—Chiapas was a perfect example—had taught me how human-scaled farms and local economies that created enjoyable and self-reliant communities were being destroyed worldwide, often with the help of trade agreements. Government subsidies to large industrial growers also allowed these corporations to expand their markets by undercutting small farmers and putting them out of business. Corn farmers in Mexico, rice farmers in Haiti, and cotton farmers in West Africa were among the many victims of globalization and subsidies. I had seen the same situation at home, too—watching small, diversified family farms that once fed their local communities squeezed out only to be replaced by gigantic plantations of mono-crops for export, leaving the rural communities with the need to import processed food. Whether farm workers or office workers, we were fast becoming serfs in a giant industrial system, and too often forced to buy from the company store.

The whole concept of large corporations shipping goods around the world makes no sense to me, especially when reducing carbons is an urgent matter. At an SVN conference in 1995, I heard localism advocate and author Helena Norberg-Hodge speak about the lunacy of our global export and import system fueled by cheap oil. On a world map, Helena showed how often the same product—such as beer, bottled water, cotton, pork, or potatoes—that was being exported from a country or state was being imported at the same time, with little benefit other than to the transnational corporations. I take delight in the story of someone pointing out how the British import sugar cookies from the Americans, and the Americans import sugar cookies from the British, and wouldn't they save a lot of money and carbon by simply exchanging recipes!

We were also, in this pursuit of limitless growth, losing our sense of place and breaking apart our communities. Most national brands have no connection to the people and natural environment of a particular place. Today most Americans no longer know who grows our food or produces our other basic needs. We've become disconnected—separated—from each other, from the land, from our own places. The butcher, the baker, the tailor—these were the relationships that once provided the foundations for strong and enjoyable community life, like the life that I experienced growing up in Ingomar. Today, most towns and cities have lost their unique identity; streets are lined with the same chain stores found everywhere or, worse, are left deserted as customers flock to big box stores on the outskirts of town. These chain stores don't have owners that the community knows and trusts, or employees who provide civic leadership the way the presidents of local department stores, banks, and manufacturers traditionally have done. And, unlike our grocer in Ingomar, they aren't throwing holiday parties for the whole town. The products in these chain stores are typically produced in sweatshops and on factory farms. The consequences are serious. Without direct relationships, few of us think about the impact of our purchases on the people, animals, and ecosystems of faraway places.

Perhaps the most threatening issue being overlooked, though, is the concentration of ownership. Clearly, real wealth creation comes from ownership, not simply jobs, so economic justice can be achieved only when business ownership is spread broadly rather than concentrated. Decentralizing our food systems, our energy systems, and the manufacturing of other basic needs creates more local ownership opportunities, as well as jobs. Importantly, decentralization increases community, self-reliance, and resilience.

Decentralizing ownership has important advantages on other fronts as well. Media is one. A decentralized media offers diverse perspectives and sources of information—not the mass-media perspective that so shocked me when I returned home from Central America to find little of what I had seen reported in the mainstream coverage of the conflicts there. We need independently owned newspapers, magazines, radio and television stations, and bookstores as well as the diversity offered by electronic social media. Local theatre, recording studios, filmmakers, and art galleries give opportunity for diverse self-expression and support local culture, languages, musicians, and artists rather than perpetuating a corporate global monoculture.

Mulling all this over, it was clear that only by decentralizing ownership to many small- and medium-size local companies could economic power reside where it belongs—in our own communities. In short, more owners means freedom, equality, and justice. More owners means a stronger democracy. Continual growth, just as I saw in the pork industry, was concentrating ownership, wealth, and political power in the hands of fewer and fewer.

More owners also means more opportunity for individual creativity and innovation, and more ways of doing things than in an economy with the uniformity and rigidity of a command-and-control corporate structure. The end result is a wider diversity of products and services with greater resilience and adaptability to change in our unpredictable future of climate change.

Rather than measuring success by continual material growth, why not measure our success by the health and well-being of our communities and the natural world? I had read about the country of Bhutan, which uses an index of Gross National Happiness to measure the impact of the economy on the country's unique culture. As an alternative to Gross Domestic Product (GDP), which uses only an economic indicator, the GNH measures social progress in more holistic and psychological terms. I doubt that America would rank high on such an index. Despite our material growth, studies show that happiness in our society began its decline in the 1950s and 1960s, when the *dominate and destroy* mentality of redevelopment we experienced on my own block of Sansom Street began decimating urban communities. At the same time, industrial agriculture and suburban development began its destruction of rural communities. As the Eskimos had shown me, it isn't material goods that bring happiness, but rather community. "It's not about belongings," a wise person once said; "it's about belonging."

My life's experience had brought me to a simple premise for meeting the many sustainability challenges that we face: A sustainable *global* economy—one that is socially, environmentally, and financially sustainable—must be comprised of a network of sustainable *local* economies. As I had envisioned in Chiapas, rather than accepting a global economy dominated by large corporations, we could build an intricate web of small-to-small, win-win business relationships—a decentralized global network of sustainable local economies comprised of independent, locally owned businesses that support their local communities and ecosystems.

It was—it is—a simple idea. But as I was coming to these conclusions at the turn of the century, this was not the prevailing model in the SRB movement. Not at all. The common belief among business owners and investors, even in our movement, was that corporate globalization was inevitable and, to be successful, business plans are made accordingly. Local economies were thought to be a utopian pipe dream.

But for me, it was just the opposite. Faced with climate change, as well as rising inequality and loss of democracy, the task of building sustainable, self-reliant local economies seemed central to our very survival. Entrepreneurs and investors would have to do more than sit back and do the best they could in a game whose rules were written by megacorporations. We would have to recognize that we have a crucial, even life-saving role to play.

When I first joined SVN in 1993, I accepted the common understanding that success in our mission of building a just and sustainable economy was about growing socially responsible companies bigger and bigger so that they could compete successfully with the large unethical corporations, proving that it was possible to do well while doing good. It's hard to argue with that model. And in our movement it was the basis of any number of successful businesses operated by talented, values-led entrepreneurs. Through their business acumen and courage to push the envelope of social responsibility, these business leaders modeled many just and sustainable business practices that the world so desperately needs. During that time in history, the growing size of these model corporations helped spread the practices of doing well while doing good and influenced thousands of other entrepreneurs, including me. I developed a great admiration for these iconic companies and their leaders. They were my heroes. But now the times had changed, and I believed the movement could find other ways to spread good business practices rather than growing companies larger and larger.

Yet when I looked at the life-threatening challenges before us and the need to change our economy as fast as possible, I couldn't help but harbor a feeling of inadequacy as a small businessperson with one little restaurant in West Philly, trying to set out in the right direction. And maybe there was still a bit of self-imposed 1950s style insecurity about women succeeding in leadership positions. This attitude was holding me back. That is, until I met David Korten.

I first met David and his wife, Fran, in the spring of 2000 at a gathering of activists they convened through their Positive Futures Network—publisher of *Yes!* magazine, which is alternative media at its best. David, author of many books but at the time best known for *When Corporations Rule the World*, is a passionate and eloquent proponent of the need to replace what he calls our "suicide economy" and reclaim our democracy from corporate tyranny. His writings brilliantly paint the big picture of an epic global struggle between greed-driven corporations and a growing self-organizing global society that values life over money. When I heard David speak, I saw that the conclusions I was drawing from my own experiences were much aligned with his views. That alone was enough to make me feel more confident about the positions I was taking at SVN. But there was more.

That fall, I visited David and Fran at their home on Bainbridge Island in Washington State. At one point David and I were standing in his kitchen and I expressed my doubts that someone like me—a small businessperson—could have enough impact to help bring about the transformation of our economy. It seemed to me that the larger companies had the most power to bring change. That's when David took me by the shoulders and gave me a good shake. "Forget about the big companies," he said; "look in the mirror. It's the *Judy Economy* you have built in your own community. That's the model we need to replicate. And we need your leadership now." It was exactly what I needed to hear.

At the time, we had no name for the new economy we were envisioning; in a speech soon after, David publicly called it the Judy Economy. Just as Ben's recognition had emboldened me seven years earlier and led me to join SVN, encouragement by David, another thinker I greatly admired, helped me to believe in myself and imagine how I could use all that I had learned to provide leadership in building this new locally based economy on a national, and even international, scale.

I affectionately call my woodland retreat in the Pocono Mountains the Wicky Wacky Woods. Like my childhood woods in Ingomar and my community on Sansom Street in Philadelphia, the Wicky Wacky Woods has become a cherished place for me, one where I feel connected and at home in the world. After all, it was here in these woods where I had first sensed the danger of climate change and was inspired to take action to protect a place I love.

Returning to the woods in my fifties I found the same freedom of being ten again—but this time I was not building forts. Rather I was building ideas and new organizations to manifest those ideas. So it was that after acquiring a modest guest cabin to accommodate more people, I began to use the Wicky Wacky Woods to convene other business owners interested in building sustainable local economies. It all started with a retreat for SVN members in the summer of 2001.

As the board chair of SVN, I was committed to our mission of building a just and sustainable global economy and our lofty goal to *transform the way the world does business.* From my experience building a local food economy in my region, I believed wholeheartedly that the place to start was in our own communities, but I needed a strategy to actualize my vision for a global network of local economies.

As I thought about this, I found my inspiration in an SVN-sponsored project to support minority-owned businesses called the Urban Enterprise Initiative (UEI). Starting in 1998, I had collaborated with other SVN members with the aim of connecting minority suppliers to large SVN companies that operated nationwide; but once we began work on the pilot project in Philadelphia it became clear that, in most cases, this was not a practical approach, because most of the suppliers we were able to identify were community-based businesses, too small to supply large nationwide companies. Our group of Philadelphia-based SVN members could see that a more effective strategy for the UEI was to connect these minority-owned businesses with companies of similar size within our own region, where we could develop authentic and trusting in-person relationships across racially separated communities.

So our group of nine or ten local SVN members began working together to build a more inclusive local economy in Philadelphia. Though most in our group had rarely connected with each other outside of SVN national conferences, we began to meet regularly in our own community and built lasting friendships while taking turns hosting dinner parties in our homes and businesses. Not only did we get to know each other and our businesses, but as a group we visited other Philadelphia businesses. All this really felt right to me—to better understand the economy of my own city and to work with like-minded peers to make it stronger. Unlike previous local chapters and gatherings in the SRB movement, our group was specifically focused on building our local economy. We were also inclusive, working with businesses that did not qualify for membership in SVN, which required a high level of financial achievement and with membership dues unaffordable to many small businesses.

It was clear that with the experience we had gained from the UEI, our Philadelphia group of SVN members now had the base from which to form a citywide business network to introduce more local businesses to triple-bottom-line practices and work collaboratively to build a whole local economy built on these val- ues—just as Fair Food had done in building our local food system. In fact, this was a model SVN members could use all over the country to build local economies.

And so, at the SVN board meeting in the spring of 2001, I proposed that we launch a new national project, which I called the Local Network Initiative, to encourage SVN members to take leadership in starting local business networks in their home com- munities. We could achieve SVN's mission for a *global* economy by first building just and sustainable local economies.

I envisioned that SVN-inspired business networks across the country would connect nationally through SVN, and eventu- ally globally through the like-minded business networks of SVN counterparts in Europe, Asia, and South America to facilitate global fair-trade relationships between local economies. The rest of the board agreed that I should try out this idea by convening SVN members interested in the Local Network Initiative at a full-day retreat that summer.

My SVN buddies responded enthusiastically to my invitation to come to the Wicky Wacky Woods, mostly because of our shared interest in local economies, but also because the name sounded like a good time—a place where, as Roman poet Virgil once said, "frolic glee seizes the woods." And such a place it was on that memorable weekend in July 2001.

I was excited that more than twenty friends and fellow entrepreneurs were traveling from towns and cities across the country—from Los Angeles to Chicago to New York City. It was enough people to fill my two cabins, a camper, and a few nearby motel rooms. Fellow board member Laury Hammel was among them. The owner of The Longfellow Clubs, a group of health clubs in the Boston area, Laury (short for Laurence) was the first person I met when attending my inaugural SVN conference in Atlanta eight years before. An exceptionally vivacious fellow, he had helped me load my luggage into a van at the airport and told me stories to introduce me to the SVN community that made me feel welcome as we drove to my first conference, beginning a long and fortuitous friendship. When the nationwide organization he had helped to launch, Business for Social Responsibility, recently abandoned its local chapters (including Laury's in Boston) in order to focus on large corporations, he had set his sights on starting a new national organization to provide a home for these local chapters of small businesses. Now, our ideas were beginning to merge.

I had asked longtime SVN member Richard Perl to facilitate the meeting, and he agreed while making another important contribution—a suggestion that we invite economist Michael Shuman, the author of *Going Local: Creating Self-Reliant Communities in a Global Age*. I soon found that Michael's invaluable book provided intellectual support for much of what I had been learning-by-doing as an activist-entrepreneur. After years of thinking and writing on issues around local economies, Michael added professional expertise to our discussions. And in turn Michael, who had previously been engaged primarily with other intellectuals, was appreciative of the passion and business experience we entrepreneurs brought to the discussion.

Most of the gang arrived on Friday night, the eve of the retreat, including Jerry Gorde, founder of an employee-owned promotional products company in Richmond, Virginia—who drove his "Good Food Camper" and volunteered to organize all the meals for the group. We prepared a delicious dinner from organic ingredients that Jerry brought up from Virginia farms, then enjoyed the amenities of the Wicky Wacky Woods—including a wood-heated cedar hot tub surrounded by a stone patio I had laid down myself. That night the lantern-lit woods were alive with splashing and laughing and the music of guitars around the campfire, where a good supply of wine and local beer was shared.

Despite the festive evening, we merrymakers were up bright and early the next morning, and after a hearty breakfast of farm eggs and oatmeal gathered in a clearing in the woods near my cottage. Above us, the towering oaks and maples provided a high-vaulted cathedral-like ceiling in a mosaic of fluttering green leaves and patches of blue. Forming a circle, our group joined hands and I began our retreat by offering a prayer:

> We are grateful for our community and the shared values that have drawn us to gather beneath these trees. Here in the stillness of the woods, may we feel the pain of those not included in our circle of prosperity—the grief of losing the family farm or Main Street family business, and the despair of young people who lack the support of a thriving community. Away from the roar of planes and rushing cars, may we hear the cry of distress from the natural world, the trees, streams, and wildlife, as well as the millions of animals confined on factory farms. We have a mighty challenge before us—to build a new economy that serves the greater good.

May nature's beauty inspire us and our joined hands give us strength. May love grow within and between us, as we begin this day with hope, commitment, and open hearts.

After arranging an assortment of cushions and chairs under the trees, we went through a round of introductions that included the reason each of us had come—belief in a place-based approach to sustainability, interest in responsible investment, support for local organic food systems, concern for low-income and minority communities, the importance of locally owned media, interest in community development, the value of mindful consumerism, the role of spirituality in business, and interest in organizing small businesses locally. Then Richard began the program with a conversation between Michael and me about what we meant by the words "sustainable" and "local." But first, true to his fun-loving nature, Laury led the group in an upbeat Hokey Pokey to get our energy flowing, and we all stood up and turned ourselves around.

Throughout the day, we discussed the questions of what this initiative would look like on the ground and how we would support its growth collectively at the national level. By the end, we had laid the groundwork for a new national organization to be incubated at SVN—a national alliance of local business networks focused on building just and sustainable local economies. Yahoo!

That day we determined important principles for this new alliance, reflecting our thinking about the structure of networks. Local business networks would be self-organized at the grassroots level, forming a "bottom up" alliance comprised of autonomous local organizations with their own names, rather than groups operating as chapters in a hierarchical national organization. Each local business network would be different according to the needs of its own community, not a one-size-fits-all model enforced from the top. Yet the networks would be connected by the common values of triple-bottom-line businesses. Our commitment was to entrepreneurship and local business ownership. We also discussed the importance of working with local government, producing basic needs locally, exchanging in fair trade, financing local businesses with local capital and, as Michael likes to emphasize, keeping capital from leaving the community by replacing imports with locally made products.

First we local economy pioneers would go home to our own communities and use our leadership positions to attract other entrepreneurs to form a local business network. Once established, local networks would send representatives to future meetings of the new alliance to further define its structure and activities. At our next meeting, during the upcoming SVN fall conference, we would recruit fellow SVN members to join our efforts.

At the end of the day, we had much to celebrate. After preparing and sharing another Jerry Gorde dinner, and finishing off the wine and beer, we capped off our big day singing around a somewhat dilapidated player piano that I pumped furiously through countless music rolls of old-time songs, starting with "Bye, Bye, Blackbird" to "My Way" and ending with a rousing rendition of "This Land Is Your Land." We were off to a roaring start. Yes, *this land is your land, this land is our land, from the redwood forest, to the Gulf Stream waters.* And we are going to protect it from the greed heads for the good of all! And yes, we will do it *our way!*

"Living economies" was a term I first heard at the SVN conference that fall of 2001, when David Korten, along with evolutionary biologist and futurist Elisabet Sahtouris, used it to describe an economy that values life over money and works in harmony with living systems. At the same conference, Michael and I made a presentation on local economies, the first of many we would do together in the coming years. Michael and I often joked that we were the yin and yang of the movement, and in a way we were—he with the more head-oriented approach of a scholar, and I with the more heart-based approach of a practitioner.

At the SVN conference, the intellectual concepts of a "living economy" developed by David and a "local economy" developed by Michael wove together, joined with the entrepreneurial energy and passion of business owners led by Laury and me, and soon resulted in the name for our new organization—the Business Alliance for Local Living Economies. BALLE for short. At our local network meeting at the end of the SVN conference, a number of SVN members jumped on board and committed to starting or supporting local business networks across North America, from Vancouver to Grand Rapids to Baltimore. Laury and I became the first cochairs of the BALLE board, with David and Michael as founding board members.

SVN provides a fertile ground where like-minded entrepreneurs share ideas and create joint ventures, and so it was the perfect launching pad for BALLE, which found an institutional home at SVN before eventually spinning off as a separate nonprofit organization. Though I remained on the SVN board, I resigned as board chair and began to devote my attention to the growth of BALLE, where we now had a concrete strategy for building a new economy.

I saw that we had created a second front in the movement for SRB. The first front, including many larger SVN companies who believe that corporate globalization with long-distance shipping is inevitable, would continue to focus on reforming the existing system, while modeling corporate responsibility, an effort crucially needed in our race to stop climate change. The new front, manifested in BALLE, was walking away from the old system to build a new economy—a decentralized global network of local living economies self-reliant in basic needs.

Our newly formed organization had a tall order to fill, but help, as was often the case, was on the way.

After winning an MBA business plan competition in 1999, Michelle and Derek Long used their prize money to launch an online company they hoped would address global poverty by providing a marketplace for fair-trade exchange. Success followed, and even President Clinton placed an order. But then they got some important feedback from the producers in the villages they were trying to help. Doing business in their local regions worked better for them, they said, than exporting to the international marketplace. So Michelle and Derek closed their new company. Their first thought was to go live in a village in a developing country to help build that local economy. But then they realized that the place to do that work was in their own community.

Around this time, the young couple, neither yet thirty years old, met Laury at a business conference, heard about BALLE, and discovered that our vision was very similar to their own. The timing was right. In the late fall of 2001, Michelle and Derek became BALLE's first national co-coordinators. Their job was to build an alliance of local business networks throughout North America, creating a bottoms-up, grassroots-based organization through which local entrepreneurs could connect nationally to learn from each other and share solutions for building local living economies. All independent, locally owned businesses were welcomed in local networks, with no requirements other than that they not be publicly traded corporations—a system driven by profit and continual growth which was not compatible with BALLE's vision.

Michelle and Derek choose the city of Bellingham, Washington, to be their home—their place in the world—and took responsibility for its well-being. From the same office where they ran BALLE, the couple soon launched their own local business network. I was thrilled to make the long trip to Bellingham in the spring of 2002 to join with David Korten as we stood before a majestic view of the bay and mountains to be the keynote speakers for the launch of Michelle and Derek's Sustainable Connections—among the first members, along with Philadelphia and Boston, of the BALLE alliance of local networks. Little did we know that in a few years' time, Bellingham would be called "the epicenter of the new economy."

Michelle and Derek understood step one in building a new economy is to be mindful of when and how we spend and invest money. Each dollar casts a vote for what businesses we want to flourish, which communities strengthened, and (ultimately) what kind of world we want to live in. Among BALLE's first success stories was Sustainable Connections' "Local First" campaign, which encourages consumers to "think local first" before spending. Surveys later showed that their campaign succeeded in shifting the purchasing behavior of three in five households in Bellingham toward choosing independent retailers and services whenever possible. Michelle and Derek developed a tool kit for launching buy-local campaigns that they shared through BALLE with other emerging networks. Soon there was a cry of "Local First" echoing across the country.

That was the first of many best practices and solutions developed by local networks or local businesses that BALLE spread to other communities through training workshops, webinars, newsletters, and BALLE's annual international conference—the first of which Michelle and Derek organized in the fall of 2003 in Portland, Oregon. It became BALLE folklore that before our first conference, Laury announced that if we didn't have at least one hundred people, he would be dipped in shellac. To make sure that didn't happen, he worked his butt off to round up attendees. We surpassed our goal, and Laury, shellacless, continued his work as a Johnny Appleseed, planting BALLE seeds around the country—as we all set forth to do.

The audacious idea that a network of local living economies will eventually replace the unsustainable corporate-controlled global economy takes a lot to imagine, but that's exactly what we localists believe. We're out to create a global system of human-scale, interconnected, local living economies that provide basic needs to all the world's people. Yes, we want them to function in harmony with local ecosystems and support just and democratic societies. But we also want the people who live in them to have joy in their lives. To put it simply, we believe in happiness.

Without prosperous local economies,
the people have no power and the land no voice.

—Wendell Berry

❦ 11 ❧
Setting the Table
for Six Billion

AFTER THE FOUNDING of BALLE, I turned my attention to my own hometown to put my ideas into practice. By the fall of 2001, our Philadelphia-based SVN members had put in place what it takes to start a BALLE business network—a committed group of local business owners who share values and a liking for one another.

The elder in our group, and a role model for the rest of us, was the remarkable Hal Taussig, who had also participanted in BETHRIC. More than twenty years my senior, Hal has been an inspiration to me. When I ask myself the question, "How much is enough?" I think of Hal. He is the most generous man I know. Others clearly agree: Paul Newman once presented him with an award for running the "Most Generous Company in America." His company, Untours, is a travel business that provides home stays for clients to live like locals in a foreign country. Hal contributes the profits to the Untours Foundation, which in turn provides low-interest loans to businesses in underserved communities. To increase funds for his foundation, Hal lives a frugal life. While most SVN members stayed in the comfortable hotel where our conferences were held, Hal always showed up on a bicycle he would ride from a cheap room at a nearby hostel, even while in his early eighties.

Hal grew up as a cattle rancher and tells a story that he can't forget, and now I can't forget either. One day when he was a young adult, the ranchers slaughtered a cow and threw her hide over a rail. When they brought the rest of the herd in for the night, the other cows gathered around the hide and let out the most mournful cries—such wailing as Hal had never heard before. Though he had thought cows had no emotions, nor feelings for each other, Hal recognized their cries as the unmistakable expression of grief. This was only one of many stories that showed him as a caring person and a lifelong learner.

Others in our group included Lynne Cutler, who runs a nonprofit that helps low-income women start and build businesses; Alan Barak, an environmental attorney; Gretchen Wilson, owner of a handmade doll company, Little Souls, which creates jobs for women in low-income communities who make the clothes and accessories for her dolls; Clemens Pietzner, at the time executive director of the Camphill Foundation, which supports an international network of residential communities for youth and adults with developmental disabilities inspired by Rudolf Steiner; and Bob Fishman, who founded the nonprofit social service organization Resources for Human Development.

By partnering with Della Clark of the Enterprise Center, Lynne's organization and others working with minority entrepreneurs, our group of Philadelphia entrepreneurs found ways to build a more inclusive local economy by doing business with minority-owned companies, mentoring minority youth, and working with something that was new to most of us—local currency.

I had not heard of local currency until Bob Fishman launched Equal Dollars in Philadelphia in 1995. As an alternative, or compliment, to government-issued dollars, local currencies provide a means to exchange locally produced goods and services without the need for traditional money. In Philadelphia, Equal

Dollars seeded its operation by enlisting many minority business owners, something that sparked trade between local businesses in Philly's diverse communities. When I started taking Equal Dollars at the White Dog in 1996, the directory helped me find a minority-owned furniture company from which to buy desks and a balloon company that for many years supplied our New Year's Eve celebration and our annual outdoor parties. Meanwhile, the owner of a popular African American radio station used Equal Dollars to pay for part of his meal when dining at the White Dog.

Though local currency can be difficult to launch in a large city like Philadelphia, a number of smaller communities in the BALLE network began to experiment with it successfully, guiding customers toward locally owned businesses. Rethinking the meaning and purpose of money became a popular conversation in the BALLE community. At our annual conferences, we included sessions on local currencies, where I learned about the oldest and largest local currency system in the country—Ithaca Hours, started in 1991 in Ithaca, New York—and the more recent BerkShares in the Berkshire region of Massachusetts. At a White Dog Table Talk, Edgar Cahn discussed his invention of Time Dollars—where hours of work, recorded in a time bank, are exchanged without the need for any other currency. So a teacher might earn credits in the time bank by contributing tutoring hours, or a doctor offering health care services, or a gardener green-thumb services. In return, they can exchange their credits (typically one credit for one hour of work) for services they need.

On a fall evening in 2001, I invited Hal, Lynne, Gretchen, Alan, Clemens, Bob, and a number of other local business owners to gather in my living room above the White Dog for the founding meeting of what I called the Sustainable Business Network of Greater Philadelphia (SBN, not to be confused with SVN!), which then became a founding member network of BALLE. SBN was the second program, after Fair Food, to be incubated at White Dog Community Enterprises, financed in part by the profits of the café. Before approving the name, Hal wanted to know if my suggested name referred to "social" as well as "environmental" sustainability. After I explained that it did, and ultimately financial sustainability, too, he concurred and generously lent us the time of his assistant Kate Duncan to help get things started, whatever that might entail.

Alan, who along with me became SBN's cochair, suggested that our initial project be holding a Social Venture Institute in Philadelphia—a program developed by SVN that deployed businesspeople, largely members, to teach emerging entrepreneurs about sustainable business practices through uniquely formatted case studies and educational workshops. We all agreed that this would be a great way to support and grow our diverse business community and build relationships.

At the end of our founding meeting, it was time to celebrate over dinner downstairs at the White Dog. Michael Shuman was the guest speaker at that night's Table Talk, so after he enlightened White Dog customers about the advantages of a local economy, I announced the founding of SBN and talked about our goals. The word was out! Now we had to come through.

As usual, I did not have a master plan, and there were no existing models, so I relied on intuition and common sense. On day one of our Philly SBN venture, I thought, *Well, what does a successful local living economy look like?* We had been building our local food system, but how about the rest of the economy? Soon I developed what I call the "building block" strategy based on identifying, connecting, and growing the various sectors, or building blocks, of a local living economy—as well as recruiting leaders from each sector to join SBN. Like my work years ago on the *Whole City Catalog*, I began by taking an inventory of what resources already existed in the city.

After some thought, I identified the following as the logical building blocks of a local living economy: food and farming, renewable energy, sustainable clothing, local manufacturing, green building, New Urbanism (Jane Jacobs's model for city planning), alternative transportation, sustainable landscape and forestry, community capital, independent retail, recycling and reuse, health and well-being, fair-trade importers, local arts and culture, and independent media.

Many of these building blocks represented important local and national movements well underway, such as the local food and green building movements, but most of the people working in them had not been collaborating across sectors. How could we make this happen? Could we get local food businesses to sign up for renewable energy, and the energy businesses to buy from local retailers, and the local retailers to adopt the principles of green building, the green builders to bank and invest locally, the local bankers to eat local food while riding bicycles? Yes, we could connect them all! Both locally and through BALLE nationally, we began to connect the dots between these important movements and their local leaders into one holistic vision for local living economies across the country.

One way I did that in Philadelphia was to identify, in each building block, a local leader who was willing to serve on our first SBN board of directors so that we could tap into the passion people felt for growing their area of the local economy. Many of the board members and building block committee leaders came from connections I had made at the White Dog—Nadia Adawi headed the Energy Cooperative, where I purchased my renewable electricity; Maurice Sampson's consulting company, Niche Recycling, had put together the White Dog's community compost center; and Jenn Rezeli's prize-winning firm, Re:Vision Architecture, designed our energy-efficient hot water system. And of course, once we got our SBN team in place, the following summer we headed on up to the Wicky Wacky Woods. It was SBN's turn for a retreat, and this time we had a trombone player.

In a clearing beneath those familiar oak and maple trees, local SBN leaders gathered in the same place SVN members had founded what became BALLE the summer before, though this time I upped the amenities by supplying fifteen matching outdoor chairs for the occasion, which we arranged in a big circle. Our group included representatives of the major building blocks—among them Bob Pierson of Farm to City, Michelle Knapik from the city's energy department, and fashion designer Cheryl Washington. After developing our strategic plan in a productive session facilitated by the late Ralph Copleman, we enjoyed an evening in the hot tub, around the campfire, and listening to a duet of piano played by community capital advocate Andrew Anderson and trombone by photographer Andy Smith. By the end of the retreat we pledged our allegiance to what we called the Merry Mecca—a community of fun and comradery, where we experience the collective joy of working together toward a shared vision for our Philadelphia community and the growth of our local living economy.

Like the White Dog had been before, SBN now became my teacher. Just as I did educational programming at the restaurant, I began to organize programs for SBN and started by asking a different building block leader every other month to teach the rest of us about his or her field, including how we could purchase a product or service in their area, whether it be renewable energy, office supplies, or green construction services. Building our local economy began with us, so at each SBN meeting, I would always ask, "How many of you purchased a product or service from another SBN member this month? How many of you purchased from a local company you never did business with before?" There was an excitement about the challenge to see how many of our supplies for both our businesses and our homes we could purchase locally. A sense of community developed as our economic exchanges increased along with our friendships. And every program put on by fellow SBN members taught me something new about my own local economy. One program advanced my thinking in ways I hadn't expected.

Sustainable landscape was a field I knew little about until Dale Hendricks, SBN board member and owner of a native plant nursery, presented a slide show with examples of both a sustainable and an unsustainable landscape. The slide of the landscape that could not sustain itself showed the plants separate from each other in a manicured style that was controlled and regimented with no wild areas between or around them. In contrast, the sustainable landscape was comprised of a wide diversity of plants growing together and sharing the same space, which created natural habitats for pollinating insects and other creatures. Here the plants were thriving year after year.

What came to mind were the similarities in other areas of our lives and economy that suffer from compartmentalization and separation and flourish with connection and diversity. On small family farms, various species comingle in the barnyards and open pastures allow grazing animals to move freely in their chosen social groups. Fields are planted in a diversity of crops and bordered by wild areas. This is in sharp contrast to industrial agriculture where row after row of identical animals, all of the same size and breed, are confined in small cages—and row after row of identical crops are grown in gigantic tracts with no wildlife habitat in sight, not even one tree.

The similarities hold true in the man-made environment of cities. The New Urbanism planning style developed by Jane Jacobs features walkable communities with a hodgepodge of residential and commercial uses. The "sidewalk ballet" and "exuberant diversity" of these urban communities are in stark contrast to the style Jacobs opposed—development that compartmentalizes commercial and residential, constructs highways that separate communities, and builds sterile high-rises and gated communities that separate communities by age and class. The jumping, joyous jumble that Jacobs valued in urban life could also describe Dale's gardens or the lively barnyard culture on a family farm.

This thinking helped me to see that our work in building local living economies is about overcoming separation by knitting together a world that has become fragmented and lonely into one that is inclusive, joyful, and strong in its diversity. Local economies are overcoming compartmentalization and reconnecting work life with community and family life, and uniting our work with our deepest values. Townspeople are reconnecting to local shopkeepers, to the farmers who grow our food, to the designers and dressmakers who make our clothes, and to the carpenters and woodworkers who build our homes and furniture. In local economies we often know who mills our flour, bakes our bread, brews our beer, distills our gin, and makes our tofu, cheese, ice cream, and candy bars—relationships that enrich community and bring greater enjoyment.

Our BALLE local business networks, or you might say webs of business relationships, attempt to reflect the greater web of life, of which we are all a part. By operating as natural systems do, our business networks strengthen rather than tear apart the web. Natural systems are cooperative and, as I had discovered in building our local food system, cooperation is also essential to building local living economies. Of course, competition is present in nature as well, and likewise, our economies have competition—but only within the bounds of a cooperative system. Restaurants engage in friendly competition to offer the best product, which results in even better food for our customers, but at the same time we cooperate in building a sustainable food system that supplies all of our businesses, and we do not compete in a way that destroys the relationships that hold our community together.

Confucius once said that all of his teachings could be condensed into one word—reciprocity. In the web of life, relationships are reciprocal, both giving and receiving, just as we breathe air both in and out. To build a sustainable economic system, we must give something back for everything we take from nature and society in our business transactions. Here are the kinds of questions we should be asking ourselves: What should we give back to the soil in exchange for giving nourishment to our food? To the forests for the wood to build our homes? To the cocoa bean pickers in exchange for the pleasure that chocolate brings us? To the dairy cows who give us cheese and ice cream?

Jane Jacobs's "jumping, joyous urban jumble" of cultural diversity is what gives strength and resilience to society and to our economy, just as biodiversity strengthens the web of life. Donella Meadows says it well, whether applied to natural or man-made systems: "A diverse system with multiple pathways and redundancies is more stable and less vulnerable to external shock than a uniform system with little diversity."

Being inclusive and finding a way for everyone to participate creates more diversity and makes the whole stronger. Ever since my experience on the softball field in fifth grade, when the girls were left out, I understood how the whole team is weakened when capable players are excluded from the game. Today, as we move from an industrial global economy to a network of local living economies, many new green businesses are needed to produce and sell goods and services locally, and this offers a historic opportunity to include more players in the game. Great strides can be taken by ensuring that communities who have been left out of the old economy have opportunities to start businesses and take jobs in the new green economy.

This concept became a greater focus for SBN after BALLE's fifth annual business conference in Berkeley in 2007, where activist Van Jones talked eloquently about connecting green job opportunities to people in low-income communities. Among those inspired by Van's talk was Leanne Krueger-Braneky, the executive director of the SBN—who brought the idea, and also Van, back to Philadelphia. After Van roused a sold-out crowd in Philly, Leanne launched a Green Economy Task Force at SBN where she convened workforce development professionals, local policy makers, triple-bottom-line business owners, labor leaders, and community organizations to develop a strategy to train and employ people from low-income communities for green jobs in

Philadelphia's growing local living economy. After developing a successful program, she shared the concept with other BALLE business networks around the country.

We also continue to make strides toward diversity in our Merry Mecca. In 2002, SBN successfully launched our first Social Venture Institute. Held annually in partnership with SVN, the SVI not only provides education but also a welcoming community. By our tenth institute, under Leanne's leadership, we had achieved our goal of having 50 percent of attendees be entrepreneurs of color, which reflects the demographics of our city. SBN is also mentoring the BALLE network in Washington DC so that they can hold an SVI in their community.

Nearly 500 members strong, SBN is a thriving organization that has made many advances since those days in 1998 when a group of us began the earlier project to build a more inclusive economy. But none of us underestimates the long way we still have to go in achieving our collective vision for economic justice. Not only do we need to make room for everyone at the Table for Six Billion, but we must find meaningful ways for each of us to contribute our true gifts in the making of the great feast.

As we worked hard to develop SBN in Philadelphia, national interest in local living economies grew quickly and, soon enough after we founded BALLE, I was on the road speaking at kickoff events for business networks and answering requests to talk about local living economies in communities across the country—from Seattle to Minneapolis to Maine.

Like many people, I once had a great fear of public speaking. So much so that when I was on a sister restaurant trip to Nicaragua, I was feeling too anxious to stand up before our group of twenty travelers to thank our tour leader. Perhaps feeling the vacuum and without any prompting, ten-year-old Grace stood up on the bus during the drive to the airport and thanked our tour leader. Then she also thoughtfully thanked our bus driver for bringing us safely over the mountainous roads. That made me see how silly I was to be fearful about something that came so naturally to my young daughter. Soon the practice of routinely introducing Table Talk speakers at the White Dog built my confidence, and gradually I overcame my fear.

Remarkably, I came to enjoy public speaking and was not only eager to share my message, but also to learn from the communities I visited. At the same time, there was much to do in Philadelphia and I was constantly pulled between the needs at home and the importance of building a nationwide movement. Our work was so exciting, but also exhausting. By 2003 I was in a frenzy trying to keep up with the three-ring circus of BALLE, SBN, and the White Dog Café. Yes, I still had a business to run. Grace had graduated from college and had become the director of community programs when Sue Ellen retired after twelve productive years to pursue a new project making jewelry out of recycled bicycle parts to raise money for worthy causes. Lawrence was off in college majoring in art and technology, so I had few family obligations. Even so, I was busier than I had ever been—so busy that I was not taking care of myself. At one point I realized I hadn't even changed my socks for what seemed like months. *Who would be so foolish as to waste time changing socks?*

My guardian angel, Cathy Berry, who had provided initial funding for Fair Food and was also the first major donor for the launch of BALLE, witnessed my hectic lifestyle (and heard about my socks) and insisted that I hire an assistant. That was something I had never even thought about: a personal assistant!

When she first entered my office, Merrian Fuller found me peering up from behind mountains of paper with a clear look of distress. Tall, graceful, and calmly composed, Merrian had come to help. Though right out of college, she was wise beyond her years and had a passion for building a new economy after seeing the forests in Thailand wasted and polluted by US corporations making toilet paper.

It didn't take Merrian long to reduce the piles on my desk—and before we knew it, she had become the first executive director of SBN, not only rescuing me, but initiating many great new ideas, such as a business plan contest. Over the next two years, Merrian grew SBN into a healthy organization before she returned home to the West Coast, leaving a good membership base for Leanne to begin her tenure as our second executive director.

Merrian and I continued to work together over the miles when she took a position on the BALLE national staff and later when she joined the BALLE board of directors. In 2009, Merrian once again rescued me. By that time, I was ready to step down from the leadership position of BALLE board chair and play a less stressful role with more time for reflection. I was trusting that the right person would come along to take my place and was overjoyed when that person turned out to be Merrian. Finally, I had time to change my socks. And, as it soon turned out, my life.

It takes a lot of capital to build a new economy. The type of low-interest loan I made to farmer Glenn Brendle for his refrigerated delivery truck is needed across the country. Yet most people, even those who want to bring social change and see the need for a more nurturing economy, invest their savings in the stock market where it perpetuates the old exploitive economy.

My own experience in learning how to invest differently began in 1999 when I suddenly became a stockholder. After my mother passed away, I inherited a stock portfolio comprised of holdings first purchased by my grandfather and kept in the family for over fifty years. I wasn't quite sure what to do with the stock. At first I hired a broker to trade my stock for what was considered "socially responsible investing," a concept where stock is "screened" to eliminate companies involved with such things as weapons, tobacco, and animal testing. But when I looked at my new portfolio, I was shocked to see Wal-Mart! I could not have stock in Wal-Mart, a company known to destroy local economies and underpay its workers—and they sold products produced in sweatshops and factory farms to boot. How could I support such a company—even if it had passed through the screens created by brokers for socially responsible investing?

That's when I realized that I did not want to participate in the stock market at all. These are single-bottom-line companies, who by law are directed toward maximizing profit for stockholders above the interest of other people and our planet. I wanted to invest in companies that were independent of the stock market and had passed through a different screen, one that can filter out all companies who are not independent, locally owned, and triple bottom line.

So in 2000 I sold all my stock and did something that my broker and all my friends in the socially responsible investment field advised against: I put most of my eggs in one basket—my local economy. My friend and mentor Hal Taussig told me about a local investment vehicle called The Reinvestment Fund (TRF), and there I invested my money to be put to work as community capital for such local needs as wind energy production, small business loans, neighborhood revitalization, and affordable housing. To the surprise of my friends, except for Hal, over a ten-year period my local investments at TRF outperformed their stock market returns.

When I discovered that the wind turbines bringing renewable electricity to Philadelphia were capitalized by TRF, I coined the term *living return*. The return on my investment was not only paid in dollars, but by the benefit of living in a healthier community. I began receiving a *living return*, and with it the happiness and satisfaction of knowing where my money is—doing good right in my own community.

As was typical, I said to myself, *My customers have got to hear this*, and scheduled a Table Talk on local investment at the White Dog with Jeremy Nowak, president of TRF. Why not inspire more Philadelphians to bring their money home—disinvesting in the stock market where we often don't know what effects our investments have on other people, animals, and the environment, and investing instead in our own economy where we have knowledge and a personal stake? That would increase the *living return* for our whole community.

I also looked into providing an option for our employer-matched IRA at the White Dog so that employees could choose to invest their retirement locally. Though I found no options for IRAs to go directly to our local community, we were able to provide an option to invest in the Calvert Community Fund, where money is invested in community development around the country. But clearly we need local financial institutions in every community to set up IRA programs through which citizens can direct their retirement savings toward building their own local economy and community rather than supporting the stock market. Thinking of all that money stuck in pension funds invested in the stock market, when we have such need for local investment in our communities, drives us localists crazy.

Capital for building local economies was central to another entrepreneur who connected to BALLE in a life-changing way— change not only for him, but also for BALLE and for the world of community capital.

Don Shaffer began his career as a partner in a skateboard design and manufacturing company, Comet Skateboards, where he and his team developed an eco-friendly resin for gluing their skateboards together. Rather than keep the formula as their market niche, Comet shared it with their competitors. Protecting the environment meant more to Don than the competitive advantage of a proprietary formula.

In 2004, Don, who was then in his early thirties, read an article in *Orion* magazine about my work to build local living economies, including the story of sharing my farm sources with my competitors. Don recognized a kindred spirit and soon he was on a plane flying from San Francisco to Philadelphia to attend the second annual BALLE business conference in 2004. Through conversations at the conference and the after-hours party in my home above the White Dog, Don found like-minded entrepreneurs who shared his values of cooperation and compassion, as well as fun. When Michelle and Derek stepped down from their leadership role at BALLE that year to focus on growing their local network as well as their family, Don became BALLE's executive director.

Tall and fair, Don has such a humble, gentle, and giving nature that I first described him as angelic (until he told me stories of his not-so-distant past as a rebellious youth). Don recognizes that the can-do focused energy of the entrepreneur is at the core of building a new economy and to be successful, entrepreneurs need capital. So Don made capital for local economies a strong part of BALLE's agenda—beginning with many speakers and sessions on community capital at our national conferences. After three years of nurturing and building BALLE, Don left the position to pursue his dream of transforming the way the world works with money as the president and CEO of RSF Social Finance, which offers investments, loans, and gifts to enterprises with triple-bottom-line values that are building the new economy.

RSF stands for the Rudolf Steiner Foundation and is inspired by the work of Rudolf Steiner, who believed that money has a deeply spiritual dimension and is a form of energy that connects one person to another and strengthens the bonds of community. Steiner's work keeps popping up in my life. It was Steiner who invented biodynamic farming (sustainable agriculture beyond organics), which is practiced at Hawthorne Valley Farm, the dairy farm I so admire for keeping calves with their mothers. The Hawthorne Valley community also has a Waldorf school, which practices Waldorf Education (sometimes called Steiner Education), an educational system with an interdisciplinary philosophy founded by Steiner in 1919. There are thousands of Waldorf schools around the world. Steiner also inspired a worldwide network of Camphill Communities—residential and working communities for disabled adults and youth, including two near Philadelphia with whom the White Dog developed projects and events. In various ways, all of Steiner's innovations recognize life's interconnections and overcome traditional separations in society, education, and finance.

Believing that financial transactions should be personal and transparent and based on long-term relationships, and in keeping with Steiner's philosophy, Don developed a unique practice that brings together RSF investors with RSF borrowers in face-to-face meetings, where investors and borrowers discuss the interest rate that the borrower pays and the investor earns, and in the process get to know each other and the businesses or projects being supported. Here is another example of how relationships that had become separated in an anonymous global economic system are being reconnected—the relationship between lender and borrower.

As a BALLE board member, Don continues to strengthen our efforts in driving investment to local economies by connecting financial resources to BALLE businesses and local networks and suggesting ideas and speakers for BALLE's monthly community capital webinars. RSF and BALLE work together with a group of innovative funders to direct more foundations and investors toward funding restorative local economies.

Additionally, once a year RSF cosponsors BALLE's national Community Capital Day along with our allies at Slow Money, an initiative launched by Woody Tasch—former CEO of Investors' Circle. The goal of Slow Money is to bring more capital to local food systems through long-term, "slow" investments in sustainable small-food enterprises. It was Woody's book, *Inquiries into the Nature of Slow Money: Investing as if Food, Farms, and Fertility Mattered*, that inspired me to approach Philadelphia's TRF (already engaged in capitalizing grocery stores bringing fresh food to inner city communities) about targeting investments toward growing the local food system in the Philadelphia region. Today, a recently hired food system analyst at TRF has already directed several loans to local farms and food enterprises, including the

Fair Food Farmstand, showing once again how my investments in TRF provide me a "living return." After serving as a Slow Money founding advisor, I watched Woody's campaign manifest in local economies around the country where many millions of dollars have been invested in farms and small-food enterprises that nurture the soil and feed their communities well. As Woody likes to say, "Let's bring our money down to earth."

I soon began to discover examples of how networks of local businesses can be ingenious problem solvers and innovators. When I read about the cooperative practices of businesses in the town of Hardwick, including making use of each other's waste products, I hopped in the car with my friend Tim Bowser and headed for Vermont. Tim had recently opened a cafe and microbrewery in central Pennsylvania and was interested in how food enterprises in other rural areas were working together. Not only did the sheer inventiveness of the Hardwick collaboration appeal to me, I knew that just as there is no waste in nature, networks of businesses need to figure out how to use the waste products from other businesses as inputs for producing their own products, and I was eager to find working models.

Tom Stearns operates a successful organic seed company called High Mowing Organic Seeds, and seven years ago he began meeting monthly with other young entrepreneurs in food and farming businesses in the Hardwick area to share ideas and soon found ways to connect their supply and waste chains. After extracting the seeds from his organic winter squash, Tom had been throwing the waste in the compost. But that was not waste to Pete's Greens, a farm with a commercial kitchen. Pete Johnson began using Tom's leftover squash to make a puree that he offered his CSA (Community Supported Agriculture) customers and sold to institutional buyers for soup, and soon was also using Tom's surplus cucumbers for making pickles.

With the need for a good restaurant in town, the group supported the planning and launching of Claire's, which now buys ingredients from the local farms and sends its food scraps to a local composting company that completes the cycle by providing compost back to the farms. Not only that, the compost company is reclaiming heat from the compost process to warm Tom's greenhouses located next door, and Tom provides trials in his greenhouse for various types of compost the company is experimenting with.

Proximity is crucial. These and many other examples of cooperation are all made possible by forming a cluster of businesses located close enough to each other to make their exchanges efficient. Plans are now in the works to build a plant to process whey, the waste from local cheese makers, to be used in producing eco-friendly floor finishing at Vermont Natural Coatings.

The twenty-five local businesses in their Hardwick network—who also make frequent bridge loans to each other and share knowledge, equipment, and storage space—have all grown and prospered from their cooperative efforts, becoming the largest employers in the region. They also started a nonprofit—the Center for an Agricultural Economy—that among other things runs a staffed business incubator kitchen, which has spawned thirty new local food businesses. I invited Tom to speak at the seventh annual BALLE business conference in Denver, where he told his story of business cooperation and the role of these young entrepreneurs in the revitalization of their town and region.

Stories like Hardwick's energize the annual BALLE business conferences—which lack the tone of one-upmanship that is often felt at traditional business events. Local economy entrepreneurs do not face the fierce competition found among companies with national brands. Rather than hide trade secrets, these community-based innovators are more than happy to share their success stories for replication in other communities. Just as I did at the White Dog, we are spreading our models, rather than our brands. And the annual BALLE business conference is one good place to do that, where presentations and conversations among entrepreneurs are focused on sharing solutions and inspiring new ideas. An entrepreneur who discovered an organic dye might recommend it to another textile company. Or a local food processor might help an entrepreneur from another community set up a similar business. Or an activist entrepreneur might share how her city council just passed an ordinance to give tax breaks to B corporations.

A relatively new development, B corporations are companies that are certified as sustainable, having gone through a rigorous review of their social, environmental, accountability, and transparency policies and practices. The White Dog was an early certified B corp, and I found that simply completing the assessment was beneficial: it encouraged me to take even further steps in social responsibility that had not occurred to me before completing the survey. A great tool for local business networks, the B corp review process can help assess the progress of their whole organization, as SBN's executive director, Leanne, explained in a BALLE conference workshop. Though SBN does not have performance requirements for admission, all member businesses are required to complete the assessment so that the sustainability status of the whole group can be monitored for progress.

Not only does certification encourage businesses along the path to sustainability, it also helps investors and consumers differentiate between those businesses that are trying to pose as sustainable businesses (a practice known as "green washing") from those that actually are. Additionally, the nonprofit B Lab, located near Philadelphia, is working to pass legislation state by state that establishes a new type of corporate entity called a "benefit corporation" which gives businesses, including those publicly traded, the freedom and legal protection to pursue the triple bottom line, rather than acting only for the benefit of stockholders—a big breakthrough for the socially responsible business movement.

BALLE conferences are gatherings we look forward to all year—a place to connect with other local economy leaders, share our stories and strategies, learn about positive solutions, eat lots of local food, drink the local beer, dance to local musicians, and come away inspired and eager to get home and try out new ideas. Hosted by a local business network in a different part of the country each year, the conference includes tours of real-life examples of a local living economy in the making, with visits to local factories producing such things as porous paving blocks made from recycled materials, or an independent retailer selling locally designed and made clothes, or projects by the local municipality, such as a city-run compost program or a solar housing development for seniors—whatever that community has to offer as successful local living economy models to share with visitors. Each year I think to myself, *This would be a great place to live*, though I always make it back home to Philly.

Each business conference begins with the recognition of the original inhabitants of the land on which we gather. The tradition began in Philadelphia when our local business network, SBN, invited a representative of the Lenni Lenape, the first peoples of our region, to offer a blessing at the beginning of the second BALLE conference in 2004. The Lenni Lenape leader led us in making a native prayer bundle that contains our hopes and dreams for building a local living economy in our region, represented by pinches of tobacco, a sacred crop to many indigenous people, wrapped in individual tiny pouches and then bundled together. Each year at the opening ceremony the BALLE community renews our intentions and the prayer bundle is passed from the host of the previous year's conference to this year's host. A representative of a local indigenous tribe ends the ceremony by sharing some history and wisdom of the tribe, and welcomes the BALLE community as we work together to restore the land and heal our relationship with nature and each other.

The uplifting annual gathering of local economy pioneers includes entrepreneurs, leaders of business networks, investors and philanthropists, and community leaders from across North America. And there are always a few from other continents, who take the concept back to their home countries to start similar organizations, as they have done in France and Sweden.

Increasingly, speakers and attendees also include cutting-edge local policy makers and economic development professionals. This is a crucial development in advancing the local living economy movement. It wasn't always so. When I initially looked for funding for our SBN in Philadelphia, my first thought was that building a local economy would be a no-brainer priority for local government. Though the economic-development officials from the state listened politely and showed interest, I was shocked to discover that the idea of building a local economy did not fit into their strategic plans. Instead the traditional strategy for economic development in local governments across the country has been to lure large corporations to the city or state with huge subsidies and tax breaks, creating an unlevel playing field harmful to locally owned businesses. Mistakenly, local governments have viewed large corporations as the major job creators.

It seems we have a tendency in our society to think that big business will solve all our problems. Even our original plan to help minority businesses in Philadelphia first relied on the idea that large nationwide corporations would save the day. Thankfully, we learned from that experiment, and so have many local governments who now work hand in hand with our local business networks across the country.

Michelle Long, who resumed her role as BALLE's executive director in 2009 after Don's departure for RSF, often hammers this point home with two simple words: *ownership matters.* A fearless and articulate champion for localism, Michelle is not someone a stockbroker or industrialist would want to take on in a debate, or they might find themselves limping home—or better yet, divesting in the stock market and putting their money into their local economy. Like other local-business evangelists, she finds she spends a lot of time showing just how many jobs, and how much community security, local businesses create.

After a report by SBN showed that 89 percent of Philadelphia's businesses are locally owned and are the city's major job creators,

Leanne accepted an award from the city's regional planning commission naming SBN as the economic development organization of the year in 2011. Times have really changed, as they have in communities across the country. Local business network leaders have transformed government procurement policies to favor local businesses in Phoenix, partnered with city government to create a recycling program in Grand Rapids, and advocated prolocalism policies in Santa Fe and Chicago. These are but a few of the growing number of examples of innovative partnerships between local government and local business networks.

Not surprisingly, at BALLE we encourage entrepreneurs who are ready to grow their companies to look at what goods or services their own community needs rather than starting a cookie-cutter replication in another community—just as I started a retail store for locally produced and fair-trade gifts in my own community, rather than another White Dog in someone else's.

My favorite example of a business modeling this notion is Zingerman's Deli in Ann Arbor, Michigan, cofounded by Paul Saginaw, a colorful character and beloved BALLE leader who typically wears a jaunty fedora and provides equal amounts of good humor and wisdom as a BALLE board member. Paul and his partner Ari Weinzweig created a new model for ownership as well as growth. Opposed to replicating their successful deli as a chain, yet desiring new opportunity for their employees, Paul and his partner work with their most motivated employees to start new businesses in their community—a bakery, a creamery to make local cheese and ice cream, a fair-trade coffee roasting company, a candy company, a full-service restaurant and several other businesses (including a farm)—which all together form the Zingerman's Community of Businesses. Not only did these businesses replace imports and increase local self-reliance, each new enterprise provided new ownership opportunities for their employees, so that Zingerman now has eight businesses and sixteen partners. Now that is a great way to reinvent growth.

To end the destructive path of continual growth, ecological economist Herman Daly promotes a "steady state economy," which maintains stable consumption within the carrying capacity of the environment. Just as I found ways to reinvent growth at the White Dog by growing in nonmaterial ways, many localists are finding ways to keep money circulating in the local economy without using up more natural resources. Some of these businesses sell ideas, events, and experiences; provide services; reuse materials; loan or lease rather than sell goods; and offer artistic expression through local arts and culture.

Another of my favorite BALLE businesses that models a way to grow deep in one's own region is Eric Henry's custom T-shirt printing company, TS Designs. On a trip to visit Eric in Burlington, North Carolina, I was first struck by the large employee vegetable garden outside his factory, including chickens that provide eggs and fertilize the garden, and hives of bees for pollinating and supplying sweetener for coffee and tea breaks. I noticed several banks of solar panels on the roof and yard, and in the bathroom lit by a solar tube I found a waterless urinal and a toilet that uses the gray water from the sink.

I was struck by how much pride Eric takes in his community, giving me a tour to see all the wonderful work his neighbors are doing: starting a biodiesel fuel business, raising beef on grass, and turning an abandoned textile mill into thriving new businesses—including a community gathering hall and a cooperatively owned store that Eric and his friends started that is chock-full of fresh local food and locally made products from tomato sauce to pickled okra to popsicles.

But most impressive is Eric's Cotton of the Carolinas project. Eric lives in cotton country. Yet the cotton he was first using in his business was imported. At the same time, 80 percent of the cotton grown in his state was exported. That made no sense to him. So he began his "dirt to shirt" Cotton of the Carolinas project, and now the entire supply chain—from farmer to ginner to spinner to knitter to finisher to cutter to sewer to print shop—happens within a radius of 750 miles compared to the 17,000-mile supply chain of the average T-shirt. Not only is Eric saving the carbon emissions of unnecessary long distance shipping, he's also so far kept over 700 jobs in his local economy. On top of that, he's building community—reestablishing the relationships that give people security and happiness. When Eric told the story of Cotton of the Carolinas at the eighth annual BALLE business conference in Charleston, South Carolina, he brought people from his supply chain along and the obvious goodwill between them and the power of their stories brought to life the advantages of keeping supply chains close to home.

But Eric never rests on his laurels. He and his group have started to produce organic local cotton and now have the most sustainable T-shirt in the whole world. Next they're working on producing natural dyes from local agricultural products, including organic tobacco. The BALLE community is waiting to hear what Eric has come up with next, and how others can learn from him.

Northern states have something to learn, too. Those of us in the north, my own state included, should take a feather from Eric's cap and start a "dirt to shirt" movement by demanding that the growing of industrial hemp be legalized in the United States, as it is in Canada, so that northern communities can break our dependence on corporate cotton producers and grow our own fiber crop appropriate for our climate. In colonial times, the northern states made many important products from the versatile hemp plant—clothing, ropes, sails for ships, paper, and fuel and food from the oil and seeds. And we could do it again.

One of the things I found in common when I visited Tom in Hardwick, Vermont, and Paul in Ann Arbor, Michigan, and Eric in Burlington, North Carolina—and people in many other communities as I traveled around the country—is that all of these entrepreneurs have a great love of place. With pride in their unique communities and gratitude for healthy natural surroundings, localists take care of the commons and look out for one another. Whether in cities, towns, or rural countryside, it is devotion to place that compels us to cooperate and share for the good of our whole community. As poet Gary Snyder advises, "Find your place on the planet. Dig in, and take responsibility from there." Whether dancing at a block party on Sansom Street with friends and neighbors or walking alone in the Wicky Wacky Woods, it has been in the places that I care most about—my main points of contact on this planet—where I have felt the exhilaration of my interconnection with all of life, and the joy that comes with it.

In 1973, I committed my first act of civil disobedience when I lay down in front of that bulldozer to protect my community from demolition and an invasion of chain stores. As a peace activist who came of age in the 1960s, it seemed odd that my first act of civil disobedience was not in opposition to the Vietnam War, but rather to defend our community and small businesses from McDonald's. But my experiences since then have now made it clear that this was, after all, an action for peace and democracy.

Globalism analyst Thomas Friedman wrote in 1999, "McDonald's cannot flourish without McDonnell Douglas, the designer of the F-15." My own experience in Central America and Southeast Asia convinced me that this is true. The United States deploys our military, or surrogates, to protect and ensure access for US corporations, which have a "grow or die mandate" for more and more natural resources, cheap labor, and new markets. Friedman went on to say, "The hidden hand of the market will never work without a hidden fist." It may be needed for globalism today, but localism has no need for a fist. As to the hidden hand, I have an entirely different perspective.

My living-above-the-shop experience gave me a sharply different interpretation to those who use Adam Smith's "invisible hand of the marketplace" as a rationale for unencumbered global trade—the economists who argue that when businesspeople seek their self-interest, unfettered by government restrictions, there emerges an invisible hand that serves the interests of society. These economists believe that as long as business decision makers have a free hand to meet the demands of the marketplace, the "invisible hand" even resolves social problems, a view aptly called "market fundamentalism."

We have seen clearly that unbridled self-interest does not serve all. Still there is something I appreciate in the concept of the invisible hand. Reimagined, it actually does work as a positive force, but only if we think of it not as the power of collective profit seeking, but rather as the power of *collective consciousness*—the shared understanding that all of life is interconnected in this beautiful world we live in.

Perhaps this was even Adam Smith's own interpretation, since in his day it was common that people lived and worked in the same community. Then the concept of our interconnection is much easier to grasp, as it was for me, when we see firsthand how our business decisions affect our community and environment and therefore those we love—and our own well-being.

If all people believed that life is interconnected, as the Eskimos and likely most other indigenous people do, then there would indeed be an invisible hand of *enlightened* self-interest guiding our decisions toward building an economy based on sharing, caring, and cooperation that would, in fact, serve the interests of society. I believe those economists are right when they maintain that business has the power to solve social problems, even world hunger and war, but only if we are guided by our desire for the common good—rather than by narrow self-interest.

After the catastrophe of 9/11 in 2001, during the time I was imagining BALLE, and when the United States invaded Iraq, I asked myself, *If we are building a new economy with a worldview of interconnection, then what is the opposing view that challenges our vision? What keeps us all from sitting down together at the Table for Six Billion?*

The opposite of *interconnection* is *separation*—a worldview that there is a *them* and *us*, and that mankind is separate from nature. World leaders with a worldview of separation—whether Christian, Jewish, or Islamic—seem to believe that there are good and evil people, and "God is on our side." Dangerously, this leads to a kill-or-be-killed mentality. With this worldview survival depends on domination over other people, animals, and nature and violence, cruelty, and degredation are inevitable.

Our traditional capitalist economic system has perpetuated this worldview of separation by teaching individualism and competition, viewing nature as a resource to be exploited, measuring success and self-worth by material wealth, and giving us the false notion that only money brings security. With this perspective, many Americans and political leaders live in fear of not having enough for themselves and are willing to use the "fist" against other people and nature to gain more material security. As I see it, greed and violence often come from a lack of faith—faith as I saw it in the Eskimo village—that the universe is abundant and can provide for everyone if we're willing to share, cooperate, and live in harmony with all of life.

In working toward such a world, local living economies are shifting consciousness by modeling these values and demonstrating that our real security, as well as our happiness, lies in strong self-reliant communities within a healthy web of life.

By building a new global economy in which every community has food and water security and locally produced renewable energy, we are creating the foundation for world peace. The British economist and author of *Small Is Beautiful*, E. F. Schumacher, put it simply: "People who live in highly self-sufficient local communities are less likely to get involved in large-scale violence than people whose existence depends on world-wide systems of trade."

Global warming brings added urgency to this work. We not ·ly need to end our addiction to fossil fuels and reduce carbons in a race against time to save our planet, but we must also prepare our communities for the inevitable consequences of climate change by ending our dependency on long-distance supply chains easily disrupted by severe weather and social upheaval. Producing basic needs locally becomes a matter of survival.

Sometimes I feel as though we are in an old-time movie where a town is preparing for a storm or a siege by an invading army. The wagons are rushing in from the countryside bringing food and supplies. The townspeople are working together passing heavy sandbags from one pair of hands to the next and stacking them in front of doors and windows. At such a time, competition is not a reasonable option—everyone is looking for ways to help, recognizing that survival depends not simply on individual self-reliance but on community self-reliance.

This concept of community self-reliance offers a meeting place for liberals and conservatives, an opportunity for a common vision in an otherwise divisive culture. While liberals value community and collective endeavors, the important role of the self-reliant entrepreneur is sometimes undervalued. Conservatives, on the other hand, value self-reliance and individualism but sometimes undervalue the importance of working collectively for the good of all. Put them together, and we have community self-reliance, not such a jump from either perspective. Perhaps this could be the basis for the "socially conscious democracy" that Martin Luther King, Jr., wrote about "which reconciles the truths of individualism and collectivism."

We can reinvent what it is to be an American. Rather than a country of rugged individuals, we can be a country of rugged communities. Perhaps we always have been.

When I walked into the kitchen that day back in 1998 and said, "Take all the pork off the menu," unknowingly I was following Gandhi and King's strategy of noncooperation. Whether it's the

Montgomery bus boycott or a refusal to go along with factory farming, once we say no to an immoral system, the next step is to build an alternative system based on values of fairness and compassion, as local living economy pioneers are doing.

The strategy Gandhi used in his nonviolent revolution to overthrow British tyranny is a good one for today in order to free our economy and democracy from corporate control. The conditions are similar. When India was colonized by the British, all the fields were planted in export crops, with the result that the Indian people lost their food security and millions starved to death. Gandhi told the people of India to plant community gardens so that villages could feed themselves. Today when citizens grow vegetables on their roofs, plant gardens in place of lawns, go to farmers markets, subscribe to CSAs, and patronize grocery stores and restaurants that buy from local farms, we are helping to build local food security, as well as strengthening our community and democracy.

Gandhi, who is often pictured at the spinning wheel, suggested that the people of India take all the clothes made in Britain, put them in a big pile, and burn them up. Then spin their own textiles. Rather than ship the Indian-grown flax and cotton off to London to be made into clothing and then shipped back for the Indian people to buy, they could make their own clothing within their local economy. Gandhi's vision for a decentralized, small-scale economic structure in India comprised of interconnected self-reliant villages governed by participatory democracy was not unlike that of the Zapatistas. As I grew to understand more about Gandhi's work, I came to see him as the grandfather of the local living economy movement, and an influence on those leaders soon to come, including British economist E. F. Schumacher.

When Eric Henry developed Cotton of the Carolinas he, too, was empowering his community and ultimately strengthening democracy. We are doing the same when we buy locally designed ' made clothes from locally owned stores. Still, even though id more clothing is being manufactured by independent local companies in many major cities and a growing number of towns, few can meet all our clothing needs locally. But buying clothes designed and made by independent companies in other communities, who pay a living wage and use sustainable fabrics and dyes also builds the green economy, increases fair trade, and supports many small fashion designers and manufacturers.

Gandhi also modeled the importance of standing up for what belongs to the commons. In the Salt March, Gandhi and his followers marched to the sea where they made salt while refusing to pay the salt tax, breaking the British salt monopoly, an act of civil disobedience that inspired millions around the world. The British attempt to monopolize salt is similar to struggles and protests today over the privatization of water, forests, and other resources—and the patenting of seeds and plants—that rightfully belong to all of us.

Michelle Long tells a remarkable story of sharing and caring among citizens and entrepreneurs in her hometown of Bellingham where a beloved natural foods store was verging on bankruptcy. After word of the store's distress was broadcast on Facebook and by the local paper, the townspeople responded by making the next few days' sales higher than any in the store's fifteen-year history. Even "competitor" stores joined in the cause, suggesting that their customers patronize the store in need. The energy grew. Fundraisers and concerts were organized overnight. Some suppliers donated product. Employees even offered to work for free.

As happened when I made the decision to cooperate with my competitors, the act of sharing transforms energy to a more powerful force that attracts others to it. This fresh, contagious energy of sharing and caring is moving us from an economy driven by profit-seeking and continual material growth to one driven by a desire to increase the well-being of our communities and natural world, where our true happiness and security lie. This is the way of beautiful business.

There are times when I feel grief for all that we have lost in our once pristine and abundant natural world and for the terrible injustices that so many people and other species suffer. I have no doubt that the years ahead will bring hardship as we face the consequences of human-caused climate change, toxicity, and resource depletion. But it's the joy and power of community and the determination to protect what we love that provides the energy to keep working toward a more just and sustainable world. Though we may tragically lose many more species, as well as human lives in the decades to come, I have hope that we will evolve as a civilization in time to keep our home on Earth from becoming uninhabitable. If we do, it will be because the world's people have joined in community with each other and with nature, and can at last sit down together to feast and celebrate at the Table for Six Billion.

Will you seek afar off? You surely come back at last,
In things best known to you finding the best, or as good as the best,
In folks nearest to you finding the sweetest, strongest, lovingest,
Happiness, knowledge, not in another place but this place,
Not for another hour but this hour.

—Walt Whitman

❧ 12 ❧

Good Night, Beautiful Business

I REALIZED IT WAS TIME to sell the White Dog Café when my travels and activities in the local living economy movement began to affect the quality of my relationships at work. After all, my philosophy revolves around my strong belief that business is about relationships. That's where the joy is. That's where the love is. But now I was neglecting my own relationships.

I thought back to the time in 2000 when I announced at our weekly managers' meeting that I was taking a national leadership position in the socially responsible business movement and would be less available to them than I had been. When I made the announcement, I felt myself unexpectedly begin to tear up. What was this about? I wasn't announcing anything important, was I? But intuitively I think I knew that when I moved my focus and passion from the business, it was the beginning of saying good-bye to the White Dog.

As time went on, I lost my comfortable sense of the right way to resolve a problem. In the old days, when problems came up, I would ask everyone's perspective and, though they might differ, I myself knew what the issues were from being in the restaurant daily, and the solutions became clear. Solving problems was fun. But gradually, with my lack of attention to the business, things changed. At some point around 2006 when I heard differing versions of a problem, I was left wondering and uncertain how to proceed. I felt bogged down. And it wasn't fun anymore. That's the moment I knew that I was no longer the one who should own and care for this precious business. New stewardship was needed.

When it first dawned on me that it made good sense to sell, I could not handle the idea. My head told me that it was the right thing to do, but my heart was not ready. Upstairs sitting alone at my desk, I was resolute in my decision to sell. That is until I went downstairs and saw the morning sun streaming through the lace curtains onto the blue-and-white checkered tablecloths and watched servers who had been with me for as long as ten years setting the tables for lunch. In the empty chairs I felt the presence of my beloved customers who had filled them over so many years—meeting with friends, blowing their horns on New Year's Eve, coming in their pajamas on New Year's Day, meeting our farmers at the Farmers Sunday Supper, discussing the issues of the day at our Table Talk lectures, and even daring to come along with me on sister restaurant trips to Nicaragua, Vietnam, and Chiapas. Then I would start to cry and run back upstairs before anyone saw me. This was repeated several times over a couple of years as I thought things through and considered my options.

With my belief that we should have more owners in our economy, my first inclination was to sell the business to the employees, and I took our financial manager, Deirdre, and another manager ⁀onference on various forms of employee ownership. I hired ⁀ho specialized in employee stock ownership pro- ⁀), and he arranged for an appraisal of the business. ⁀mployees know my intention, and hired consultants to assist with introducing various forms of self-governance, I did not see what I was looking for among the staff—the willingness and capability to step up and take responsibility for the whole. Kevin had left as chef to start his own restaurant, and it soon became clear that I had not spent enough time cultivating the leadership necessary to take our places in running the White Dog.

I was also concerned about whether the values and sustainable practices of the business I had developed over the years would continue without me, no matter who bought the company. The White Dog stood for something important to my customers and the community as well as the employees, and I wanted the business to stay true to those values even after I was gone. For years, I had rolled my own share of White Dog profits into the foundation, taking only my salary for myself and my family—something I could do because I owned the real estate that housed my business and the rent from the White Dog, or whatever business followed it, would provide my retirement income. Able to live only on that rental income if necessary, the thought occurred to me that I could simply close the business and have it disappear into memory like a Tibetan sand painting I had blown away.

But then I thought about the farmers who depend on our orders, the employees who may want to stay on, and this beautiful block on Sansom Street that I had helped save so many years ago. The White Dog is a large part of the neighborhood's identity and a place where a community of loyal customers had been coming for twenty-five years. I had to find a way for the business to continue.

During my early trial and error days of building the White Dog, I discovered a creative process that I describe as simultaneously holding two different energies. On one hand a sense of taking control with determination—using my will power to forge ahead in a focused way. And on the other hand, a sense of letting go—surrendering to something beyond my control while remaining highly aware, not knowing where I was being drawn, but having no doubt I should go anyway. I have come to call this dichotomy of two different yet mysteriously connected energies "grace and will" (not to be confused with the TV show *Will & Grace*). While I use my will to accomplish something with intention, at the same time I surrender in acknowledgement that I am an imperfect human without all the answers and am guided by grace. When I try to describe this feeling, I am reminded of my youthful experiences as a Girl Scout canoeing down a river, where I used my paddle with intention to make strategic moves and at the same time went with the flow of the current to take me safely through the rapids.

Just as I opened myself to both will and grace when I created and ran the White Dog, I let these dual energies work in me during the years when I was wrestling with how to transition from the company. I did not jump immediately into making a grand plan, but rather waited until I felt the time was right, while staying open and alert to all the possibilities that might come my way.

When the trademark for the name *White Dog Café* came up for renewal, I intuitively took the ownership of the name from the corporation to my personal ownership. The name of the business was so closely associated with me as a person that it seemed the right thing to do, though I wasn't exactly sure why. A couple of years later the idea finally occurred to me. Why not sell the corporation, but not the name? Then I could lease the name to the new owner along with a contract that outlined the business practices that must continue in order to use the name. I was onto something!

I had little idea how to go about negotiating the sale of the business. I thought of my friend Jerry Gorde, who had brought his Good Food Camper to the retreat in the Wicky Wacky Woods seven years before when our band of merry friends had founded what became BALLE. Jerry has a deep understanding of financial issues and is great at making deals. And as fellow SVN members, we shared the same values. I called Jerry to ask his advice, and he told me that what I was talking about was not leasing the name, but rather licensing, and that I needed a licensing lawyer to draw up an agreement. He knew the right person, also an SVN member, and advised me that I needed three documents—an agreement of sale for the corporation, a lease for the commercial property, and a licensing agreement that would include my idea for a contract, which he suggested we call a "Social Contract."

With a plan in mind, I no longer had any hesitation, nor sentimentality. It was time to get on with it and I set out to find a buyer. Within only a few weeks I had two strong prospects and after another week, I made my choice—a restaurateur with a good reputation for running several fine places in the area. When I met Marty Grims, I liked him right away. He saw the White Dog Café as a beloved Philadelphia institution that he would be proud to care for and hoped to bring to even greater success. With a long track record for good hospitality, Marty had the credentials I was looking for to provide leadership and the financial capacity to invest in our aging physical plant to make sure that the White Dog was prepared for another twenty-five years of service. And thankfully, he didn't balk at signing the Social Contract.

Jerry negotiated the financial terms for the sale and the licensing of the name. We needed a corporation to own the White Dog Café brand, and after I found my first choice of "Legal Beagle" was already taken, Jerry came up with a most suitable name of "Perpetual Pooch LLC." Refusing to accept any payment for his essential work on my behalf, Jerry allowed me to make a contribution in his name to his favorite nonprofit, the Bainbridge Graduate Institute, where he and I have both lectured to business students earning a sustainability-based MBA.

While Jerry handled the financial negotiations, I wrote the Social Contract, a six-page document that begins with this preamble:

> The White Dog Café brand is trusted by our customers for our high ethical standards. Chief among these is our commitment to purchase only humanely raised meat, poultry and eggs and sustainably harvested fish and seafood, as well as many fair trade imported products. The White Dog is a leader in the local economy movement,

especially in support of locally raised food and sustainable agriculture. White Dog models many green practices, leading the way in addressing the challenges of global warming and natural resource depletion. This document outlines most of the practices that have made the brand locally and nationally known, respected and admired, and which must be sustained and improved upon in order to hold the trust of our constituency and maintain the value of the brand.

The contract went on with the details: seafood choices must be approved by the Monterey Bay Aquarium Seafood Watch and fair-trade items must include coffee, tea, vanilla, cinnamon, and chocolate—the last of which is particularly important to me because of the pervasive use of slaves in picking cocoa beans. All electricity must be purchased from renewable sources, water preheated by solar, all nonmeat food scraps composted, and so on through the practices developed over twenty-five years. The agreement also allows for the brand name to be used in additional locations provided that 51 percent of the ownership lives within fifty miles. No chains!

The downside of this exit strategy is that the sale price was reduced to less than 20 percent of the appraised value. But the good news is that over the fifteen-year period of the contract, I would recoup that difference through licensing the name, and importantly the values I cared so much about would be maintained. The agreement could not require that these practices be followed forever, but I hoped that in fifteen years most of the practices would become mainstream as the new local living economy came into being. That was our audacious plan.

So, in January 2009, the same month the business celebrated its twenty-sixth birthday, I sold the White Dog Café with no regrets or sadness. That month I held my last White Dog event, the twenty-second annual dinner in memory of Martin Luther

King, Jr. It was fitting to end that way—with the special event that had been my very first at the White Dog and my favorite.

Though it was time for me to say, "Good night, beautiful business," I was also saying "Good morning" to a whole new economy of beautiful businesses springing up faster than I could ever have imagined.

People often asked me how the White Dog got its name. Did I once have a white dog? It wasn't that simple.

Everything started with a knock on the door that came around midnight just after moving onto Sansom Street in 1973 ten years before I started the White Dog. I opened the door to find a dark-haired, middle-aged woman who seemed a bit strange and agitated. "Is this the home of the great Madame Blavatsky?" she asked.

"Who?"

"Is this 3420 Sansom Street?" she asked impatiently.

"Yes, but there's no Madame here," I replied hesitantly.

"No, no, of course not, she lived here in 1875, but would you mind if I came in for a minute, just to see where it was she once lived?"

I swung open the door, and she tore around the house, explaining how this was where Madame's bedroom had been, and this was her parlor, and oh, how disappointing it was that the rooms had been so altered. Then she was off, and I went back to bed, wondering if I had been dreaming.

Several months later, I was looking out the window of a bus when I noticed a small message board in the window of an elegant building near Rittenhouse Square, a popular well-kept park in central Philadelphia, which read, "Who was Madame Blavatsky?" Exactly! That's what I wanted to know, too. I quickly hopped off the bus and ran into the building, which turned out to be the Theosophical Society. It was White Lotus Day, which I learned meant the society was celebrating the life of its founder, Madame Helena P. Blavatsky.

Then I began to learn the story of the remarkable woman who had lived in my house one hundred years before I did. A Russian noblewoman turned world-traveling vagabond, Madame Blavatsky first came to the Americas in 1851 to study the history and philosophy of Native Americans. She became a US citizen predicting that an advanced society would develop in the future because in the United States the races and nationalities of the world would come together. During a delirium caused by an illness while living on Sansom Street, she developed a vision of a world united by universal brotherhood through the belief that all beings evolve from the same Source or Universal Spirit. After her recovery, she founded the Theosophical Society, an organization established to reconcile all nations and religions through a common understanding of ethical truths, to investigate the laws of nature, and to develop the divine powers latent in humankind.

Often credited for bringing Eastern philosophy to the West, Blavatsky was also among the first to state openly the understanding that all religions are branches that originate from the same trunk—one of ancient truths. Though a common idea today, this was considered blasphemy at the time, and Blavatsky was attacked and marginalized. Recognizing that organized religions actually separate people, often pitting them against each other, Madame Blavatsky, when asked what religion she belonged to, would reply that she belonged to all.

In addition to her bold vision of universal brotherhood, I also appreciated that Madame Blavatsky was not self-righteous. An eccentric character with an irreverent sense of humor, she once had a job as a bareback rider in a circus and allegedly smoked hashish.

A few years after the stranger knocked on my door to see the house where Madame Blavatsky once lived, I noticed another stranger—this time taking photos of my house. When I asked the man what his interest was, he told me he was researching for a major motion picture about the life of Gandhi and had heard that a woman who had once lived in my house had been an important influence in Gandhi's life while he was a student in London. Gandhi's days in London were eventually edited out of the movie, but years later Gandhi's own words in his autobiography verified the stranger's account. While a young law student, Gandhi had met Madame Blavatsky in London, and her ideas inspired in him a desire to embrace his native Hinduism, which he had all but abandoned during his secular education. That renewal turned him toward a more spiritual life. It was hard to imagine that a woman who had lived in my house had influenced the life of my hero. Yet another reason to honor Madame Blavatsky and appreciate her work.

Years later, I also learned that she had been an important influence on Rudolf Steiner, whom I had come to greatly admire. After ten years of leading the German section of her Theosophical Society, Steiner became disillusioned with the direction the society took following Blavatsky's death and broke off in 1912 to found anthroposophy, a philosophy consistent with Blavatsky's but one that promoted practical innovations like biodynamic farming, Waldorf School, Camphill Communities, social finance, and ethical banking.

Ten years after the midnight knock on my door, I started the café and decided to name it after Madame Blavatsky to recognize that this great woman had once lived in my house. But I did not want to call it *Blavatsky's Café*. I looked for ideas in her own letters, reading through a published collection of those that had my return address—3420 Sansom Street. In one of these letters dated June 12, 1875, Blavatsky explained to a friend that she had been seriously ill with an injured leg. The doctors had urged amputation to save her life, but she would have none of it.

"Fancy my leg going to the spirit land before me," she exclaimed in the letter, "and have my obituary read 'gone to meet her leg.' Indeed!" So she shooed off the doctors and cured herself, the letter goes on, by having a white dog lie across her leg, healing all in no time.

Whether there actually had been a white dog, or the dog was a symbol of the healing power of faith and good humor, I'll never know. Since dogs for me have always represented the qualities of friendship, trust, and fun that I wished for the café, the name suited. I drew the logo as the silhouette of my beloved beagle dogs—Peppy, Pooie, and Newman. The dog of the logo was not a white Labrador as most people guess, but the ghost of my tricolored friends.

After many years of travel, Madame Blavatsky moved to England, where she lived until her death in 1891. During this time, she was a leader in the nascent antivivisection movement to stop experimentation on live animals, something that had concerned me since I was ten years old when I had discovered that beagles, with their trusting and gentle nature, are primary victims of these experiments. Like Gandhi, who was also a staunch antivivisectionist, Madame Blavatsky had great compassion for all people and all beings that suffer. This beautiful passage, which continues to hang above my desk for inspiration, is from her book *The Voice of the Silence*:

> Let thy Soul lend its ear to every cry of pain
> like as the lotus bares its heart to drink the
>   morning sun.
> Let not the fierce Sun dry one tear of pain
>   before thyself
> hast wiped it from the sufferer's eye.
> But let each burning human tear drop on
>   thy heart and there remain,
> nor ever brush it off, until the pain that
>   caused it is removed.

As though fate had brought me to the house in which she had lived and then to the organization she had created, I discovered that my own belief in the fundamental interconnectedness of all life was also at the core of Madam Blavatsky's philosophy. And for her, compassion was the highest principle—the dynamic force that can move the world.

I had built a business as best I could based on caring relationships—a business I had named in honor of the extraordinary woman who had lived in my house one hundred years before me. An intellectual and scholar, Madame Blavatsky worked to bring the world together through the study and teaching of ancient truths. With the same goal in mind, I took a different route—building a compassionate economy that would reflect the spiritual and environmental interconnection of all living things.

When I first moved to the university neighborhood in 1970 to start Free People's Store, I was twenty-three. Forty years later when I was sixty-three, it seemed that everyone around me was getting younger and younger! Because the White Dog was a favorite gathering place for many ages, I hadn't noticed that I lived in a neighborhood that had become almost totally inhabited by college students.

As I moved through the process of selling the White Dog, it was not easy to think of leaving the Sansom Street block where I had begun my career as a waitress at La Terrasse and which I had helped save from demolition. I had lived in my home for thirty-eight joyous years, raising two wonderful children and throwing many great parties with friends, customers, and employees—parties in the restaurant, in my home, in the street, and even on the roof, once resulting in a civil complaint from my law-school-student neighbors that I was running on their roof at night while playing loud music and throwing firecrackers. I denied the firecrackers!

My children had grown and moved from the house. Now I wanted to find a new neighborhood within Philadelphia—one that was not too far away, but closer to where my friends lived. A new special place in my life. I felt a strong desire to be part of a community, and work with my own neighbors in addressing climate change and building our local living economy. I was ready to move from an activist entrepreneur to an activist citizen.

I closed the Black Cat after a twenty-year run, gradually selling down the merchandise over a six-month period to make an almost-perfect landing as an almost-empty store on its last day in business. The upper floors of the house had been used in the last years by White Dog Community Enterprises, which I closed when I sold the business. The two projects we had incubated—Fair Food and SBN—had become their own strong nonprofit organizations. I sold the Cat House, as we liked to call the brownstone housing the Black Cat, separately, keeping the other three houses for the White Dog—and used the Cat House funds to buy a new home for myself.

After some searching, I chose a row house only ten blocks from the White Dog, but across the river in a residential neighborhood of mixed ages where many of my friends live—a walkable community with easy access to shops, three farmers markets, the train station, and cultural attractions on a picturesque town square with plenty of nearby open space to walk and ride bikes along the river. And there was even a big dog park!

When I began renovations on my new house, I was excited to use many of the new green companies I was discovering. The son of an old White Dog customer started Greensaw, a construction company specializing in reclaimed wood. They even reused the beams removed from my third-floor ceiling to build my kitchen cabinets. Other building materials came from a young company called Greenable, much like a small and eco-friendly Home Depot, selling sustainably made tile, flooring, and paint. My rain barrel out front was locally manufactured by Shift_Design. It was inspiring to see so many beautiful businesses popping up across Philadelphia.

To my delight, all these companies, and almost five hundred more, are members of SBN—the organization I had started in my living room ten years before and housed in an office off my bedroom that had now grown up and out to a high-rise center-city office building. What's more, the work of these local green companies and nonprofits in Philly is being highlighted in a new monthly publication, *Grid* magazine. I was so pleased when the young publisher, Alex Mulcahy, told me that he had been inspired by the programs at the White Dog to start *Grid* so that he could tell the stories of all these people who were building a sustainable Philadelphia.

I experienced an even stronger sense of what my past had become in the spring of 2012 at the first Philly Farm & Food Fest organized by Fair Food, still led by Ann Karlen, and the Pennsylvania Association for Sustainable Agriculture's eastern district, headed by Marilyn Anthony, who had learned about local farms while working at the White Dog. I was surprised and delighted to find that over three thousand local-food-loving people (otherwise known as locavores) had shown up at this event. It was a dream come true for me to see over one hundred exhibitors displaying locally made products from cheese to chocolate, including herb-scented body lotions and so many types of honey that you could choose it by zip code.

In truth, it was like a White Dog Café reunion. There was Wendy Born, our first manager, and James Barrett, our former pastry chef, standing behind a display of the crusty artisan breads from their popular Metropolitan Bakery, now eighteen years old. When James left the White Dog in 1994, I thought I would die without a daily dose of his house-made olive bread, but when Wendy and James opened Metropolitan Bakery, the White Dog became its first wholesale customer, and I was able to keep enjoying their exceptional breads every day. James and Wendy not only use local organic ingredients as much as possible and sell local cheeses, jams, and other local products in their five retail stores, their bakery also employs and trains recent parolees and mentors at-risk high school students.

Then I spotted John Doyle behind a table of John & Kira's chocolates. I had met John when he approached me in a hallway of the White Dog and told me that he had read about me in Ben & Jerry's book *Double-Dip* and had taken the train down from New

York to find me, because he wanted to work in a socially responsible company. He would gladly quit his Wall Street job if I would hire him. I was intrigued and hired him on the spot, figuring I would find a way to fit him in. After a few years of working in our office helping to upgrade financial systems and other projects, he left to start his chocolate company, which featured flavorful fillings with a social story about each ingredient. Some candies are named for the ingredients purchased from longtime White Dog suppliers—Farmer Glenn's Raspberry and Mut Vitz Coffee. Another is Garden Mint, which uses mint grown by students in an inner city school where the White Dog had sponsored a garden project.

I could see that so much of what we had all accomplished together at the White Dog lived on in many other beautiful businesses. When Kevin left as White Dog chef/partner in 2004, he soon started his own successful restaurant, Farmicia, on the east side of Philadelphia, specializing in healthy food from the farms. And the White Dog itself was continuing to thrive under new ownership. In fact, Marty had opened another location near his own home in the suburbs, in keeping with our agreement that any additional locations be within fifty miles of the principal owner's residence. When I went to the new White Dog Café in Wayne, Pennsylvania, about twenty miles from Philly, I was delighted to observe the care that Marty and his team had put into the comfortable and eclectic design, complete with many dog portraits. Most of all, I was happy that the second location meant more business for our local farmers, sustainable fish vendors, and fair-trade supply chains. When I was leaving, an old White Dog customer greeted me, saying how happy he was to have a White Dog in his own neighborhood. A second location was also cutting down on the carbon of driving into the city. I hadn't predicted that outcome!

My move from activist entrepreneur to activist citizen was not automatic. In the old days, when I learned of a problem facing our community or society, I would hold a program at the White Dog with speakers to educate us. Or I would organize a tour to observe firsthand the problem or solution. Or off we would go to Washington DC with a busload, or two or three, of our customers to protest a problem. When I was a business owner, I had the powerful voice of business that I used at our press conference in Mexico and in congressional testimony in favor of government supported health care or keeping the estate tax. Or when I collected the signatures of hundreds of fellow business owners around the country for a full-page ad in the *New York Times* calling on President Bush to sign the Kyoto Protocol.

Now, without the vehicle of the White Dog, when confronted with a problem I felt powerless. I kept thinking, *What could I do as only one person?* Then my girlfriend, Kitsi Watterson, responded, "But Judy, you have always been only one person." Of course, she was right. So why should I feel powerless now?

So when Bill McKibben called for people to come to Washington DC in August 2011 to commit mass civil disobedience in front of the White House to protest the Keystone pipeline, I did not hesitate to hop on the train. This proposed pipeline would bring oil from the Canadian tar sands across the United States to a Texas port and would not only endanger the aquifers of our Midwestern states and add to the destruction of indigenous lands in Canada, but burning all this oil would also be the death knell in warming the planet beyond its capacity to sustain life as we know it. Bill, who first alerted the public to the dangers of climate change in his classic 1989 book *The End of Nature*, has been working tirelessly to stop the use of fossil fuels through 350.org, a grassroots campaign he organized to address the climate crisis. Though Bill is a writer, husband, and father who enjoys living a quiet, low-carbon life in the woods of Vermont, he has devoted his life to traveling, speaking, and organizing to save our planet. How could I not do my part?

My arrest in DC that hot summer day was my first act of civil disobedience as an activist citizen, rather than an activist entrepreneur. My focus remains on creating an alternative new low-carbon economy and preparing our communities for the growing crisis of climate change, but I don't think we'll get there if we don't help change public policies to curb the burning of fossil fuels and support the growth of renewable energy systems. In this urgent time, our federal government, as the representative of our collective will, is the only force large enough to stand up to corporations at the national and international levels. It will take active citizens to help wrestle government back from the bribers and lobbyists and turn it in the right direction to stop the fossil-fuel-driven machine of greed and destruction.

A couple of months after the Keystone protest, in October 2011, I continued my activist activities and went to Zuccotti Park in New York City to join the Occupy Wall Street movement for economic justice. Curious passersby stopped to read my big sign: MOVE YOUR MONEY FROM WALL STREET TO MAIN STREET. SHOP LOCAL, BANK LOCAL, INVEST LOCAL, MAKE LOCAL. I was happy to serendipitously run into several friends from SVN and see that supporters of this youth-led movement were of many ages. I was impressed with how the Occupy community walked their talk in "being the change" by the cooperative, generous, respectful, and caring way they treated each other. That evening I attended an Occupy "Alternative Economy" working group meeting to let people know about BALLE and our work to build local living economies. A few of our BALLE communities partnered with local Occupy groups in Bank Transfer Day to move money from large commercial banks to credit unions and small local banks.

It was no surprise to soon find myself in cahoots with my old friend Ben Cohen in helping to raise money for Occupy endeavors. Ben has focused in on the Occupy cause of getting money out of politics by joining the movement for a constitutional amendment to overturn the US Supreme Court decision *Citizens United*. Last time I saw Ben he was busy stamping dollars with the phrase CANNOT BE USED TO BRIBE POLITICIANS as part of his Stamp Stampede campaign.

My principal role as an activist remains with the local living economy movement, and I continue my frequent travels to speak anywhere people want to hear my story and message about building a new economy, a mission that has taken me around the country and as far as Europe, Australia, and India. In 2006, I was thrilled to accept the invitation of internationally acclaimed local food advocate Vandana Shiva to speak on Gandhi's birthday in Delhi, near the place where he spent the last years of his life.

And BALLE is thriving! At last count we have eighty local business networks in the United States and Canada comprised of thirty thousand local independent businesses. Last year's 2012 conference held in Grand Rapids, Michigan, was our tenth since that first one in Portland when Laury vowed he would be dipped in shellac if we didn't have one hundred attendees. No chance of taking a shellacking now. Under Michelle's passionate and energetic leadership, our conferences now number six to seven hundred attendees. Though I serve each year on the conference committee, my role has rightfully gotten smaller as new energy and innovations come forward, and I am happy to sit comfortably in the audience watching with wonder all that our movement has become.

I continue to serve actively on the BALLE board of directors, which is now skillfully and lovingly led by board chair Sandy Wiggins, a dear friend and passionate defender of nature, who helped create the standards used in green building and works tirelessly in the areas of sustainable development and ethical banking to create a healthy future for his children and grandchildren—and the children of all species. Michelle and the BALLE board are like family to me. It seems as though, across the thousands of miles that separate us, we live in the same house—a house of shared commitment and affection for one another.

I have a belief about social transformation—that it comes when two or more generations share the same values and vision and transfer knowledge intergenerationally. Largely because of the Vietnam War as well as the conformity of the 1950s, our 1960s generation was often at odds with our parents and consequently were unable to bring forward all the change that we had hoped for. But it's not too late. Now I see how many boomers are working in alignment with our grown children's generation to bring greater peace, justice, and sustainability to the world by building a new economy. In Philadelphia, the twentysomethings and thirtysomethings are not only starting their own green companies, they are also taking leadership in local government and nonprofits to build our local living economy and address climate change.

Among the creators of green companies is my own daughter, Grace, who founded an organic urban gardening business, Graceful Gardens, that designs and installs edible and ornamental gardens in courtyards, on decks, on rooftops, and in window boxes in Center City Philadelphia, including an herb and vegetable garden on the roof of the Four Seasons Hotel. To get around town, her first commercial vehicle was a bicycle cart made from an old bunk bed frame by the Neighborhood Bike Works, the nonprofit founded by our friend and former White Dog program director Sue Ellen Klein to help inner city youth learn how to repair bikes and earn the money to buy their own. I'm proud of Grace's prosperous company and happy that she did not go into the restaurant business as she once contemplated, though her experience growing up in the White Dog clearly had an influence—as I could see by reading her website: "Utilizing organic gardening techniques, I combine my love of nature, people, food, design and healthy urban habitat to serve the Philadelphia community." Another beautiful business!

Making my new life, I discovered that I had become old enough for younger people to take me under their wing sometimes. Having drinks after a board meeting, SBN's executive director of eight years, Leanne, asked me what I was wearing to a SBN fund-raiser called the SustainaBall. "Just the same old black cocktail dress I've been wearing for thirty years," I replied.

"But, Judy, as our founder, you should be wearing a locally made dress from a member-owned dress shop," suggested Leanne.

So I went to SA VA, a clothing company Leanne introduced me to, run by a young woman, Sarah Van Aken, who has spoken at our BALLE conferences about her model business—where 90 percent of the clothes are made in their garment center upstairs with fabric that is always fair trade and often eco-friendly. SA VA fills their living-wage garment worker jobs through partnerships with local nonprofits assisting women coming out of poverty. I found a skirt that appealed to me, but the fabric was not dressy enough. "No problem," said Sarah, "I can make the same skirt in a beautiful purple taffeta"—and began to take my measurements. "But the ball is tomorrow night," I exclaimed. "No problem; I'll have it for you."

The next day back at SA VA, only a seven-block walk from my house, I found that the beautiful purple skirt fit me perfectly. I was thrilled, and Sarah refused to allow me to pay for it. This was a community effort to get me looking good for the ball!

That night, feeling terrific in my new skirt with a black top and new black shoes from a locally owned shoe store, I met a man about my age named Craig Johnson, who was the most terrific dancer. After we started dating, I asked him what had first attracted him to me. "It was that purple skirt you were wearing—*caliente*!" Now that's a benefit of buying local I hadn't expected!

After all my traveling to spread the word about localism, I felt a strong desire to apply my knowledge and activist nature to my own neighborhood—to go hyperlocal in my work to build sustainable communities. So not long after I settled into my new neighborhood, I founded a new project with some old friends, which we named

Sustainable 19103, to work on greening the neighborhood within our zip code. Soon we began announcing bimonthly bring-your-own-wine-and-cheese events with panel discussions on sustainable practices, encouraging our fellow residents of 19103 to plant gardens and eat local food, sign up for weekly compost pickup, install rain barrels, buy renewable electricity, and paint roofs white—or better yet, install solar panels. I was up to my old tricks!

And, as always, we had fun, too. I couldn't help but organize a Sustainable 19103 party for Bastille Day after celebrating July 14th for almost forty years on Sansom Street. Over thirty people from the neighborhood showed up for our potluck picnic dinner along the river—old friends like Sandy Cadwalader and Ollie Cherniahivsky whom I had met when I was waitressing at La Terrasse in 1972 and who had come to White Dog's very first New Year's Eve party, and new friends like Sophie and Ed Bronstein who arrived on a tandem bicycle decked out in red, white, and blue. I could tell they were my kind of people. There were no poodles released from the Bastille by French revolutionaries to do the cancan, but I turned up the volume on my boom box to play French cabaret music as Craig and I spread our blanket on the grass and popped open a bottle of champagne. The same French flag I had used on Sansom Street on many a Bastille Day waved nearby, but this time I was not worried about staging a big production for hundreds of customers. I simply enjoyed a leisurely time laughing with friends and sipping champagne, while listening to Édith Piaf singing "La Vie En Rose" in the glow of the setting sun. I had sold the business but kept the community.

One day on the sidewalk near my new home, soon after I moved into it, a young woman—tall, blonde, with very long slender legs in tight jeans and high heels, and walking a tiny, brown, Chihuahua-like dog—asked me out of the blue if I had worked at La Terrasse. Very surprised, I replied, "Why, yes, many years ago."

"My father used to work for you. He has passed away, but maybe you remember him." Not only did I remember her father, Tom Slenzate, the young blond man who had been my property manager at La Terrasse, but I remembered the day about thirty years ago when Tom had proudly brought his newborn daughter to the restaurant to meet us. Though he seemed so young, Tom was the first of my employees to have a child. Four years later he had tragically died. This was that little baby Tom had so adored. This was his daughter Violet.

I knew I must have pictures somewhere of Tom holding his baby daughter. I had given Tom and his wife a reception at my house on Sansom Street to welcome the baby and had taken several photos, including some I remembered of one-year-old Grace patting the infant Violet's head. I spent hours looking through many boxes and albums—I had tens of thousands of photos of most every employee and many of my customers during my forty-year career in the restaurant business, times I cherished and wanted to remember. Finally, I found the ones I was looking for and had copies made. It turned out that Violet lived only a couple of doors down from me on Panama Street, and one evening I brought the photos to her house. Violet told me that she had not seen pictures of her father in the La Terrasse days, and she looked carefully through the photos: Tom at his desk, attending a wine tasting, dancing at a staff party, and finally her father holding her as a baby in his arms, beaming with love and joy.

Violet told me that she was engaged to be married and had been so sad to think that her father would not be at her wedding. The photos of Tom helped her remember her father and made him a bigger part of her life. She recalled a time as a four-year-old when her father had helped her climb the long stairway to see his office above La Terrasse. It must not have been long before his death. I pictured Tom now, as he would be today, the proud father of the bride, beaming again with love and joy.

Soon after meeting Violet, I attended my first neighborhood block party, a thirty-year tradition on Panama Street. Violet sang while another neighbor, Jerry Amari, sang and played the guitar. The duo did so well together that they began performing at a local bar and restaurant, and Violet began developing her career as a singer/songwriter. Craig and I are among the many neighbors—including of course Violet's husband, Sharif Alexandre—who regularly come out to hear Violet and Jerry at the neighborhood café. After all, this is another important part of growing a local living economy—supporting our local artists and musicians.

One night just as Craig and I entered the room, Violet and Jerry began singing a song they knew was our favorite, Neil Young's "Harvest Moon." As Violet and Jerry sang and Craig and I danced, and Sharif took photos of us all, I felt as though things had come full circle. The love I had shown to my employee Tom and his newborn daughter so many years ago had circled back to me. As neighbors in the same community, relationships span generations. Life goes on. The music and fun go on. My new neighborhood had become another special place in my life—a place to belong to and come to know. Most every place can be special when we care for it and make it so.

Acknowledgments

My dream since childhood was to write a book. Yet after graduating from college with a degree in English, there was nothing I felt compelled to write about. I needed more living under my belt. Thirty-six years later, in 2005, it came as a surprise and an exciting challenge to be invited by Chelsea Green publisher Margo Baldwin to write a book about the White Dog Café and my work in building a new economy. I'm thankful to Margo for recognizing that I had a story to tell and for her patience over the next seven years, during which I constantly reassured her that I really was going to write this book.

Writing a full-length manuscript was much harder than I had imagined, and perhaps I would have given up on my dream and hired a ghostwriter if it hadn't been for the help of editor Harris Dienstfrey, whom I began working with in 2011, and Chelsea Green editor Joni Praded. Harris and Joni brought order, asked the right questions, and made insightful suggestions. I'm eternally grateful for their wisdom, guidance, and support, which made this a better book.

I'm also thankful to Patricia Stone, Melissa Jacobson, Eric Raetz, Eileen Clawson, Shana Milkie, Shay Totten, and the whole team at Chelsea Green—a triple-bottom-line company that is now employee-owned. Chelsea Green not only publishes work around sustainable living, but also practices it. I'm grateful to have a publisher that shares my values and proud to be a Chelsea Green author.

Thanks to the readers of my manuscript who gave me good advice and encouraged me onward—Jean Brubaker, Linda Goldstein, Mark Nicolson, Grace Wicks, and Sandy Wiggins, and especially Kitsi Watterson, who not only made important suggestions, but also inspired a breakthrough for me at the writer's workshop she teaches.

Thanks to Craig Johnson, my life-partner and geezer squeezer, who supported me with meal cooking, dog walking, wise recommendations, and patience during the final year when I was glued to the computer, constantly promising him that life would be different when I finished the book.

There are many people throughout the years who influenced my life in ways that made this book possible, and I am grateful to them all:

My parents, the late Jack and Betty Wicks, who gave me both the love and the freedom to be who I am. And the other parents, teachers, and citizens of my hometown of Ingomar, who created a community where children could thrive.

The Eskimos of Chefornak, Alaska, who showed me a beautiful way of life and demonstrated the power of community, cooperation, and sharing.

Dick Hayne, my first husband and business partner, who was my companion as we set out into the world and launched our careers as entreprenuers.

Elliot Cook, who led the effort to save and restore Sansom Street, which gave me the opportunity to buy the house where I founded the White Dog Café and lived for almost forty years, and who provided my entry into restaurant management.

The late Neil Schlosser, my former husband and father of my children, who renovated our two houses for our home and business and helped me start the White Dog Café.

My children, Grace and Lawrence, who endured a childhood during which their mom was constantly busy with the restaurant, and more recently was often unavailable while writing this book. They are among my best teachers and my life's greatest joy.

The White Dog Café including our loyal clientele; our farm suppliers, especially Glenn, Karen, and Ian Brendle, Mary

Corboy, Mark and Judy Dornstreick, Bill and Helen Elkins, Joe and Angie Evans, Phil Landis, Ivan Martin, Dougie Newbold, Torrey Reid, Paul Tsakos, and the Amish farmers represented by Lancaster Farm Fresh Co-op; the thousands of employees of the White Dog and Black Cat over the past thirty years who contributed to our success, especially James Barrett, Wendy Born, Alisa Green, Kevin Klause, Sue Ellen Klein, Deirdre MacDermott, Long Pham, and Eric Tucker.

The new White Dog Café, especially principal owner Marty Grims and chefs Eric Yost and Zach Grainda, who are carrying on the values around healthy, locally sourced food, and Ron Gordesky and Jerry Gorde, who assisted in the sale.

Ben Cohen, who discovered me, connected me to a community of like-minded entreprneuers that changed my life and has generously supported BALLE and my other nonprofit work over many years.

The late Happy Fernandez, who paved the way for women leaders in Philadelphia. She recognized the importance of my work in practicing business from the heart and nominated me for my first award, which led to the initial funding of my nonprofit projects.

My friends at Social Venture Network who answered my call to come to the Wicky Wacky Woods to launch what became BALLE, including Jerry Goode, Richard Perle, Doug Hammond, Jim Slama, Stephen and Patricia Blessman, Larry Bohlen, Aliza Gravitz, Terry Mollner, Gretchen Wilson, Alan Barak, Mark Lighty, Reed Glidden, Aleyne Larner, Wendy Brawer, and Martha Shaw.

And especially BALLE cofounder Laury Hammel, whose leadership as cochair in the formative years of BALLE was crucial to our success.

The staff and board of Social Venture Network where BALLE was incubated, especially Deb Nelson and Mal Warwick. And the SVN members who helped build BALLE in the early days by founding or supporting local-business networks in their own communities, including Guy Bazzani, Ted Rouse, Matt Bauer, Joel Soloman, Peter Strugatz, and Andy Shallal.

And the many other local leaders in the BALLE community across North America who have been working on the front lines of the movement for local living economies, among them Sarah Bishop, Andrea Dean, Dan Finn, Anthony Flaccavento, Beth Geagan, Jamee Haley, Christine Hanna, Elissa Hillary, Kimber Lanning, Mickki Langston, Derek Long, Karen Marzloff, Vicki Pozzebon, Jessie Radies, Wendy Siporen, and Kimberlee Williams.

My colleagues who served on the board and staff of BALLE over the first ten years as we worked together to build the organization and the movement, including Baye Adolfo-Wilson, Alissa Barron, Matt Bauer, Merrian Fuller Borgeson, David Korten, Derek Long, Michelle Long, Derrell Ness, Jamilla Payne, Paul Saginaw, Don Shaffer, Ellen Shepard, Michael Shuman, and Sandy Wiggins. And our funders and supporters, especially Cathy Berry, Jennifer and Peter Buffet, and Bob Dandrew.

My colleagues in Philadelphia who worked with me to build our local living economy as the board and staff of White Dog Community Enterprises, Fair Food, and the Sustainable Business Network during our first ten years, including Nadia Adawi, Andrew Altman, Andrew Anderson, Marilyn Anthony, Frank Baldassarre, Alan Barak, Leslie Benoliel, Ben Bingham, Merrian Fuller Borgeson, Tim Bowser, Ralph Copleman, Bridget Croke, Lynne Cutler, Amy Dalton, Kate Duncan, John Eshlemann, Susan Firestone, Lindsay Gilmour, Lori Glass, Elizabeth Guman, Iola Harper, Dale Hendricks, Monica Hennessy, George Hoguet, Ann Karlen, Sue Ellen Klein, Michelle Knapik, Linda Knapp, Leanne Krueger-Braneky, Antje Mattheus, Marian Metner, Kim Miller, Bob Pierson, Bill Reddish, Jenn Rezeli, Hassen Sakar, Maurice Sampson, Andy Smith, John Smith, Charlie Szoradi, Hal Taussig, Cheryl Washington, Steve Weinberg, Jeremiah White, Erin Wieand, and Sharon Wilson.

And the dogs in my life, including Peppy, Pooie, Augie, Newman, Douglas, Emily, Alice, Dee-Dee, and Jack who taught me to be a better human, kept me company through joys and sorrows, and in recent years waited patiently for me to take a break from writing this book, so that we could enjoy our favorite activity—walks in the woods.

.

Index

NOTE: JW refers to the author, Judy Wicks. Page references with *ci* refer to photographs in the color insert section.

H

Hamilton, Dorrance ("Dodo"), 196

Hammel, Laury, 215, 217, 219, 220, 221, 269

Handley, Jim, 170, 178

Hardwick, Vermont, local business collaboration, 238–39

Harris, Bill, *ci6*, 180, 181, 182, 183

Hawthorne Valley Farm, 197–98, 236

Hayne, Richard, 4, 17, 18, 50–51, 85–86. *See also* Chefornak, Alaska experience; Free People's Store

Heinregle, Joe, 5

Heldring, Frederick, 78

Hendricks, Dale, 228

Hendrix, Jimi, ix

Hennel, Bob, 167

Henry, Eric, 244–45, 250

High Mowing Organic Seeds, 238–39

hog farming, 186–87, 193–97

Hog Summit conferences, 193–97

humane farming
balance of efficiency and nurturing in, 107, 199–200
beef and dairy production, 188–89, 197–98
pork production, 188
poultry production, 189–90

I

Imhoff, Dan, 126

industrial food system. *See also* factory farms
communism and capitalism similarities, 139
misguided efficiency of, 199
need for transformation of, xi–xii, 205, 207

Ingomar, Pennsylvania
JW fort building, 1–4
local businesses, 4–6, 9, 10

Inquiries into the Nature of Slow Money: Investing as if Food, Farms, and Fertility Mattered (Tasch), 237

investment, local
JW experiences, 233–35
Shaffer, Don work, 235–37
Tasch, Woody work, 237–38

Investors' Circle, 204

invisible hand concept, 246–47

Iocca, Pasquale, *ci2*, 71, 73, 74, 98

Iran-Contra affair, 124

Isaac (musician), 68–69

Israel-Palestine conflict, 135

Ithaca Hours local currency program, 224

J

Jacobs, Jane, 57–58, 228, 230
Jensen, Derrick, 18
Jessica (dog), 34
John & Kira's chocolates, 265–66
Johnson, Craig, 271, 272, 274
Johnson, Pete, 238
Jones, Van, 230
Jung, Carl, 145, 150

K

Karlen, Ann, 191, 192, 198, 265
Katzive, David, 48
Kennedy, Robert F., Jr., 195–96
Keystone pipeline protest (2011), 267–68
King, Martin Luther, Jr., 108–9, 137, 249, 258–59
Klause, Kevin, *ci6*
  animal product sourcing, 188, 190
  chef role, 110, 111, 112
  holiday party advice, 168, 169
  sister restaurant trips, 135, 140, 141
  start of own restaurant, 255, 266
  stock in White Dog, 116
Klein, Sue Ellen, 127, 128, 167, 191, 270
Knapik, Michelle, 227
Korten, David, 211–12, 218, 219, 220
Korten, Fran, 211–12
kospoks (dresses), 24–25
Krueger-Braneky, Leanne, 230–31, 233, 240, 243, 271

L

LaBelle, Patti, 189
Lappé, Frances Moore, 37, 126
Las Abejas group, *ci6*, 168, 175
La Terrasse restaurant, *ci2*, 52–86
  becoming the manager, 59–66
  celebratory events, 72–73, 113–14
  community outreach work, 77–82
  innovations as manager, 67–75
  leaving, 84–86
  Sansom Committee role, 56–59, 66–67, 82–83
  waitressing role, 51, 52–55
Leadership, Inc., 78
Le Bec Fin restaurant, 119
Leg Lifter Lager, 102
Lenni Lenape people, 241

❧ T ☙

Wicks, Judy, *ci1–2, ci4–7. See also* Business Alliance for Local Living Economies (BALLE); Chefornak, Alaska experience; Free People's Store; La Terrasse restaurant; Social Venture Network (SVN); Sustainable Business Network of Greater Philadelphia (SBN); White Dog Café
  childhood businesses, 11–12
  childrearing years, 76–77, 88–89, 93–94, 145, 147
  civil disobedience acts, ix, 66–67, 167, 246, 267–68
  cottage, *ci7*, 147–48, 212–13, 214–18, 226–27
  feminine energy embracing, xii, 15–16, 17, 150, 199, 200
  food memories, 6–8, 98
  fort building, 1–4
  grace and will process, 255–56
  Hayne, Richard relationship, 4, 17, 18, 50–51, 85–86
  hometown memories, 4–6, 8–10
  lessons from pets, 16, 185–86
  local investing, 233–35
  new neighborhood, 263–64, 271–74
  Sansom Street home, 53, 82, 83, 142–45, 259–61, 263
  Schlosser, Neil relationship, 57, 75–76, 83, 91–92, 94, 147
  school days, 12–17, 64
  Sustainable 19103 project, 271–72
  transition from entrepreneur to citizen, 266–69
Wicky Wacky Woods cottage, *ci7*, 147–48, 212–13, 214–18, 226–27
Wiggins, Sandy, 269
Willis, Paul, *ci5*, 194–95, 196
Willis Free Range Pig Farm, 194–95
Wilson, Gretchen, 223, 224–25
Women of Dignity cooperative, 183
World Trade Organization (WTO) protest (1999), 201–3

❦ Y ❧

Yanoff, Shelly, 128
Yuengling Brewery, 101

❦ Z ❧

Zakarevicius, Romas, 139

About the Author

AN INTERNATIONAL LEADER and speaker in the local living economies movement, Judy Wicks is former owner of the White Dog Café, acclaimed for its socially and environmentally responsible business practices. She is also cofounder of the nationwide Business Alliance for Local Living Economies (BALLE), as well as founder of the Sustainable Business Network of Greater Philadelphia and Fair Food—both incubated at the White Dog Café Foundation and supported by the restaurant's profits. In her retail career, Judy was founder and owner of Black Cat, which featured locally made and fair-trade gifts for twenty years. In 1970, Judy cofounded the original Free People's Store, now well known as Urban Outfitters.

Her work has earned numerous awards, including the James Beard Foundation Humanitarian of the Year Award, the International Association of Culinary Professionals Humanitarian Award, and the Women Chefs and Restaurateurs Lifetime Achievement Award.

She lives in Philadelphia. Continuing her work to build a new economy, Judy mentors the next generation of entrepreneurs and consults for beautiful businesses. She can be reached at www.judywicks.com.

the politics and practice of sustainable living

CHELSEA GREEN PUBLISHING

Chelsea Green Publishing sees books as tools for effecting cultural change and seeks to empower citizens to participate in reclaiming our global commons and become its impassioned stewards. If you enjoyed *Good Morning, Beautiful Business*, please consider these other great books related to socially responsible business and social justice.

LOCAL DOLLARS, LOCAL SENSE
*How to Shift Your Money from Wall Street to
Main Street and Achieve Real Prosperity*
MICHAEL SHUMAN
9781603583435
Paperback • $17.95

WHAT THEN MUST WE DO?
*Straight Talk About
the Next American Revolution*
GAR ALPEROVITZ
9781603584913
Hardcover • $27.95
9781603585040
Paperback • $17.95

INQUIRIES INTO
THE NATURE OF SLOW MONEY
Investing as if Food, Farms, and Fertility Mattered
WOODY TASCH
9781603582544
Paperback • $15.95

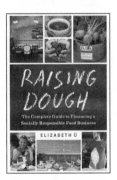

RAISING DOUGH
*The Complete Guide to Financing
a Socially Responsible Food Business*
ELIZABETH Ü
9781603584289
Paperback • $19.95

the politics and practice of sustainable living

For more information or to request a catalog,
visit **www.chelseagreen.com** or
call toll-free **(802) 295-6300**.

the politics and practice of sustainable living

CHELSEA GREEN PUBLISHING

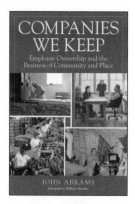

COMPANIES WE KEEP
*Employee Ownership and
the Business of Community and Place*
JOHN ABRAMS
9781603580007
Paperback • $17.95

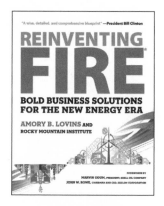

REINVENTING FIRE
Bold Business Solutions for the New Energy Era
AMORY LOVINS AND
ROCKY MOUNTAIN INSTITUTE
9781603583718
Hardcover • $34.95

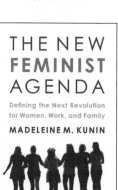

THE NEW FEMINIST AGENDA
*Defining the Next Revolution
for Women, Work, and Family*
MADELEINE M. KUNIN
9781603584258
Hardcover • $26.95
9781603582919
Paperback • $17.95

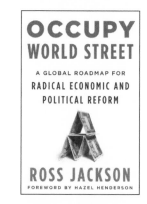

OCCUPY WORLD STREET
*A Global Roadmap for Radical
Economic and Political Reform*
ROSS JACKSON
9781603583886
Paperback • $19.95